POSTCARD HISTORY SERIES

St. Augustine in the Gilded Age

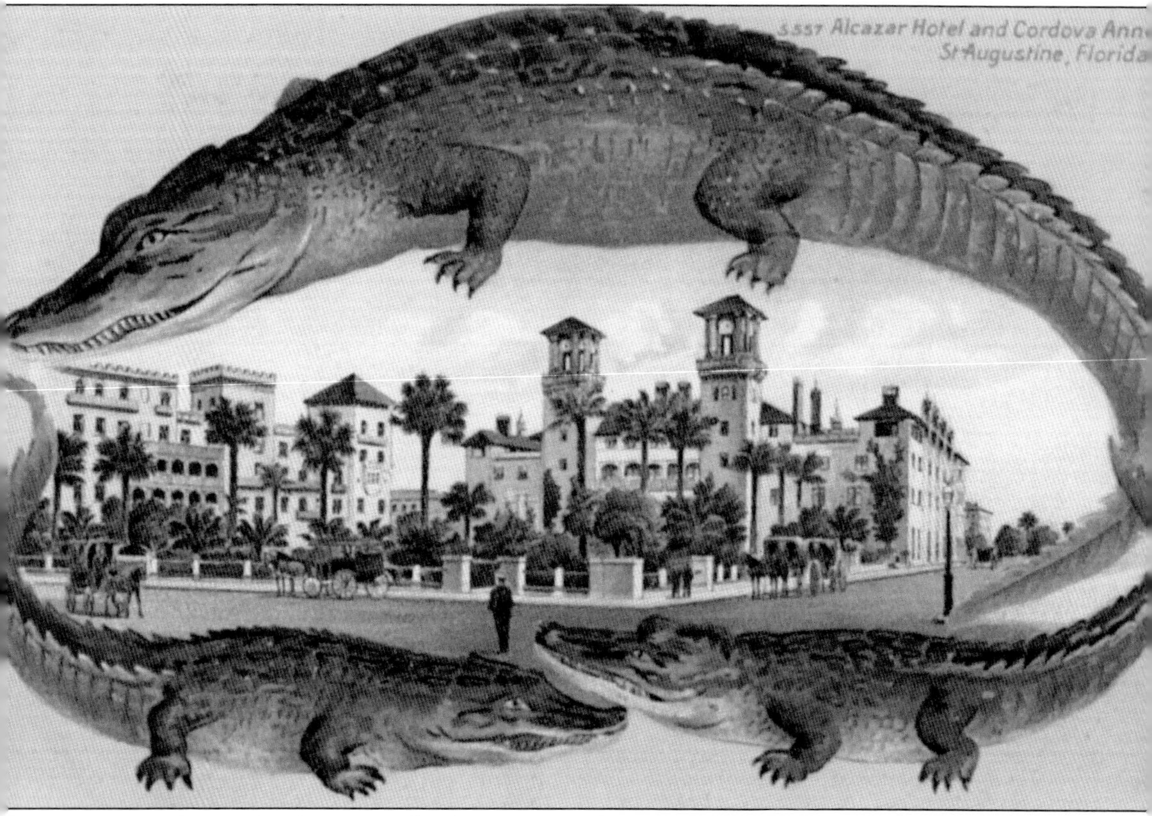

This alligator-border postcard published by the Langsdorff Company of New York shows the Alcazar Hotel at the center with the Cordova Hotel on the left. The Alcazar now houses St. Augustine's city hall and the Lightner Museum, and the Cordova is the Casa Monica Hotel.

On the Cover: The Monson House, located on Bay Street (today's Avenida Menendez) and overlooking the Matanzas River, was one of St. Augustine's most popular hotels. At the center of the postcard is the "Red Devil," the first automobile owned by a St. Augustine resident. The early car belonged to Judge James W. Henderson, whose family was the last to occupy the Oldest House as a residence. The postcard was published by R. B. Allen, St. Augustine, and printed in Germany.

Postcard History Series

St. Augustine in the Gilded Age

Beth Rogero Bowen and
the St. Augustine Historical Society

ARCADIA
PUBLISHING

ISBN 978-0-7385-5342-9

Published by Arcadia Publishing
Charleston, South Carolina

Printed in the United States of America

Library of Congress Catalog Card Number: 2008920716

For all general information contact Arcadia Publishing at:
Telephone 843-853-2070
Fax 843-853-0044
E-mail sales@arcadiapublishing.com
For customer service and orders:
Toll-Free 1-888-313-2665

Visit us on the Internet at www.arcadiapublishing.com

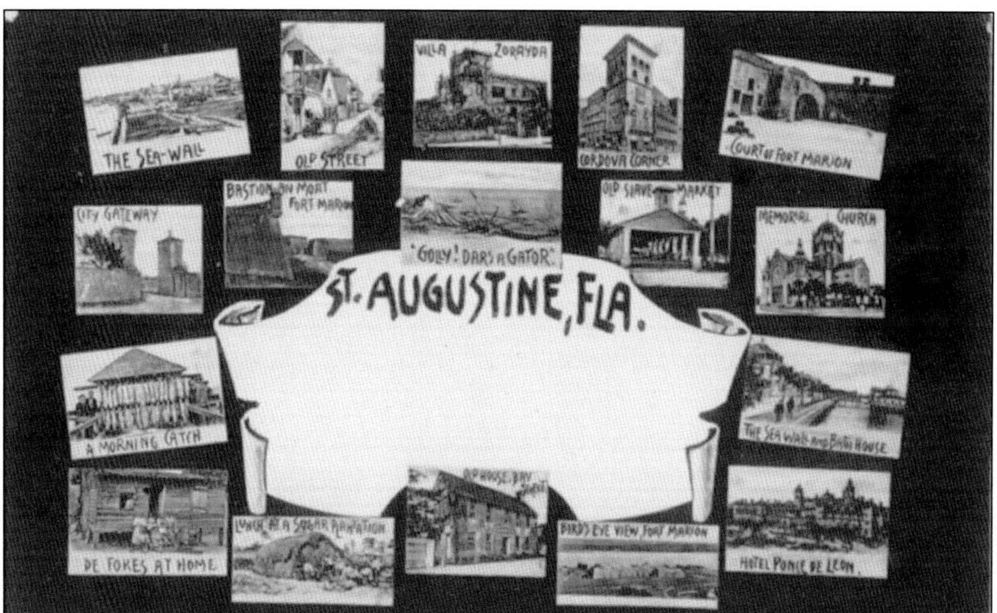

This multiview postcard contains 17 scenes of St. Augustine from around 1905. A brief message could be written in the space on the front of the card, as the back was reserved solely for the address.

Contents

Acknowledgments

The author wishes to thank Charles Tingley, library manager of the St. Augustine Historical Society Research Library, for his help gathering information for the book, identifying postcards, and proofreading the text. His knowledge of the people and events that shaped St. Augustine's history is unsurpassed, and his editorial comments, support, and confidence in me as a first-time author have been invaluable.

Also thanks to Dr. Susan Parker, executive director of the St. Augustine Historical Society, for her technical advice and proofreading of the text; Jack and Nadine Connahey for the loan of several postcards included in the book; Dick and Yvonne Punnett for information on Florida photographers and early aviation pioneers; Ken Barrett for the use of his notes on St. Augustine photographers; Robert Goller for information on W. J. Harris and the copy of the Fish Scale House postcard; and Judith Foxworth, library associate, and Judy Drapeau, library assistant at the St. Augustine Historical Society Research Library, for all their help in retrieving and copying information from the society's collections.

And to my husband, Jerry Bowen, special thanks for his continual support, his help formatting and proofreading the text, and his much-welcomed interest and encouragement.

Unless otherwise noted, all postcards used in this book are from the authors' collections.

INTRODUCTION

The term "Gilded Age" was coined by Mark Twain and Charles Dudley Warner in their 1873 book, *The Gilded Age: A Tale of Today*, to describe the period of opulent self-indulgence of America's upper class. St. Augustine's Gilded Age was the era of Henry Morrison Flagler, wealthy partner of John D. Rockefeller in Standard Oil. It began in 1885, with Flagler's first business dealings in St. Augustine, and ended soon after his death in 1913.

Henry Flagler first traveled to St. Augustine in the 1870s but was not impressed with the quaint town. Travel was difficult, accommodations were poor, and most visitors were invalids or consumptives. Flagler returned to St. Augustine in the winter of 1885 with his second wife, Ida Alice Shourds, and found the place much improved. He stayed at a new luxury hotel, the San Marco, and his fellow visitors were now well-heeled members of society. Less involved with his business interests in Standard Oil, Flagler needed a new project and conceived the idea of turning St. Augustine into a winter resort for the wealthy. He set about buying up properties and hired a pair of young architects, Thomas Hastings and John Carrere of New York, to give substance to his vision of a grand resort. Flagler purchased the small railroad that ran from south Jacksonville to St. Augustine, converted it to standard gauge, and bridged the St. Johns River, thus enabling passengers to travel straight through to St. Augustine from northern cities.

The Flagler era brought profound changes to St. Augustine. To provide a location for his two luxury hotels, the Ponce de Leon and the Alcazar, Flagler filled in Maria Sanchez Creek, whose marshes had extended as far north as King Street. A Methodist church stood on his hotel site; he purchased it and built Grace Methodist Church on Carrera Street for the congregation. Flagler built a second church, Memorial Presbyterian, in memory of his daughter, and donated the land for a third, Ancient City Baptist. The jail on Cordova Street was too close to Flagler's upscale hotels, so he had a new one constructed north of town. He built a city office complex on Hypolita Street and leased it to the town for a modest annual fee. The Alicia Hospital (later renamed Flagler Hospital), Florida East Coast Hospital, the YMCA, and a new bell tower for the Roman Catholic cathedral were all the results of Flagler's largesse. Streets were paved, public utilities installed, buildings repaired and enlarged, and the town spruced up for the affluent winter visitors. By the early 1900s, St. Augustine looked dramatically different from the sleepy village that had existed before Flagler's arrival.

For a short time, Flagler's dream of St. Augustine as a winter Newport was realized. But warmer weather drew visitors farther south, and Flagler extended his hotel and railroad empire all the way to Key West in 1912. The wealthiest visitors now spent only a few days in St. Augustine on their way to and from destinations farther south. But tourists of more modest means still came to St. Augustine for the winter, and smaller hotels and guesthouses sprang up to accommodate these less affluent visitors.

In the midst of St. Augustine's Gilded Age, the United States was swept up in a postcard craze that began in Europe several years earlier. This fad reached almost fanatical proportions, and postcard collecting soon became a popular pastime.

The first U.S. postcards were "postals," issued by the Post Office in 1873, with a 1¢ stamp printed directly on the card. The first picture postcards in the United States were souvenirs of the Columbian Exposition, held in Chicago in 1893. These were extremely popular, and on May 19, 1898, Congress authorized the use of privately produced postcards, called Private Mailing Cards, with the same 1¢ rate as the government postal cards. The backs of these cards were reserved solely for the address, and manufacturers left a margin around the image on front for a short message. On December 24, 1901, postal regulations were changed to allow private printers to use "Postcard" or "Post Card" on their products. These cards are referred to as "undivided backs," as the reverse was still used just for the address. On March 1, 1907, new regulations divided the back of the postcard between the address and a message, and the front of the card was now used entirely for the view.

The golden age of American postcards was the decade from 1905 to 1915. During this time, photography and printing technology improved to the point where high-quality cards could be mass-produced very cheaply. Just as important, the U.S. Post Office began Rural Free Delivery, so that by the early 1900s, all but the most remote households had mail delivered right to their door. By 1913, over 900 million postcards were mailed annually in the United States, at a time when the population of the country was only 88 million.

To meet this high demand, large national publishers hired photographers who traveled the country supplying images of famous landmarks. Most postcards were printed in Germany, where scientists had perfected the best inks and color separation processes. Many local businesses, such as drugstores and souvenir shops, sent their own negatives to Germany to be printed as postcards. In St. Augustine, postcards were published by R. B. Allen, Rogero and Pomar, W. H. DuBois (owner of El Unico), Foster and Reynolds, Usina Brothers (Oscar F. and Leonard A.), Herbert J. Usina, and William J. Harris.

In 1902, the Eastman Kodak Company developed photographic paper with mailing information printed on the back. Postcards could now be made directly from negatives, allowing photographers to make and sell "real-photo" postcards. St. Augustine's premier purveyor of these photo postcards was William J. Harris, who produced thousands of images of tourists posed in front of local landmarks. Other St. Augustine photographers producing real-photo postcards in the early 1900s were Lewis W. Blair, Fred C. Brown, Albert A. Cummins, Charles E. Gray, Willis A. Kugler, A. D. Thrasher, and Phillip A. Wolfe. Today these real-photo cards are especially prized because they show much greater detail than printed postcards and often picture scenes and subjects that do not appear in mass-produced postcards.

After 1915, the collection fad declined and so did the quality of postcards, as World War I cut off access to the German printers who had produced so many of the high-quality views. During the second decade of the 20th century, the telephone replaced the postcard as a convenient way to keep in touch. As more families acquired automobiles, distances shrank, and the need to stay in contact by mail was much less compelling.

St. Augustine in the Gilded Age offers views from the beginning of the postcard era up to 1914, when a disastrous fire swept through the downtown area. The book features the mass-produced postcards of the large national companies, as well as postcards printed by local publishers. But special emphasis has been given to the real-photo postcards produced by local photographers, as these offer unique glimpses of life in St. Augustine during its Gilded Age.

One

Hotels and Guesthouses

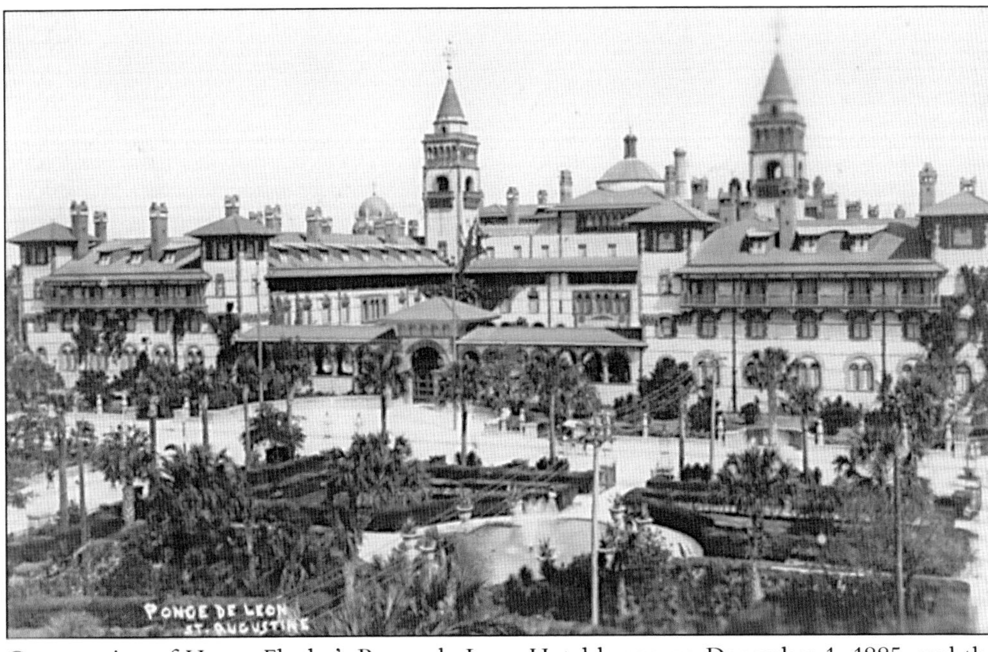

Construction of Henry Flagler's Ponce de Leon Hotel began on December 1, 1885, and the hotel opened January 10, 1888. A pair of young architects, Thomas Hastings and John Carrere of New York, designed the Spanish Renaissance hotel to reflect St. Augustine's heritage and sparked an architectural style still prevalent in Florida today. Flagler hired the construction firm of James A. McGuire and Joseph McDonald, builders of the San Marco Hotel (located just north of the City Gate) and many other wooden hotels in Florida. A new construction material, Portland cement, was combined with local coquina shell to form the Ponce de Leon's poured concrete walls. Some of the most noted artists and craftsmen of the day created the hotel's interiors, with stained-glass windows by Louis Comfort Tiffany and ceiling paintings by Virgillo Tojetti.

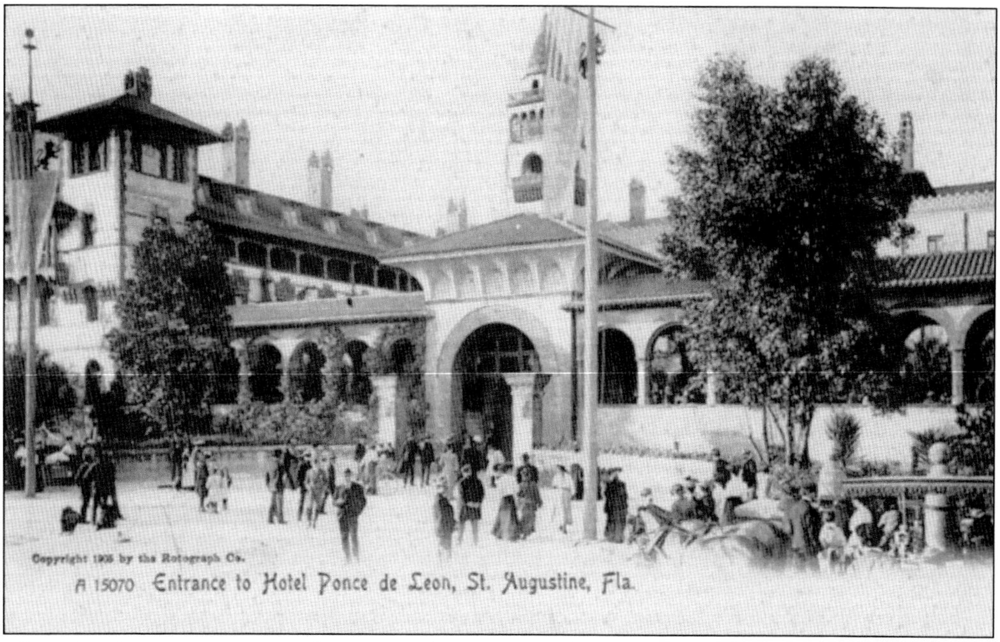

The King Street entrance to the Ponce de Leon Hotel was a scene of much activity, as shown in this 1905 view by the Rotograph Company. Guests arrived from the depot at the front door, while their baggage was unloaded at the carriage entrance in the rear and sent directly up to their rooms. No luggage was allowed to clutter the hotel's magnificent lobby.

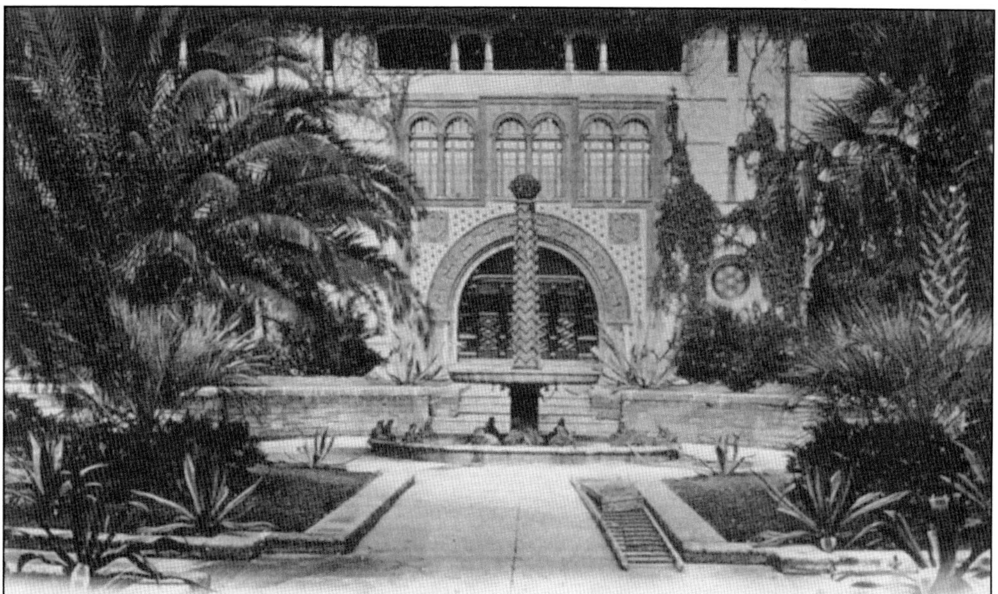

The centerpiece of the Ponce de Leon's tropical courtyard was a large fountain, surrounded by water-spewing terra-cotta frogs. Novelist Henry James visited St. Augustine in 1905 and wrote of the Ponce De Leon: "it breaks out into circular arches and embroidered scenes, into courts and cloisters, arcades and fountains, fantastic projections and lordly towers, and is . . . the most amusing of hotels."

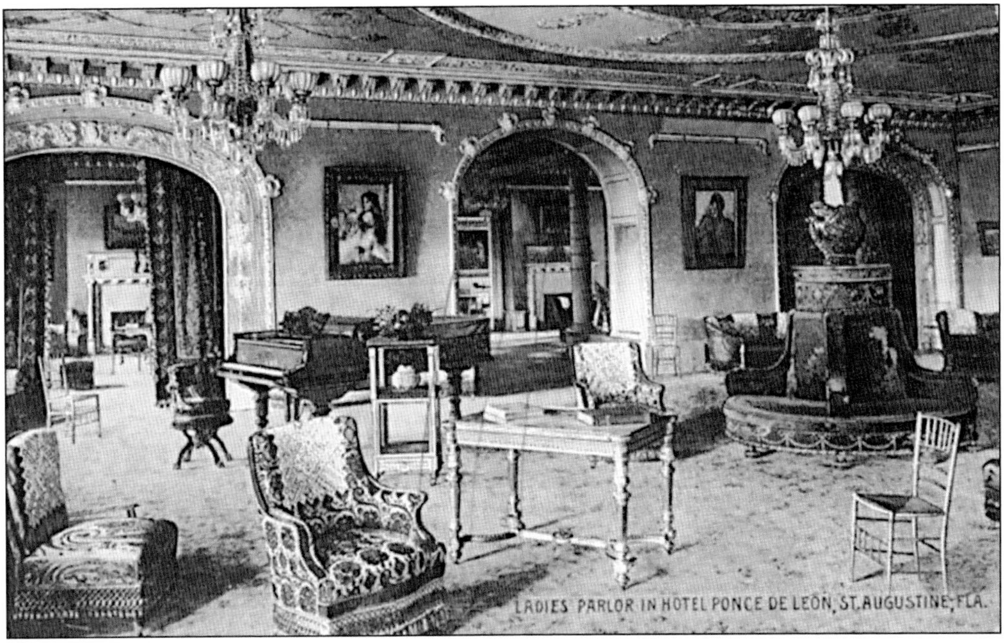

The walls of the Ponce de Leon's grand parlor, located at the west end of the first floor, featured paintings by many prominent artists. Flagler invited artists to take studios in a series of lofts facing Valencia Street at the rear of the hotel. The best known of these artists-in-residence were Martin Johnson Heade, Frank Shapleigh, George Seavey, H. A. Dyer, Felix de Crano, and W. Staples Drown.

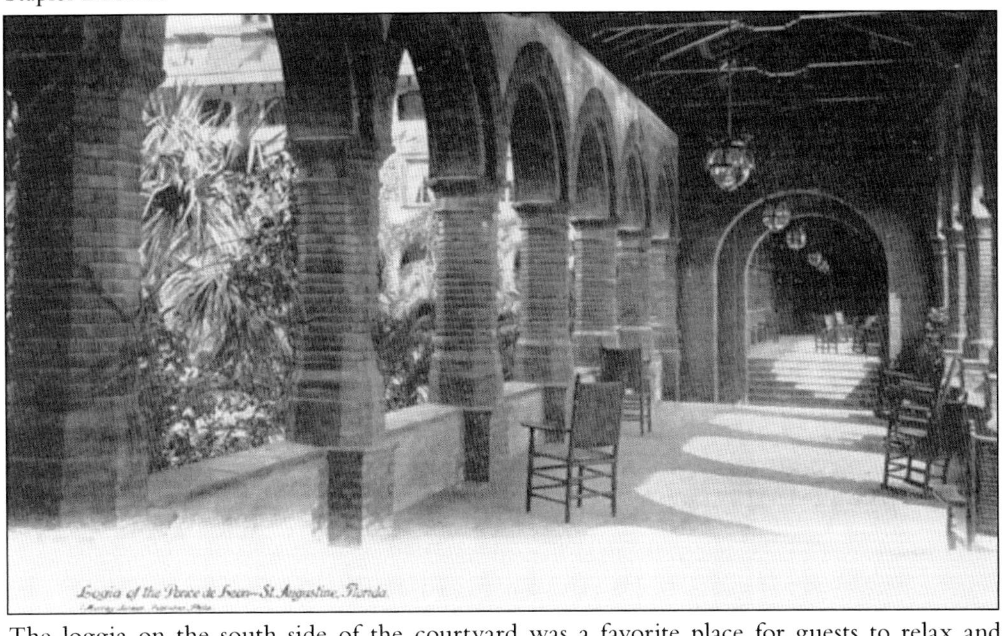

The loggia on the south side of the courtyard was a favorite place for guests to relax and enjoy the sun. After World War II, attendance at the Ponce de Leon continued to decline, and the hotel closed at the end of the 1967 season. Flagler heir Lawrence Lewis Jr. was the driving force behind the establishment of Flagler College, which opened in September 1968 in the former hotel.

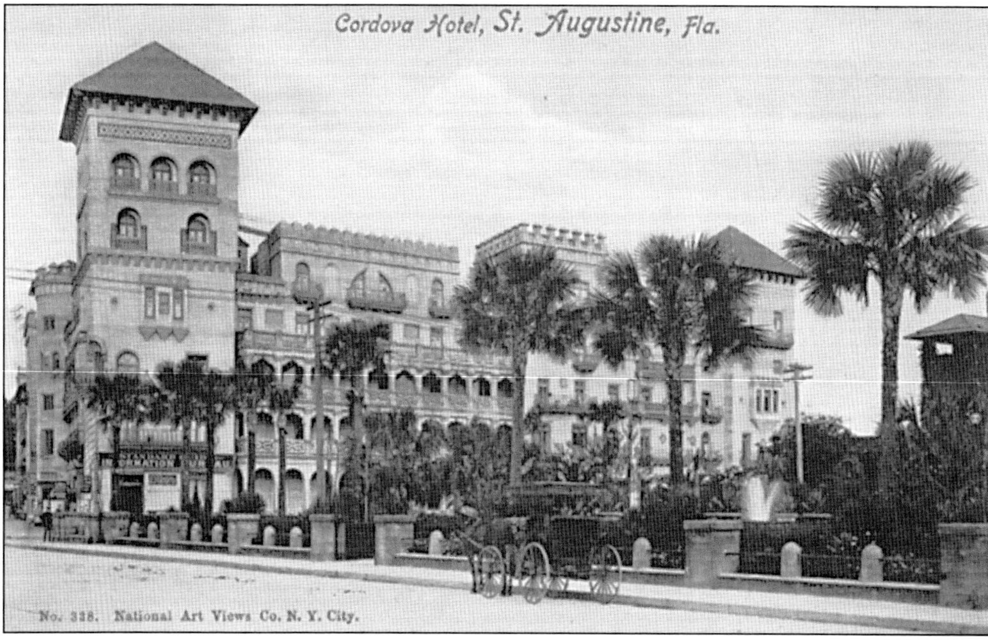

Franklin W. Smith opened the Casa Monica Hotel in January 1888. It was a financial failure after only four months' operation, and Smith sold it to his competitor, Henry Flagler, who renamed it the Cordova Hotel. The hotel closed in 1932 and was remodeled in 1968 to serve as the St. Johns County Courthouse. It has now been returned to its original use as the Casa Monica Hotel.

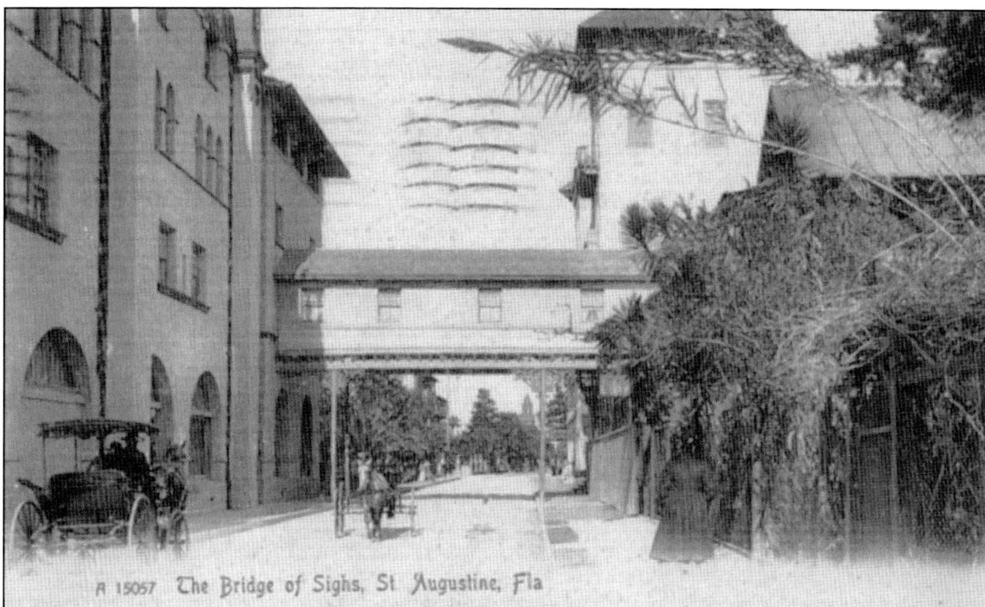

In 1903, a bridge was constructed over Cordova Street linking the Alcazar and Cordova Hotels, and the Cordova became the "Alcazar Annex." The bridge was removed in 1947, but its outline can still be seen on the northeast corner of the Alcazar, which now houses St. Augustine's city offices and the Lightner Museum.

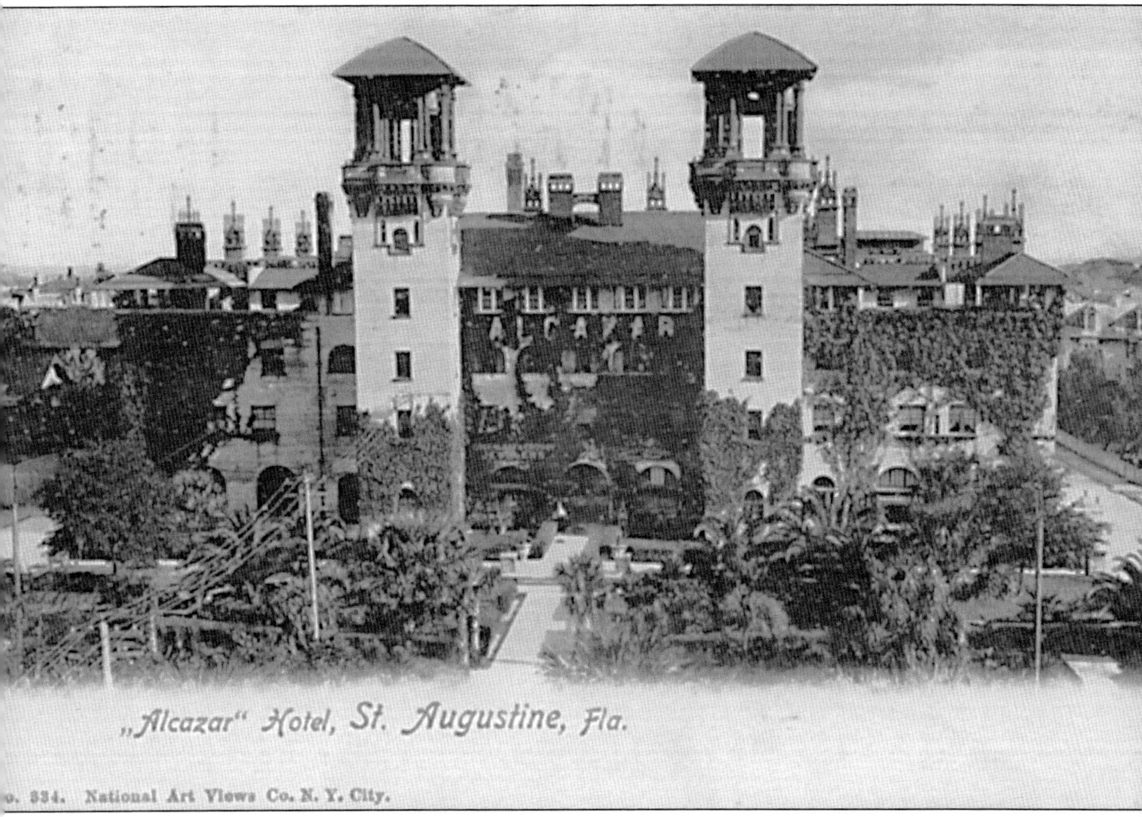

The Alcazar Hotel was built by Henry Flagler to be a more modest and less formal hotel than the Ponce de Leon. Construction began in May 1887, using the same poured concrete techniques as the Ponce, and the Alcazar opened on Christmas Day 1888. At first, the Alcazar had a small café that served only breakfast, but the hotel proved to be so popular that a formal dining room was soon added. The Alcazar was originally designed to have an ellipse of shops in front of the hotel. This was never constructed, although the foundations were laid and are still in place. Greenleaf and Crosby Jewelers can be seen just to the left of the Alcazar entrance in this 1905 postcard. This firm specialized in high-end souvenirs and had branches in Jacksonville, Daytona, Palm Beach, Miami, Nassau, and Hot Springs, Virginia.

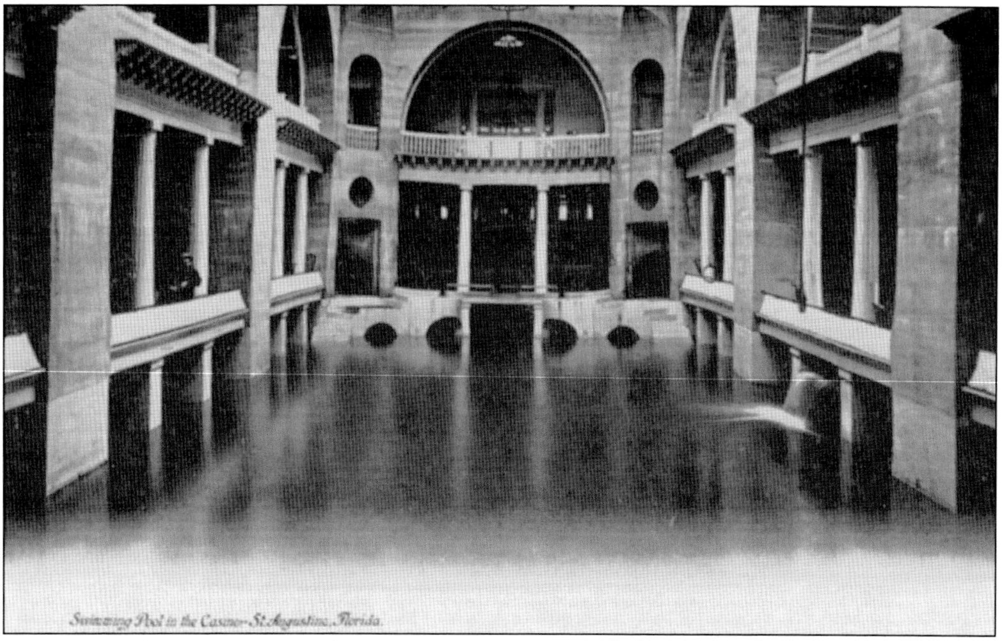

At the rear of the Alcazar was the casino, with a pool, gymnasium, and health baths for hotel guests. Water for the Alcazar pool came from a 1,400-foot artesian well that maintained a temperature above 80 degrees but smelled of sulfur. The pool was 120 feet long, 50 feet wide, and covered by a glass roof that could be opened. A café and several antique shops now occupy the pool area.

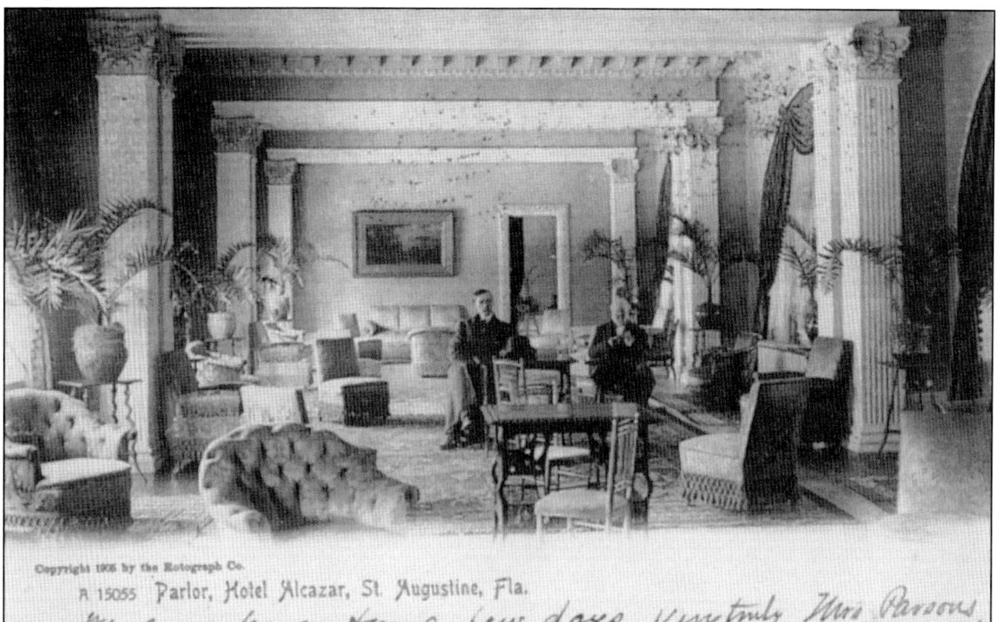

The first-floor parlor of the Alcazar was a popular spot for guests to relax. The Alcazar was closed in 1932 and stood vacant until Otto Lightner purchased the building in 1947 for his Museum of Hobbies. In 1971, the hotel was renovated to serve as offices for the City of St. Augustine, and this parlor is now the city commission meeting room.

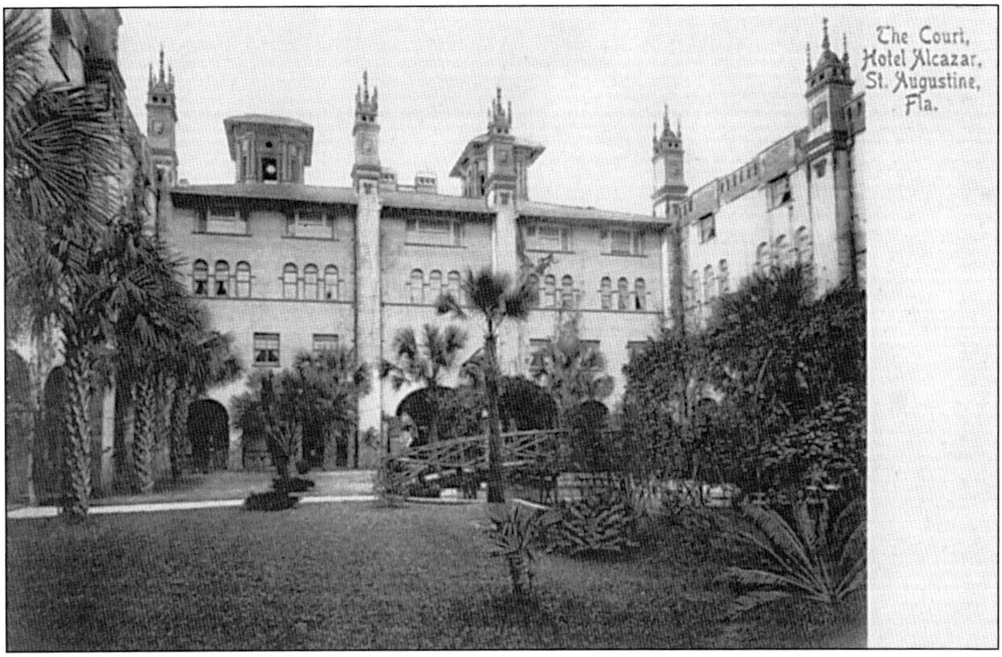

The central portion of the Alcazar contained an open courtyard, with an arcade of shops on the ground floor. A rustic wooden bridge spanned the pond in the center of the courtyard. The wooden bridge was replaced by a stone structure in 1948, soon after Otto Lightner purchased the vacant building to house his collection of hobbies.

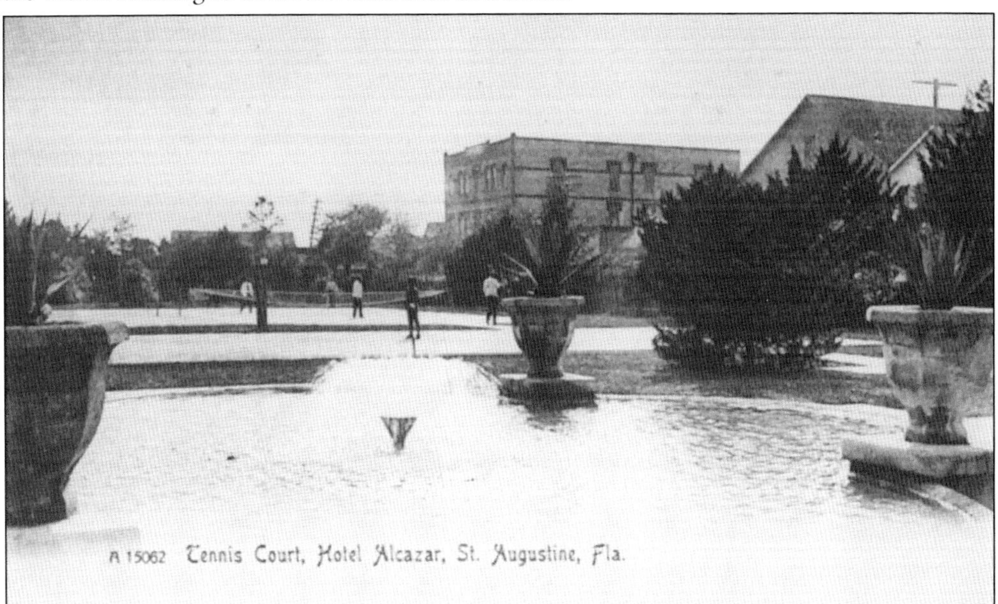

Four asphalt tennis courts were constructed behind the Alcazar Casino, and Henry Flagler sponsored the Tropical Tennis Tournament beginning in 1888. The tournament drew many of the top-ranked players in the country to contest for a fabulous trophy—a huge sterling silver replica of the City Gate. Bicycling became a popular craze, and the tennis courts were also used as a bicycle academy for instruction of the Alcazar's guests.

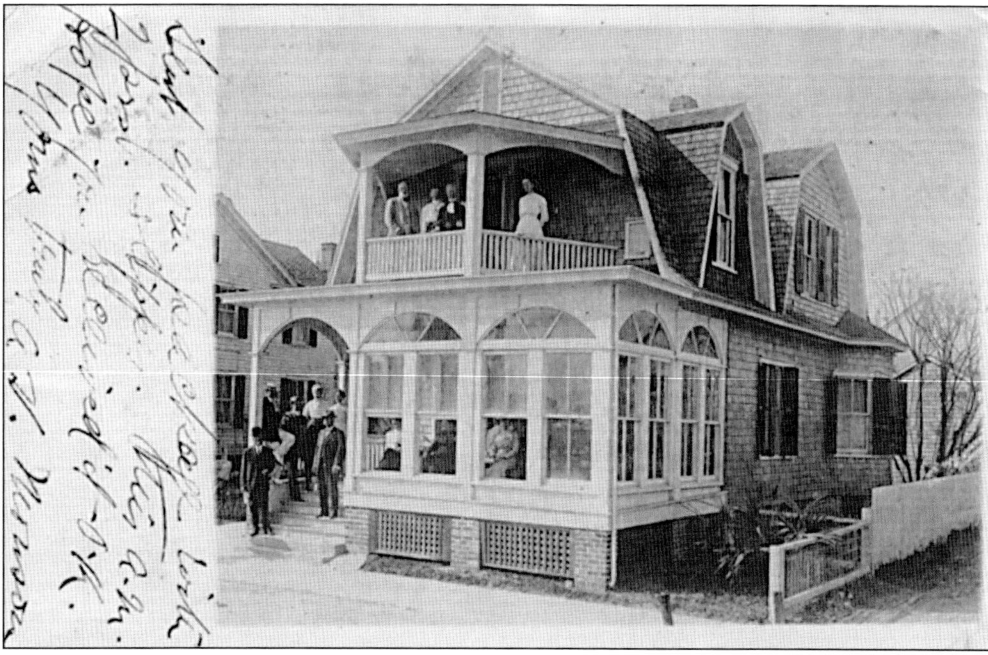

This is the second Monson House, located at 26 Bay Street (Avenida Menendez), the first having fallen victim to fire in 1895. Owner A. V. Monson used this postcard to write a forgetful guest: "Sent your package with 2 prs. slippers this A.M. Hope you received it O.K."

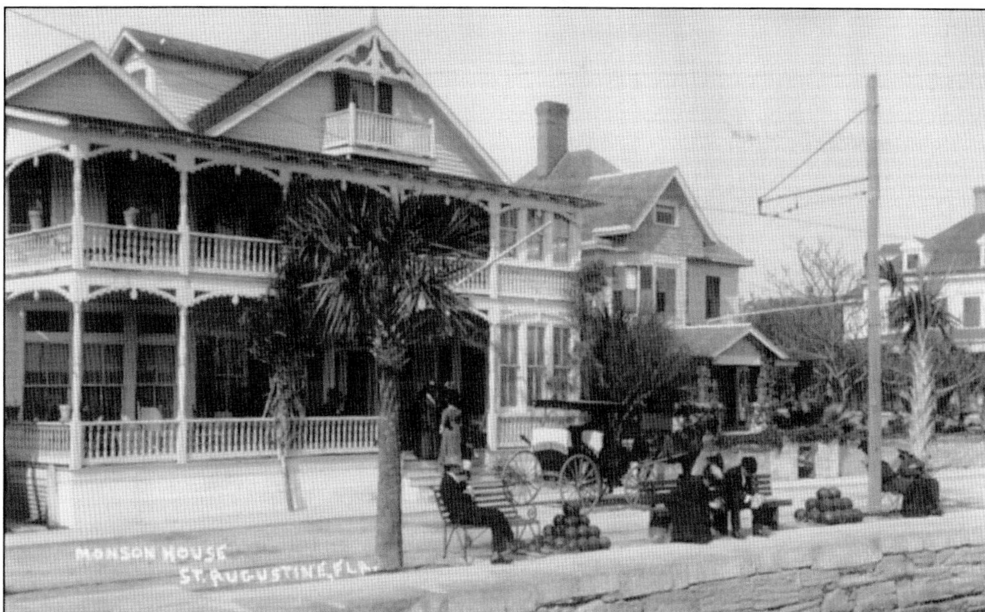

The Monson House became a very popular waterfront hostelry and was enlarged in 1901. It was destroyed in the April 2, 1914, fire and replaced by a masonry structure in 1915. The Monson Hotel would remain one of St. Augustine's landmarks until 1960, when it was razed and replaced by the Monson Motor Lodge. This motel and its pool were the site of 1964 civil rights demonstrations led by Dr. Martin Luther King Jr.

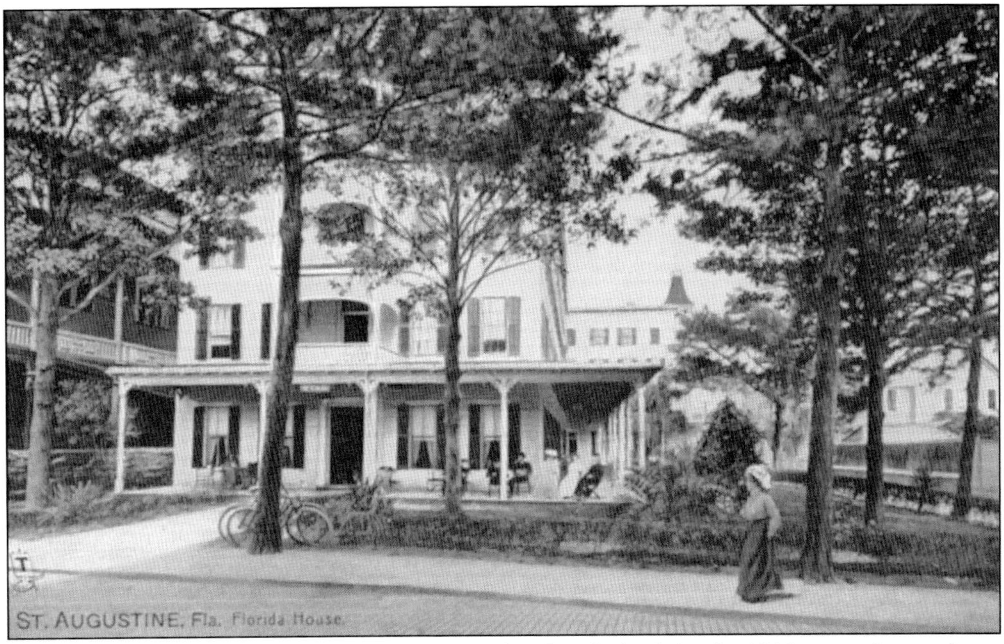

The Florida House was one of St. Augustine's first hotels, built in the 1830s near the northeast corner of St. George and Treasury Streets. In this view, a woman is walking north on St. George Street with Treasury Street to the right. The disastrous fire of 1914 began in the Florida House, and the hotel was completely destroyed in the blaze.

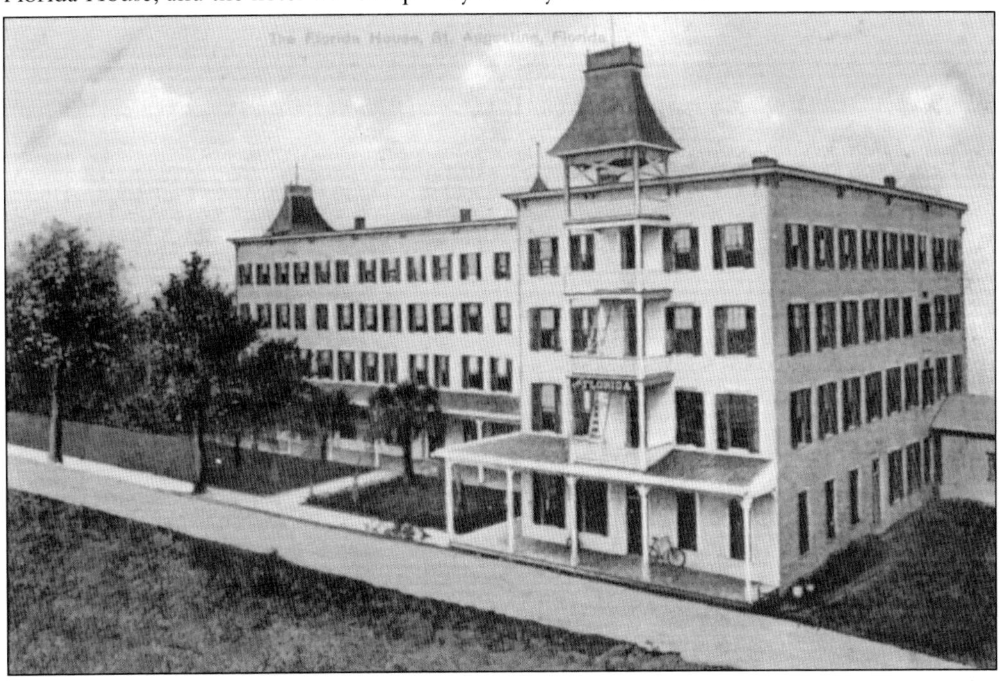

In the 1870s, the Florida House was enlarged with an addition to the east, as shown in this view along Treasury Street. A 1910 advertisement touted the Florida as having "more southern exposure than any hotel in the city." From 1907 until 1912, the hotel was managed by John B. O'Connor and had rates of $2.50 per day and up.

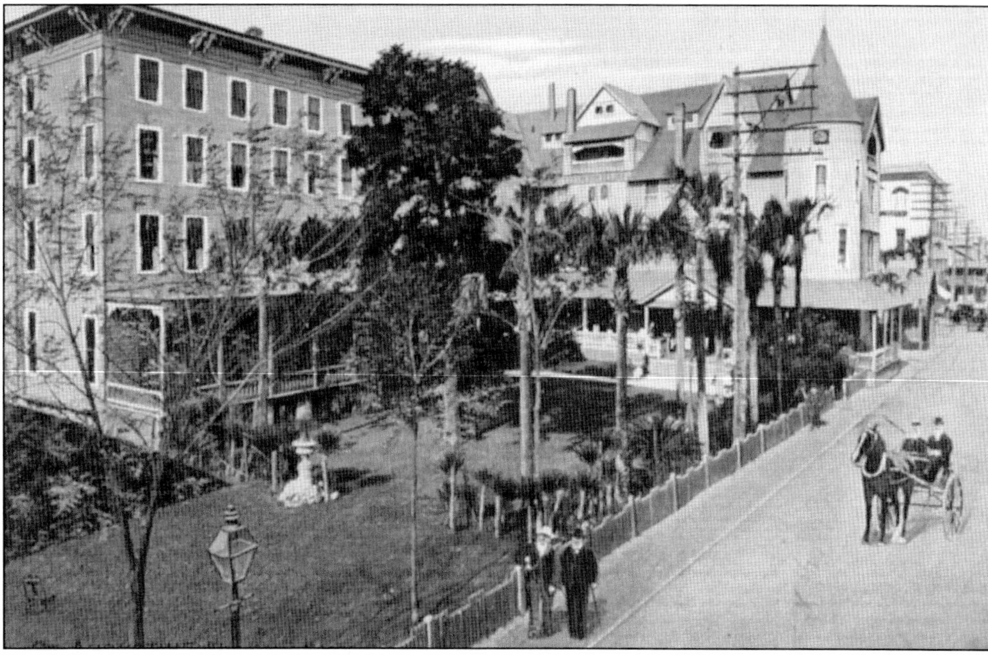

Burroughs E. Carr built the Hotel Magnolia in 1847, near the southwest corner of St. George and Hypolita Streets. Originally constructed in a territorial style, the Magnolia evolved through a variety of architectural styles and additions. This view shows the hotel around 1910, after the Magnolia was enlarged and remodeled in Queen Anne style with a large round tower overlooking St. George Street.

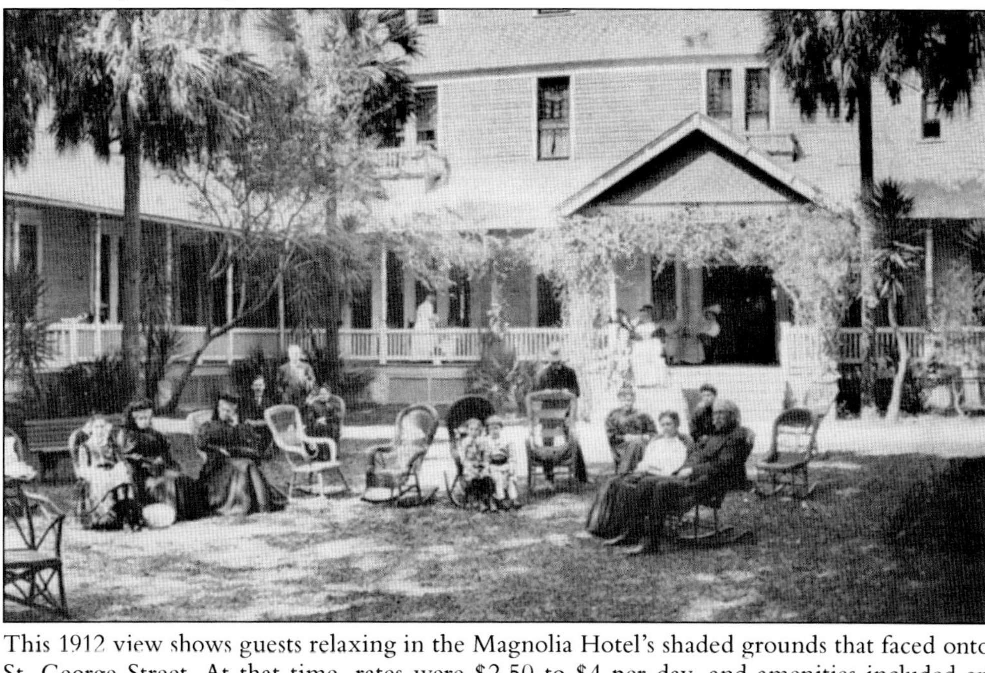

This 1912 view shows guests relaxing in the Magnolia Hotel's shaded grounds that faced onto St. George Street. At that time, rates were $2.50 to $4 per day, and amenities included an orchestra that played twice daily. The hotel burned on December 26, 1926, and the site is now occupied by retail businesses at 100 through 110 St. George Street.

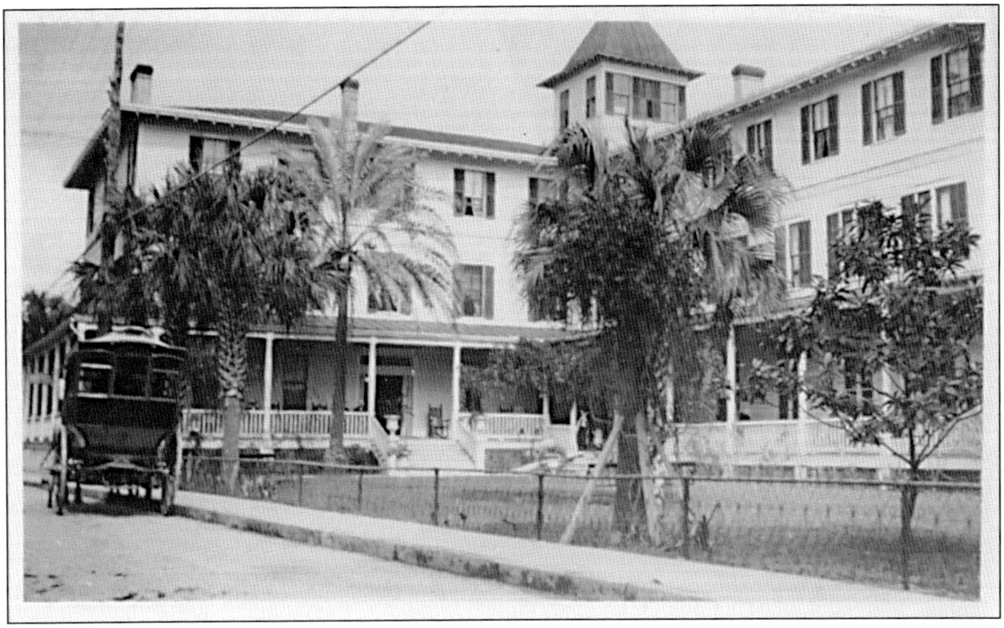

The Hotel St. George was located at 207 St. George Street between Trinity Episcopal Church and Artillery Lane. L. H. Tyler began operating his residence as a family hotel in the late 1800s and later enlarged it to become the Hotel St. George. A 1902 newspaper advertisement lists F. S. Tyler as the proprietor and manager, offering "rooms for 150 guests at $2.50 per day and up."

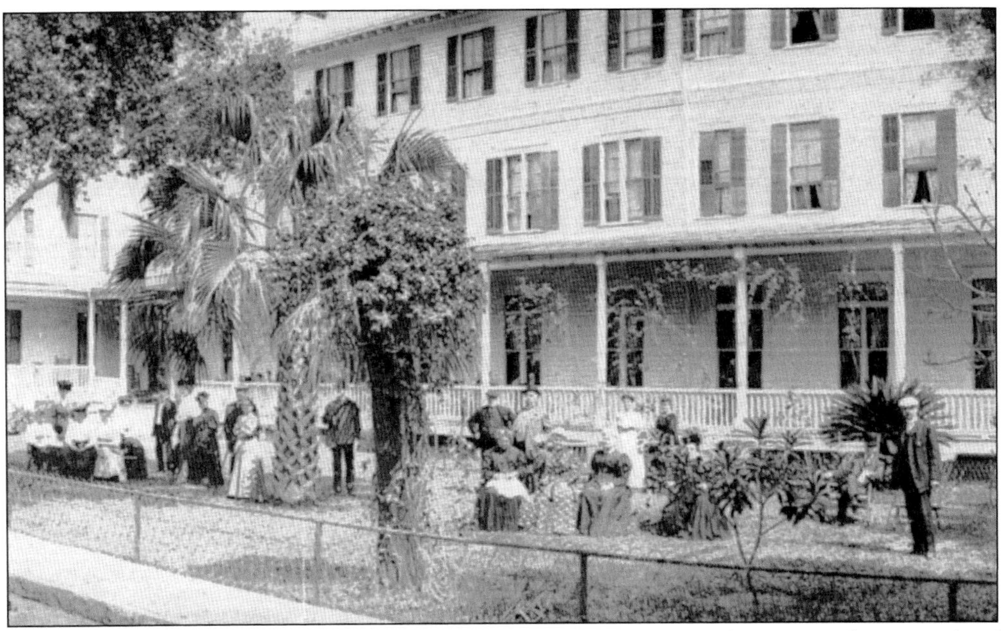

This 1907 view looking north toward King Street shows guests relaxing on the grounds of the Hotel St. George. In 1941, Trinity Episcopal Church purchased the property and razed the hotel, uncovering the coquina foundations of an earlier structure that was once the home of the Angulo family. The site is now the parish hall of Trinity Episcopal Church.

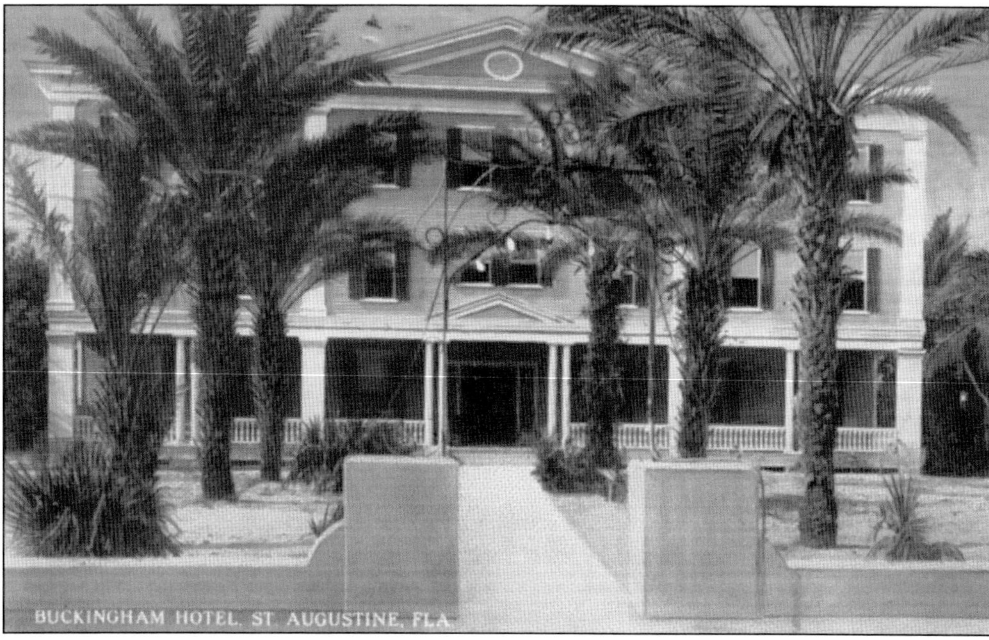

The Buckingham Hotel at 16 Granada Street was built in the 1870s as a nursing home for blacks, at the bequest of Buckingham Smith, a diplomat and historian from St. Augustine. In 1883, it became an industrial school for blacks and was then leased as a hotel after 1894. Closed in 1964, the Buckingham is now the site of the Flagler College gymnasium.

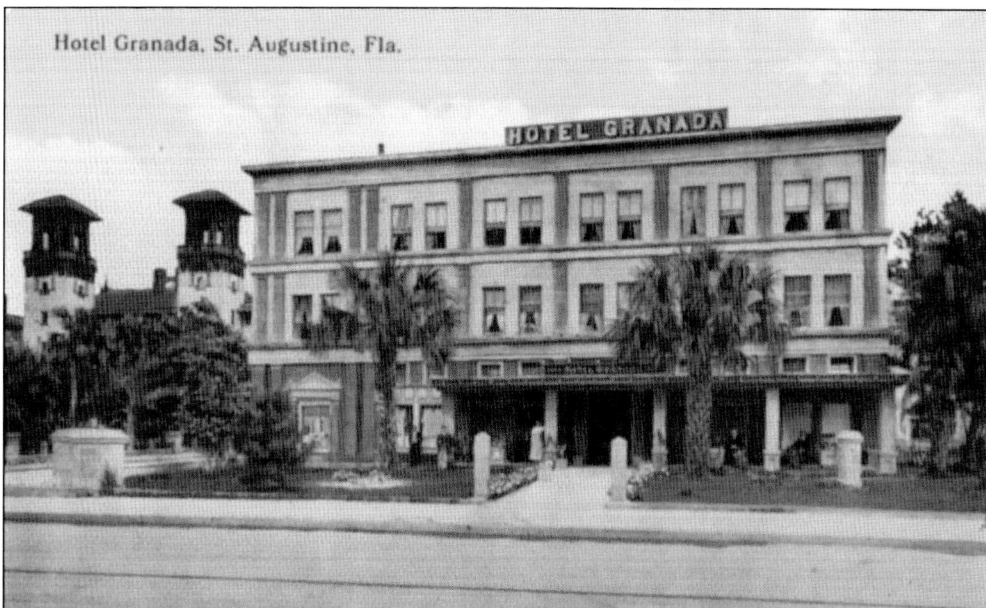

The Hotel Granada opened in February 1895 at the southwest corner of King and Granada Streets and was one of the few hotels in St. Augustine that operated on a year-round basis. The Mussallem family purchased the hotel in 1913 and changed the name to the Hotel Alhambra. The hotel was destroyed by fire on September 21, 1954, and the site is now a bank and shopping complex.

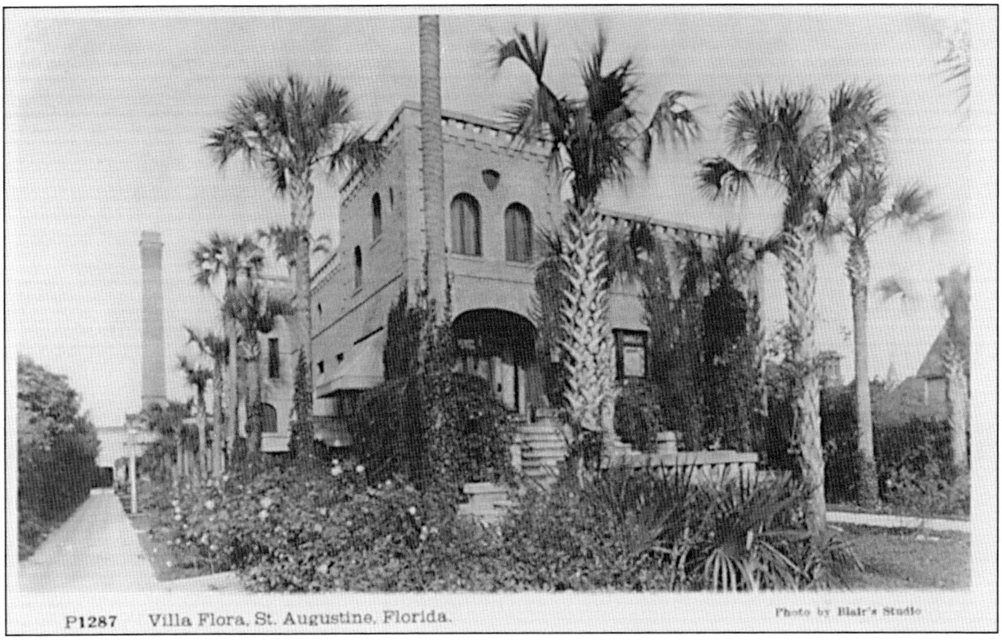

Rev. and Mrs. Olaf A. Weenolsen, winter residents from Minneapolis, built the Villa Flora at 234 St. George Street in 1898. After 1906, Bessie O. H. Wood operated it as a hotel for many years. The Sisters of St. Joseph bought the house in the 1940s, using it as classrooms for St. Joseph's Academy, and today the Villa Flora is a residence hall for nuns.

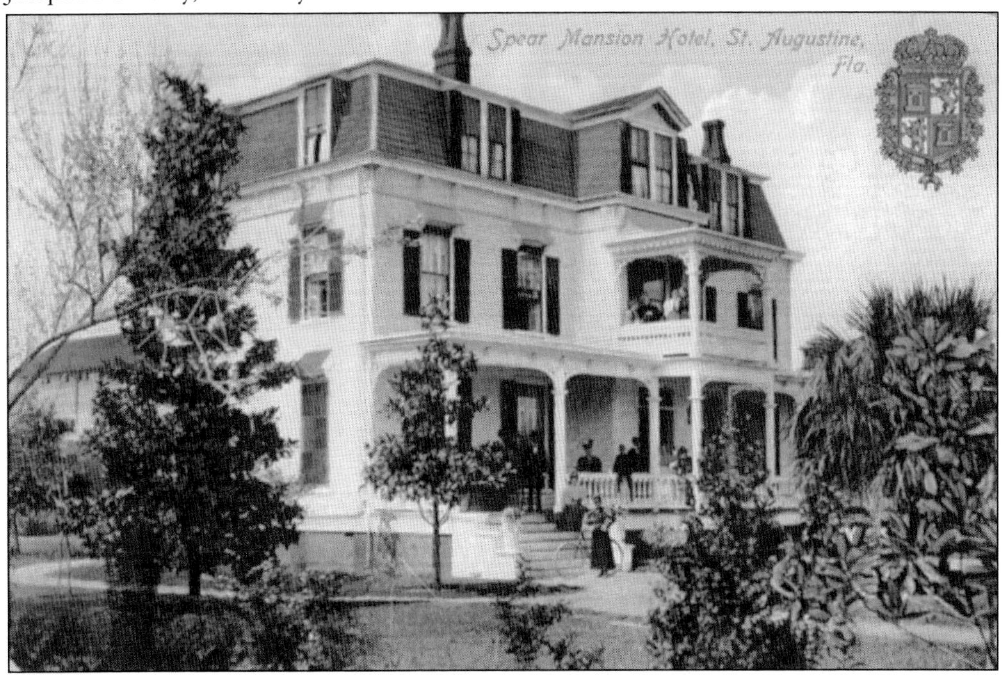

Capt. Thomas F. House, who also built the Lorrillard Villa and Sunnyside Hotel, constructed the Spear Mansion at 240 St. George Street. It was the home of John Howard; later his daughter, Julia Spear, operated it as a hotel. In 1938, the Sisters of St. Joseph purchased the property and demolished the mansion. They built tennis courts on the site, and now use it as a parking lot.

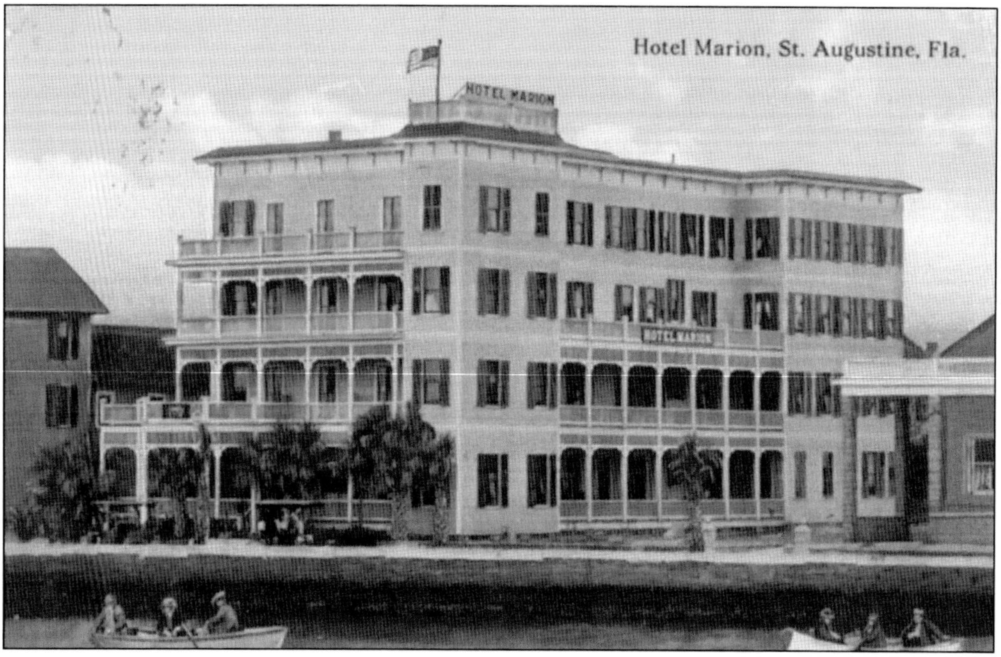

Owner Henry Mueller doubled the size of the Hotel Marion at 128 Bay Street (Avenida Menendez) with the 1910 addition shown in this postcard. A fourth story was added, and the building enlarged westward along Bravo Lane to Marine Street. The Hotel Marion was torn down in 1962 and replaced by the Marion Motor Lodge.

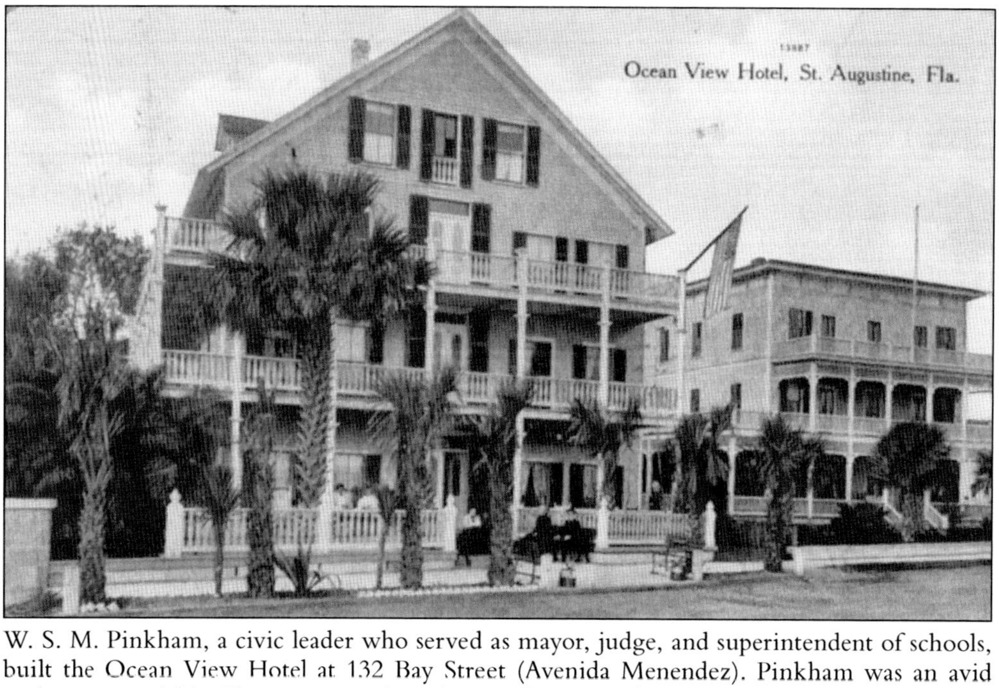

W. S. M. Pinkham, a civic leader who served as mayor, judge, and superintendent of schools, built the Ocean View Hotel at 132 Bay Street (Avenida Menendez). Pinkham was an avid yachtsman, and his *Cheemaun* was the winner of many sailing regattas on the bay. Around 1911, Henry E. Hernandez purchased the Ocean View, and the site is now the location of the Bayfront Inn.

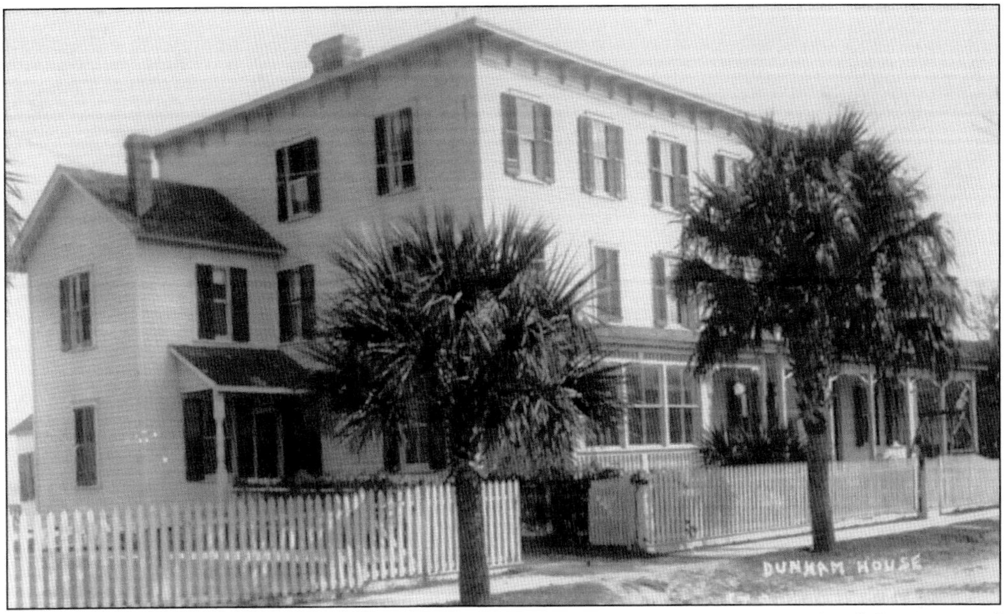

The Dunham House was located on the bay at 131 Marine Street, just south of the National Cemetery. Owners Donald and Lillie Dunham operated it during the winter season and also ran the Dunham House in Waynesville, North Carolina, in the summer months. In 1911, it featured "modern sanitation," with rates of $1.50 to $2 per day. The site is now occupied by a home constructed shortly after World War II.

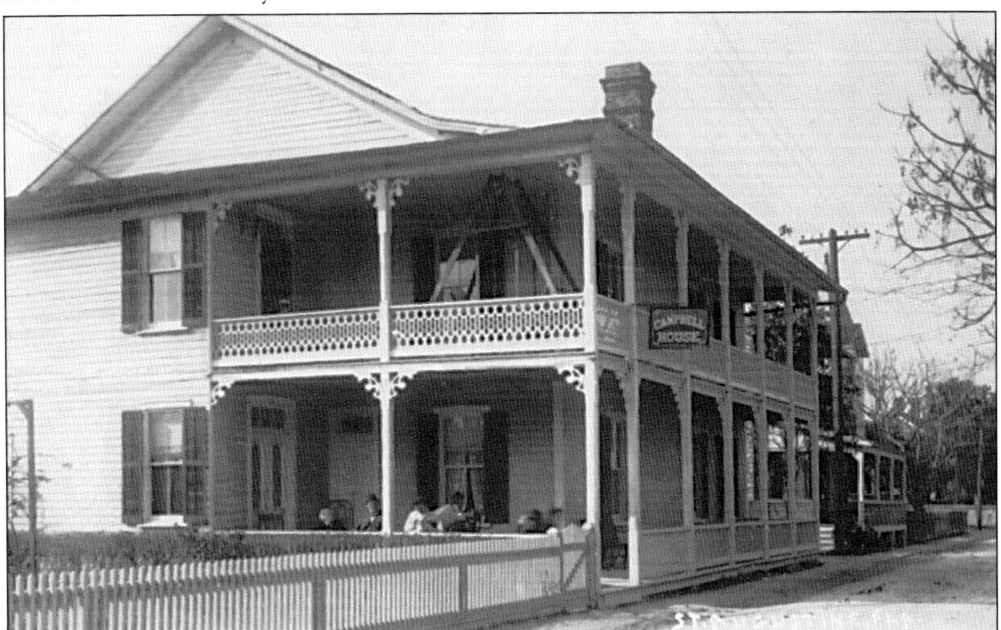

John T. Campbell operated this guesthouse at 50 Marine Street. In 1912, it advertised "perfect sanitary arrangements, central location, and excellent cuisine, with rates of $2 per day." It also boasted "overlooking bay and ocean"—but it was one block from the bay and a considerable distance from the Atlantic! A modern home has been constructed on the site of the Campbell House.

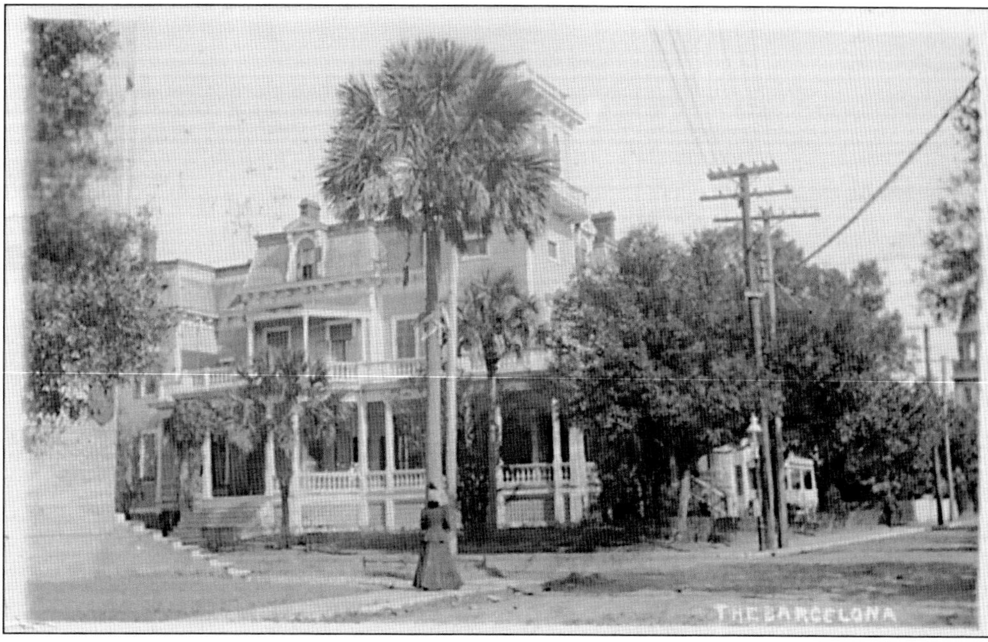

The Barcelona Hotel was built in 1874 as the home of Henry Ball, a wealthy New York jeweler. The house was originally located at the site of 20 Valencia Street but was moved around 1890 to the northeast corner of Sevilla and Carrera Streets and enlarged to become the Barcelona Hotel. It was demolished in 1962, and the site is now the parking lot of the Ancient City Baptist Church.

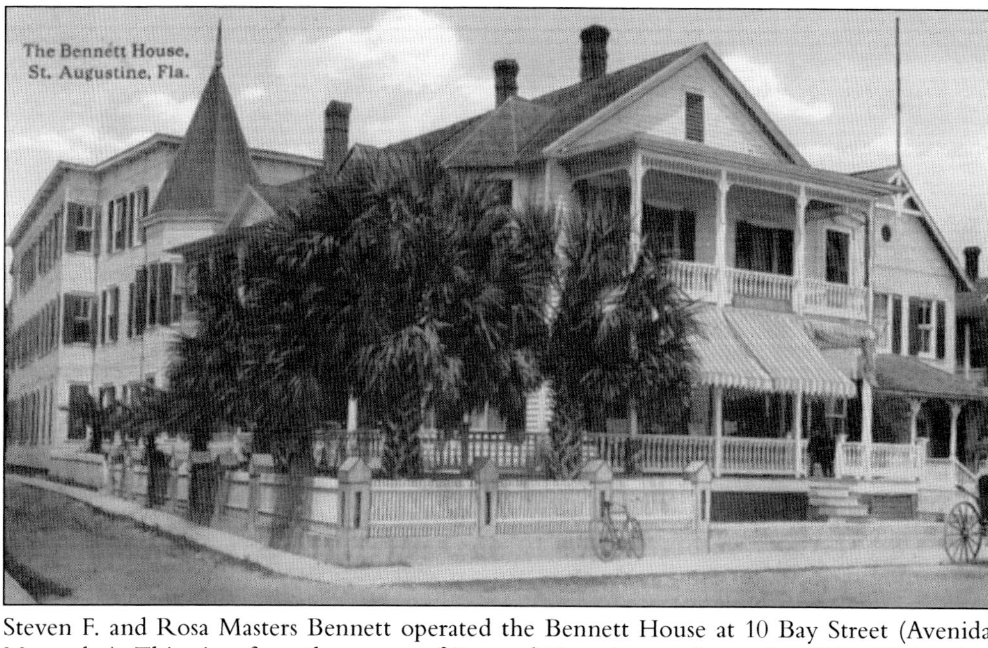

Steven F. and Rosa Masters Bennett operated the Bennett House at 10 Bay Street (Avenida Menendez). This view from the corner of Bay and Cuna Streets shows the 1911 addition that expanded the Bennett west to Charlotte Street. The hotel was demolished in 1961 when the National Park Service purchased the property to reroute Fort Marion Circle and enlarge the visitors' parking lot at the fort. (Connahey collection.)

Looking north toward the City Gate, the Abbey Hotel at 21 St. George Street is the large building on the right with the tower. Originally owned by Mrs. A. B. Abbe, it later became the Northern Hotel and then the New Arlington Hotel. It burned in the 1920s, and the site is now the reconstructed Gallegos House in the Colonial Spanish Quarter.

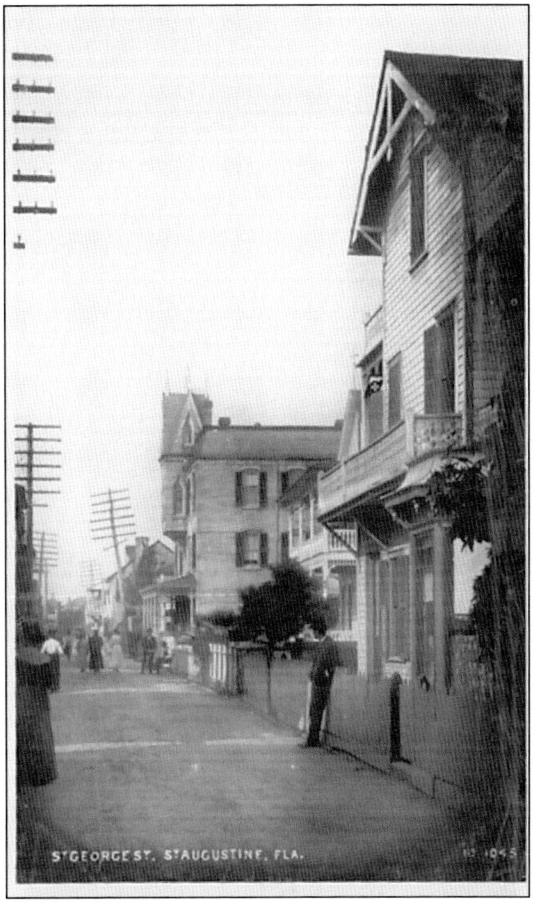

The hotel at 11 King Street occupied the entire block between Hospital (Aviles) Street and Charlotte Street. In 1899, it was operated by C. F. Cox as the Algonquin Hotel. By 1907, it was the Hotel Chautauqua and operated by Margaret Crittenden, who ran the Colonial Cottage at Chautauqua, New York, during the summer season. The State of Florida reconstructed a territorial-style building on the site in 1964.

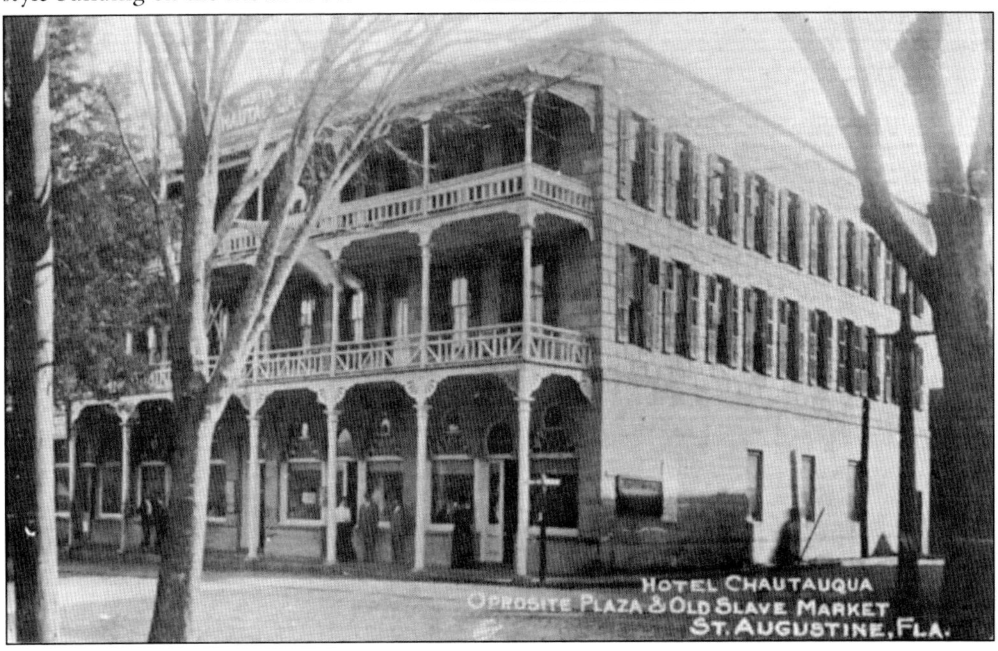

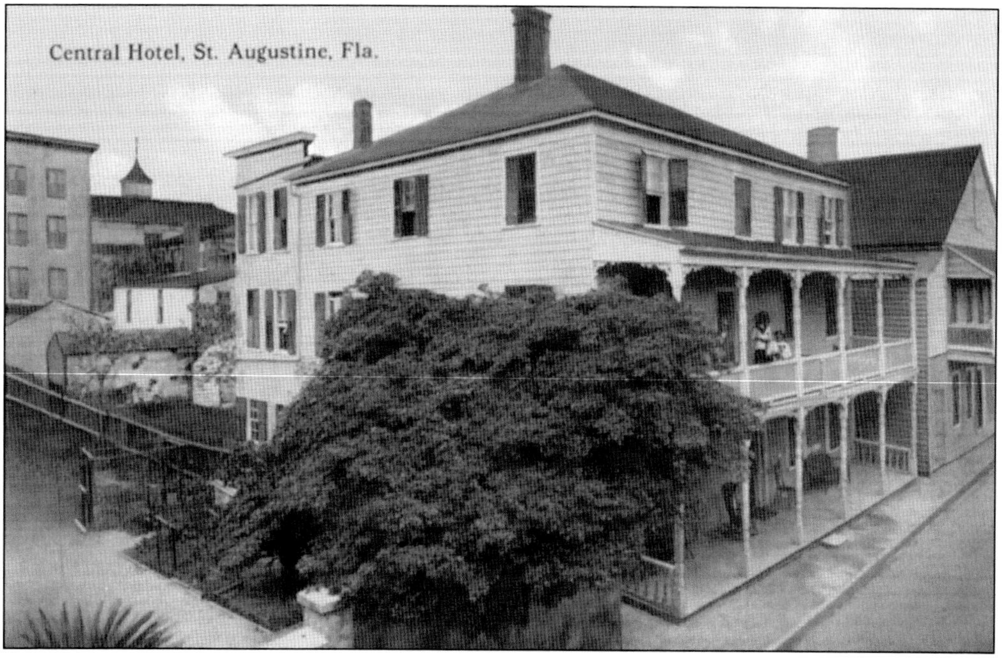

The Central Hotel was located at 84 Charlotte Street, just north of the intersection of Treasury Street. Henry E. Hernandez owned the hotel until around 1910, when he sold it and purchased the Ocean View Hotel. The Central was one of six hotels destroyed in the 1914 fire. (Connahey collection.)

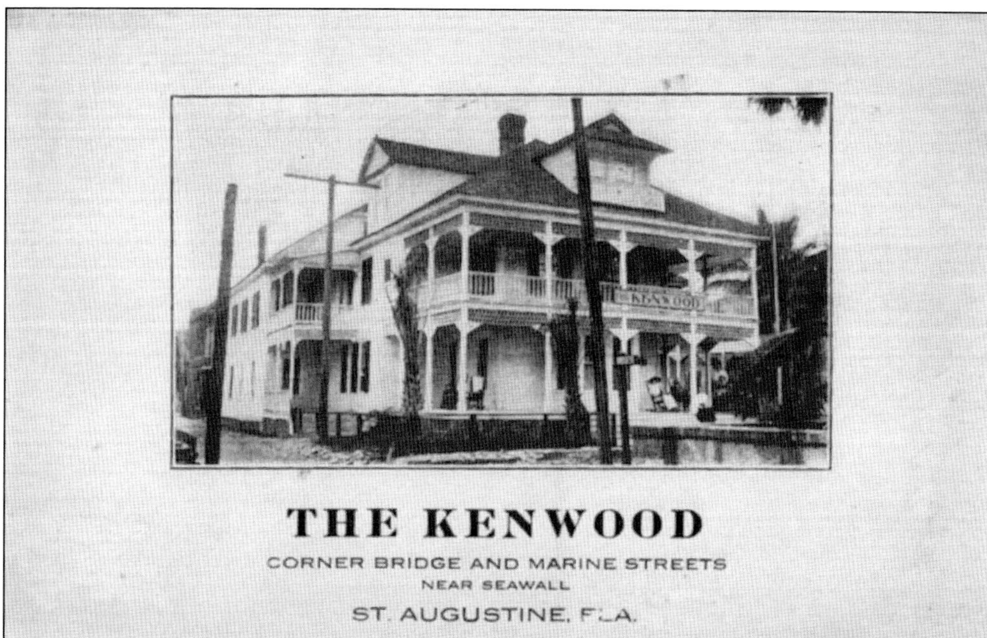

The Kenwood, built in 1886 at the northwest corner of Bridge and Marine Streets, was known as the Hotel La Borde until around 1910, when it was sold to Margaret Morgan. It is still in operation today as a bed-and-breakfast at 38 Marine Street. (Connahey collection.)

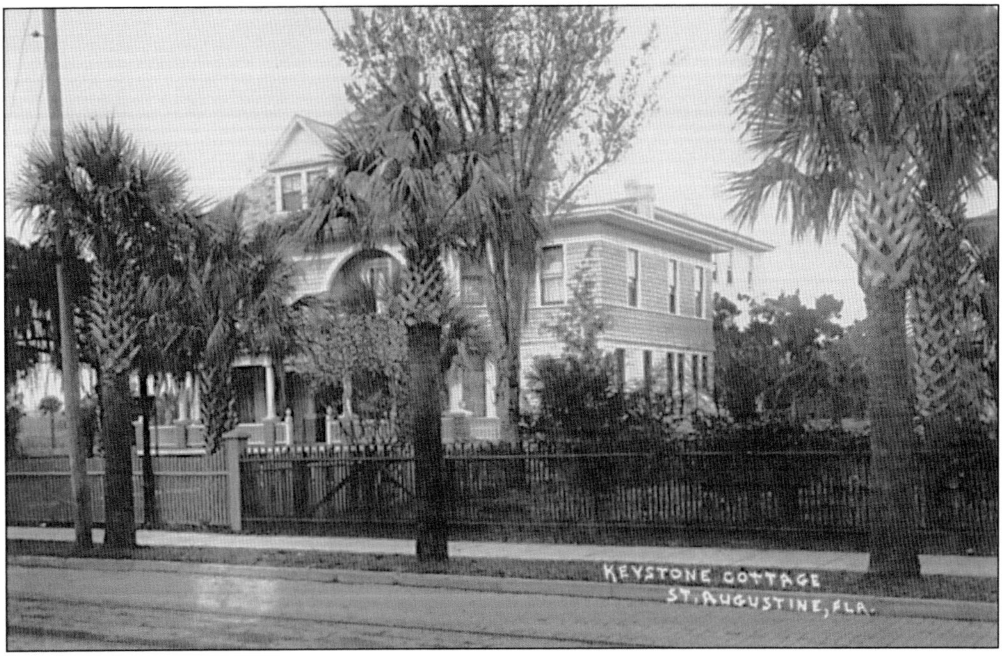

Lou J. Boyes operated the Keystone Cottage at 112 King Street; it was later remodeled and enlarged to become the Keystone Apartments. In 1913, the Keystone advertised "tasteful rooms and a trolley stop at the front door." The site is now the parking lot on the east side of the First Methodist Church.

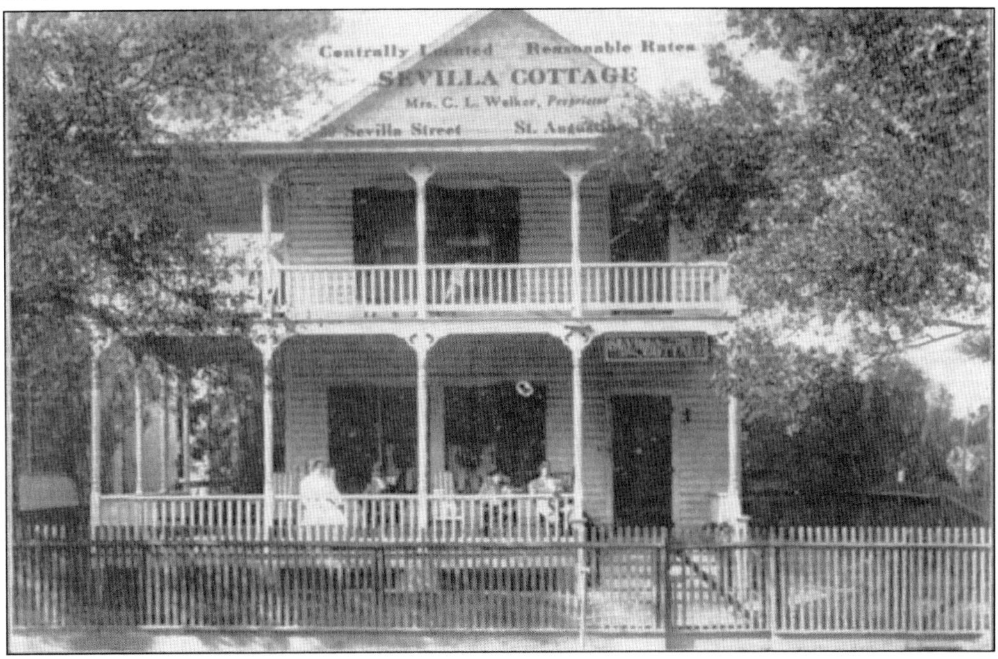

The Sevilla Cottage was operated by Charles L. Walker and offered furnished rooms at 30 Sevilla Street. It was located next door to the Ancient City Baptist Church, and by 1940, it was used as the Sunday school building for the church. The building was razed, and the site is now part of the educational complex north of the church.

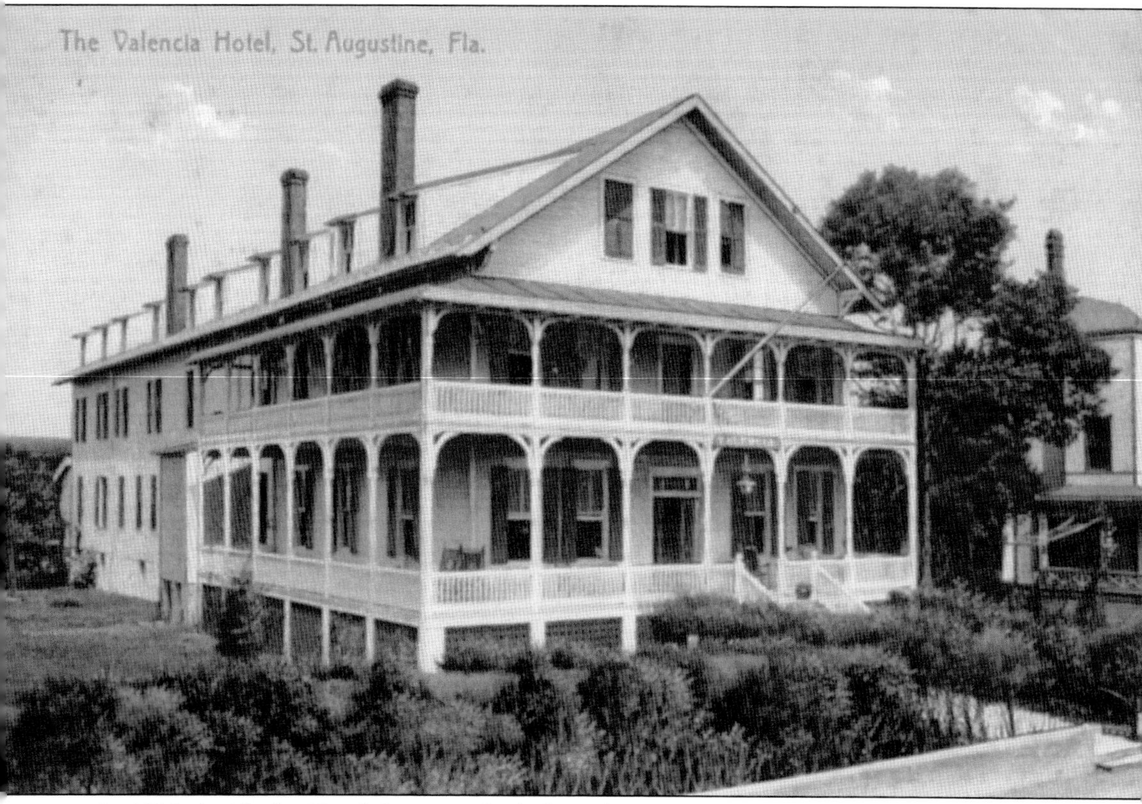

In 1892, the Flagler Hotel Company built the Valencia Hotel as an annex to the Hotel Ponce de Leon. Carrere and Hastings, architects of the Ponce de Leon, also designed the Valencia, and the door hardware matched that of the Ponce. The decorative molding used on the ceilings in the lounge and foyer was left over from the construction of the larger hotel. The Valencia's most famous guest was Pres. Theodore Roosevelt, who was feted at a seafood dinner on October 21, 1905. In later years, the name was changed to the Alencia Hotel, to avoid confusion with the Valencia Apartments. The location at 276 St. George Street is now the parking lot for the St. Francis Inn, but the low concrete wall and iron gate of the Valencia still stand. Two of the cottages from the Valencia, named Wendy and Peter, still survive. (Connahey collection.)

Two

Churches and Schools

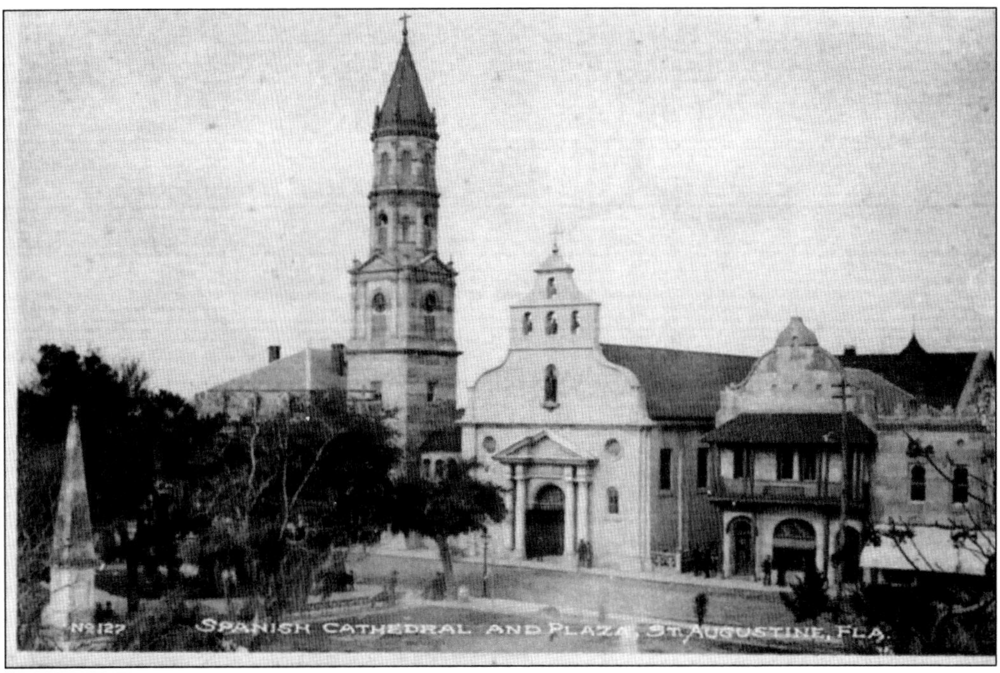

Construction of the Spanish mission–style cathedral was begun in 1793 and completed in 1797. On Tuesday, April 12, 1887, the cathedral was gutted by a fire that also destroyed the nearby St. Augustine Hotel. The thick coquina walls and facade of the church were relatively unharmed, and the church was rebuilt with the help of architect James Renwick, who happened to be staying in St. Augustine at the time of the fire. Renwick was the architect of St. Patrick's Cathedral in New York City and offered his services in the restoration. He designed the beautiful bell tower, which was a gift from Henry Flagler. Renwick removed the clock from the facade of the cathedral to create a niche for a statue of St. Augustine, and a new town clock was installed in the bell tower.

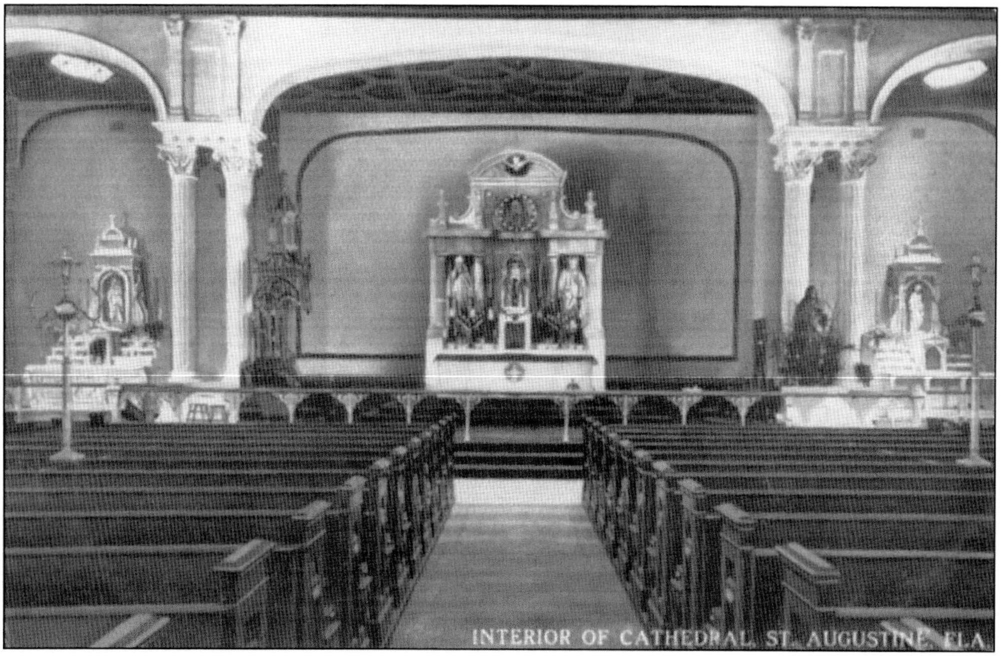

This postcard shows the interior of the cathedral around 1910. It would remain essentially the same until 1965, when the cathedral was remodeled for the 400th anniversary of the founding of St. Augustine. The wooden ceiling seen here was removed and the roof jacked up, and an open-truss system was used to give a loftier appearance to the interior.

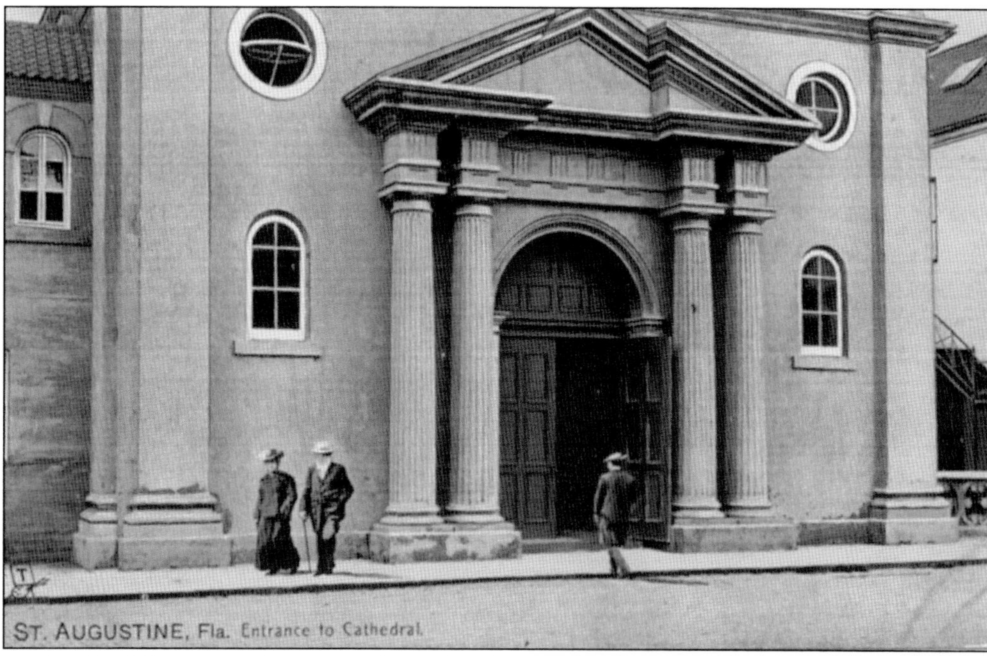

Notice the fish-eye windows on either side of the entrance to the cathedral, one of which is open for ventilation. These were removed when the church was remodeled in 1965, but their outlines are still faintly visible on the front wall. The parish records of the cathedral are the oldest written church records of American origin in the United States.

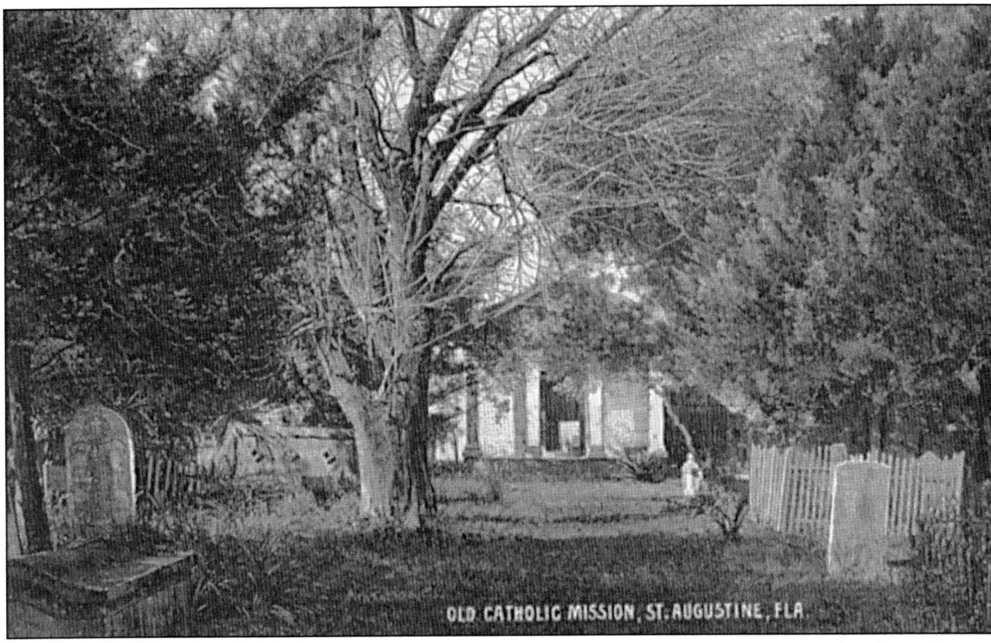

This view entitled "Old Catholic Mission" is the Tolomato Cemetery on Cordova Street. The site was originally a Native American village and Franciscan mission. During the British period, Catholics used it as a cemetery, and it served that purpose until closed in 1884. Cuban patriots built the mortuary chapel, shown here at the rear of the cemetery, for Fr. Felix Varela, who died in 1853.

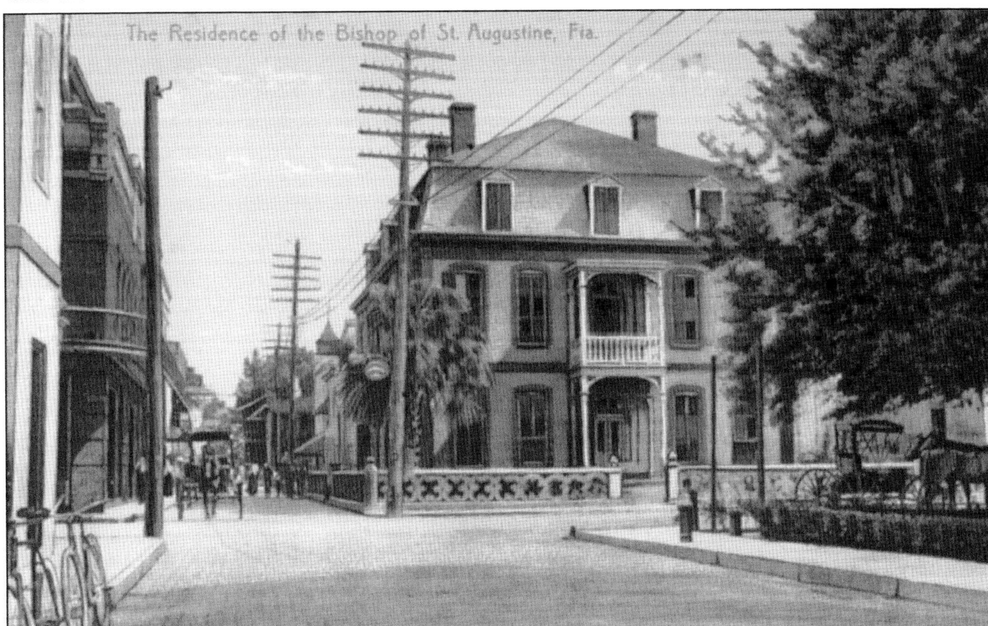

The bishop's house and rectory was built in the 1870s on the west side of the cathedral, at the corner of St. George Street and Cathedral Place. Architect James Renwick designed the distinctive concrete fence that surrounded the property. The bishop's house was demolished in 1965, and a portion of Renwick's fence is now in front of a home at 262 St. George Street.

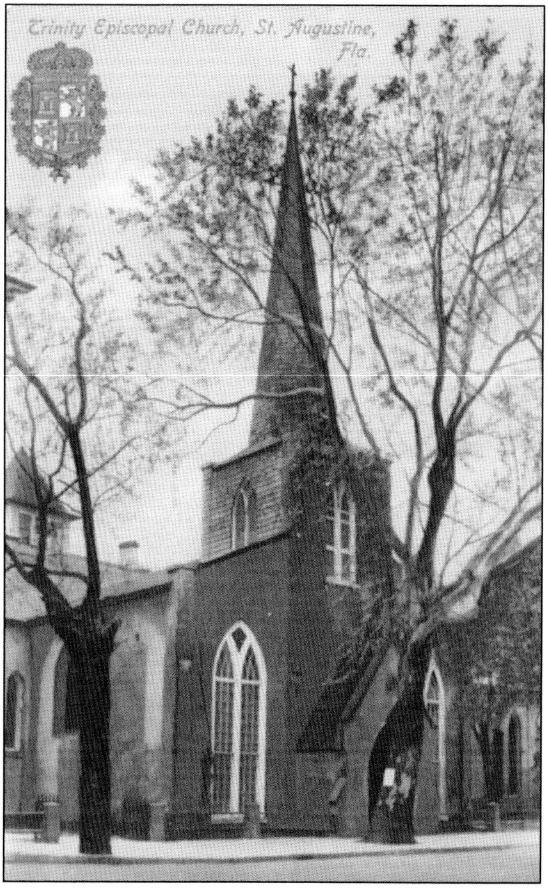

Trinity Episcopal Parish was established in 1821, soon after Florida became a territory, and is the oldest Protestant church in the state. The original building was constructed in 1830–1831 and is an early example of the Gothic Revival style. The church faced King Street, and the building was oriented in a north-south direction. This view from King Street shows the original entrance to the church with its familiar spire.

In 1902–1903, Trinity Episcopal Church was remodeled and enlarged to its present cruciform structure. The main entrance now faces St. George Street, with the nave running in an east-west direction. The church contains 28 stained-glass windows, including one signed by Louis Comfort Tiffany in St. Peter's Chapel, the north section of the original building.

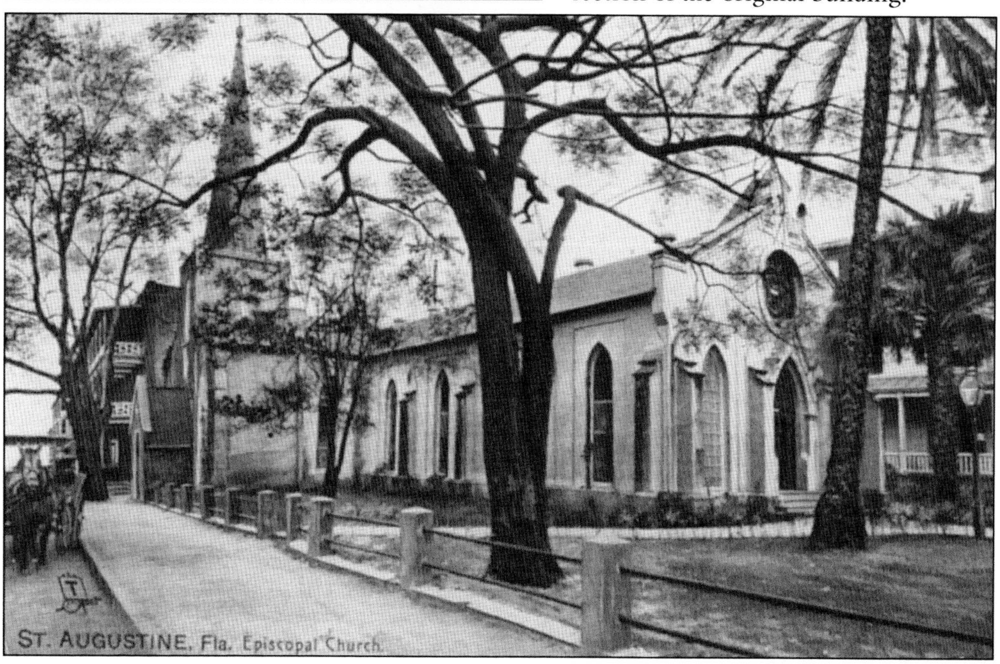

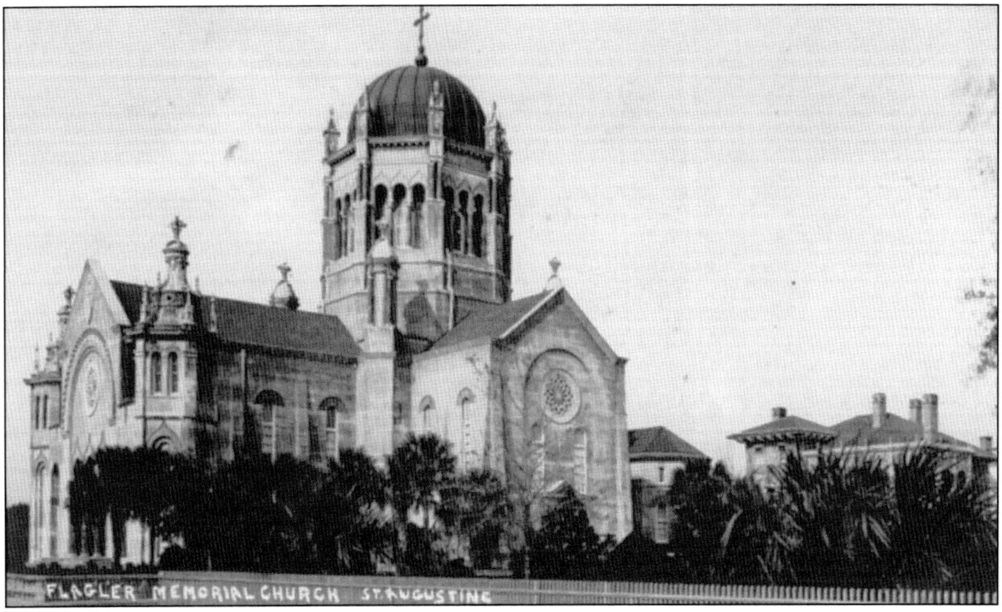

Henry Flagler built the Memorial Presbyterian Church in memory of his daughter, Jennie Louise Benedict, who died in 1889 soon after giving birth. The Venetian Renaissance Revival church was designed by Carrere and Hastings, architects for Flagler's Ponce de Leon Hotel. Contractors Maguire and MacDonald completed the building in less than a year, using the same poured concrete construction techniques employed in the Ponce de Leon.

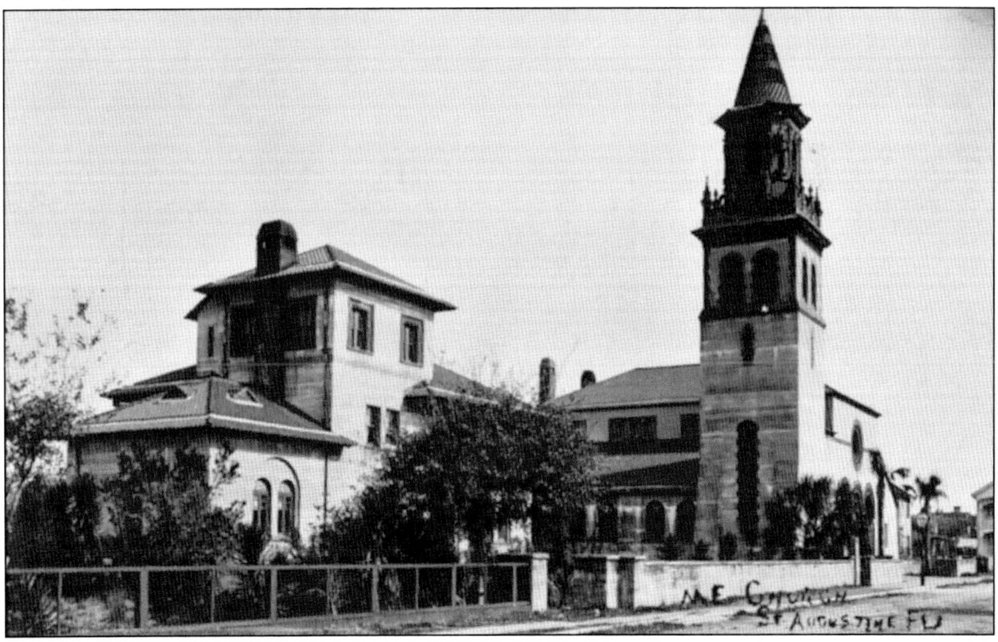

The Olivet Methodist Episcopal Church was located near the corner of King and Tolomato (Cordova) Streets, on land that Henry Flagler needed to build his Alcazar Hotel. He purchased the Olivet Church and built in exchange the Grace Methodist Episcopal Church, shown here, at 8 Carrera Street. The new church was designed by architects Carrere and Hastings, constructed by Maguire and MacDonald, and opened its doors for worship on January 1, 1888.

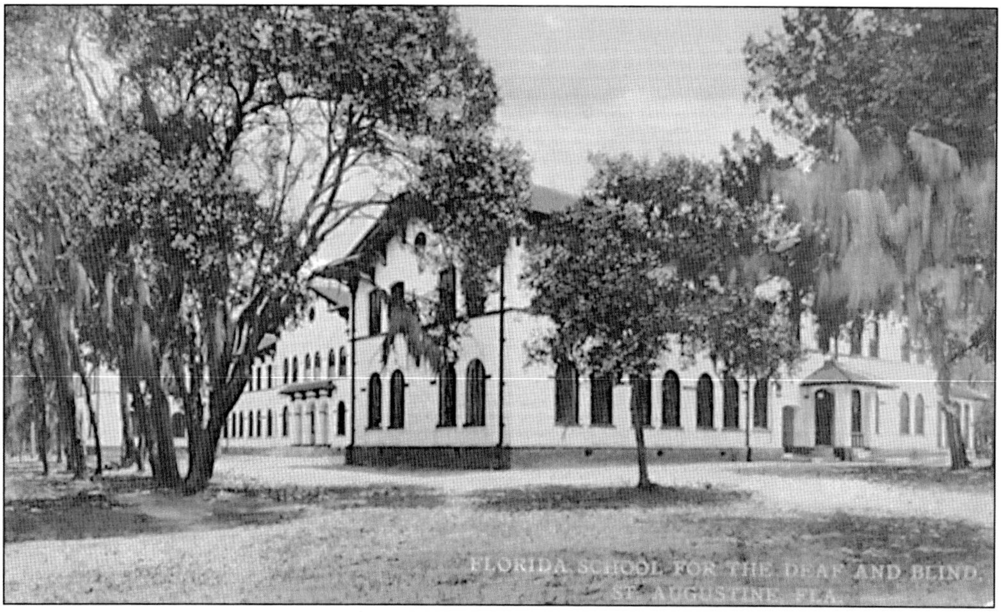

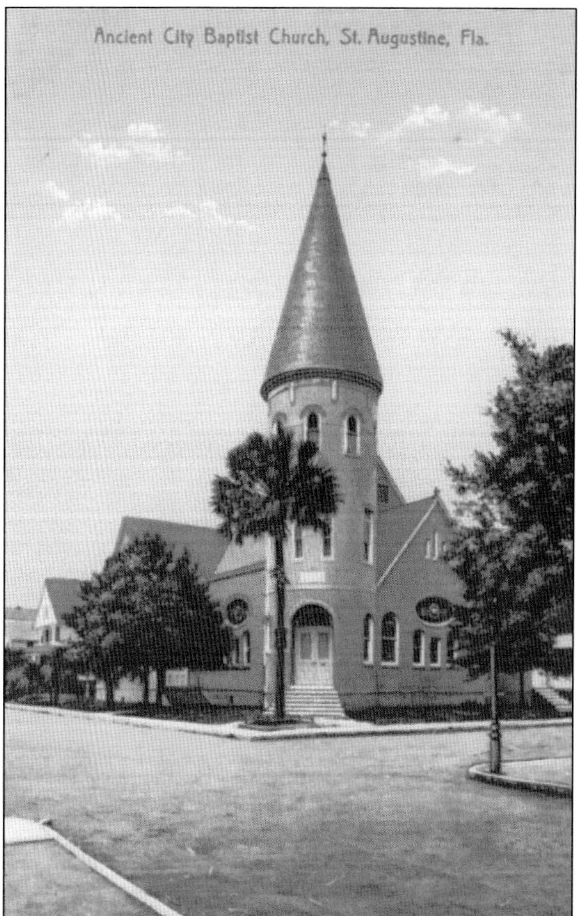

The Florida School for the Deaf and Blind was established north of the city on five acres of land donated by Capt. Edward E. Vaill, owner of the St. Augustine Hotel. Three wooden buildings were completed in 1884, and the first class graduated in May 1898. Two members of that class, Artemas Pope and Cora Carlton, later married and were the parents of state senator Verle A. Pope from St. Augustine.

Ancient City Baptist Church was built on land donated by Henry Flagler, with the stipulation that the church be constructed within two years and the building be worth at least $10,000. The Romanesque Revival church was completed in 1895 at the northwest corner of Sevilla and Carrera Streets.

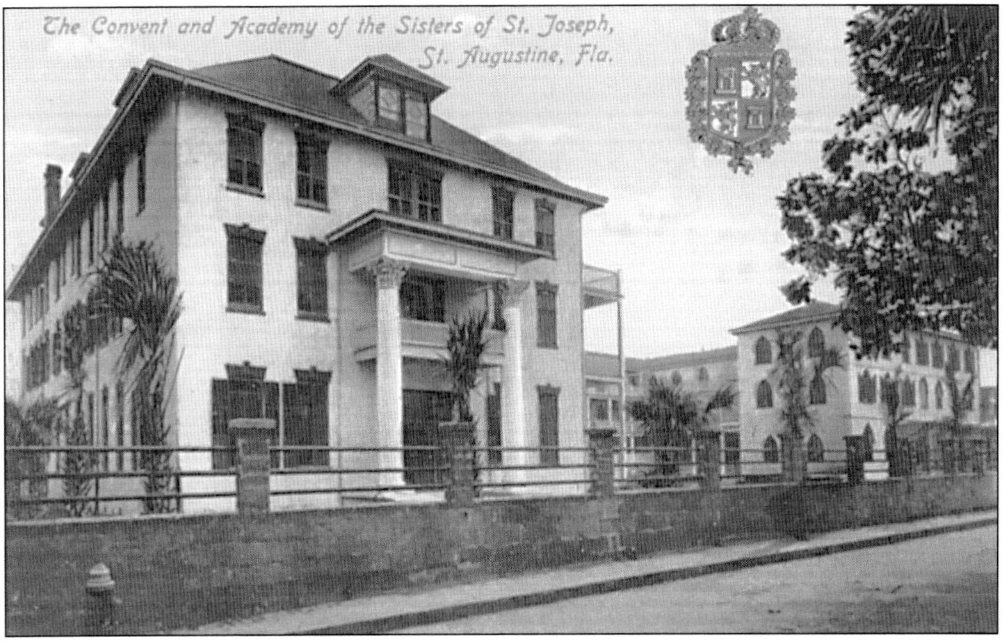

The Sisters of St. Joseph arrived in St. Augustine in 1866 from LePuy, France, summoned by Bishop Augustin Verot from his hometown to educate the black children of the city. Their convent at 241 St. George Street was built on land bequeathed to the church in 1812 by Fr. Miguel O'Reilly, whose house is located behind the convent at 32 Aviles Street. The convent was built in 1874–1876, and was one of the last major structures in St. Augustine constructed of coquina quarried on Anastasia Island. The academy buildings were built between 1904 and 1910 and remained in use until 1980, when a new campus was constructed west of the city. The academy buildings were demolished in 1982, but the convent remains on the site.

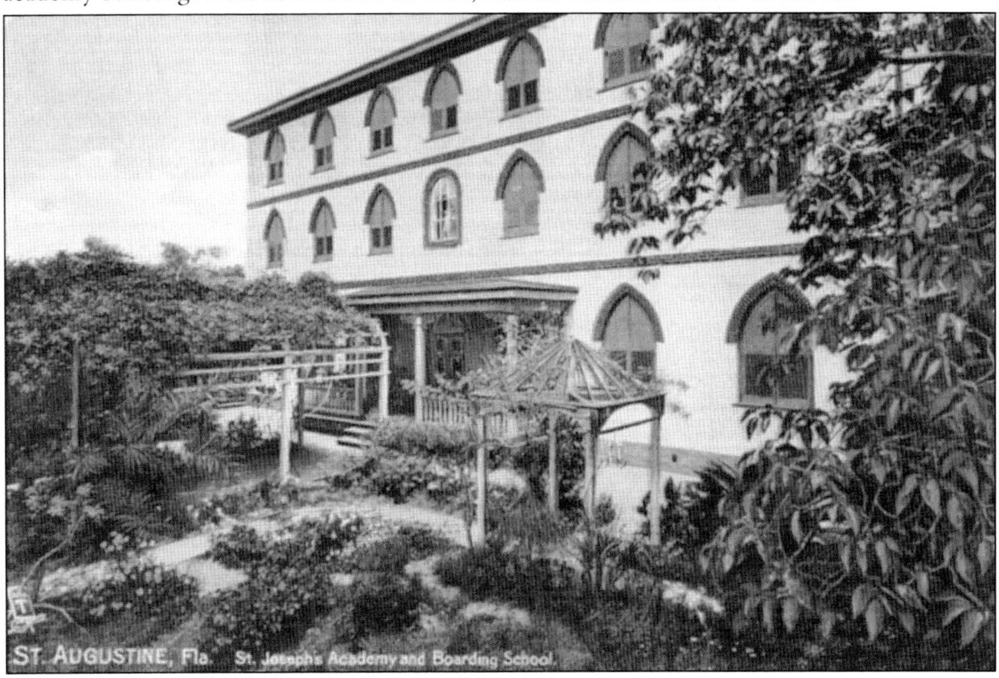

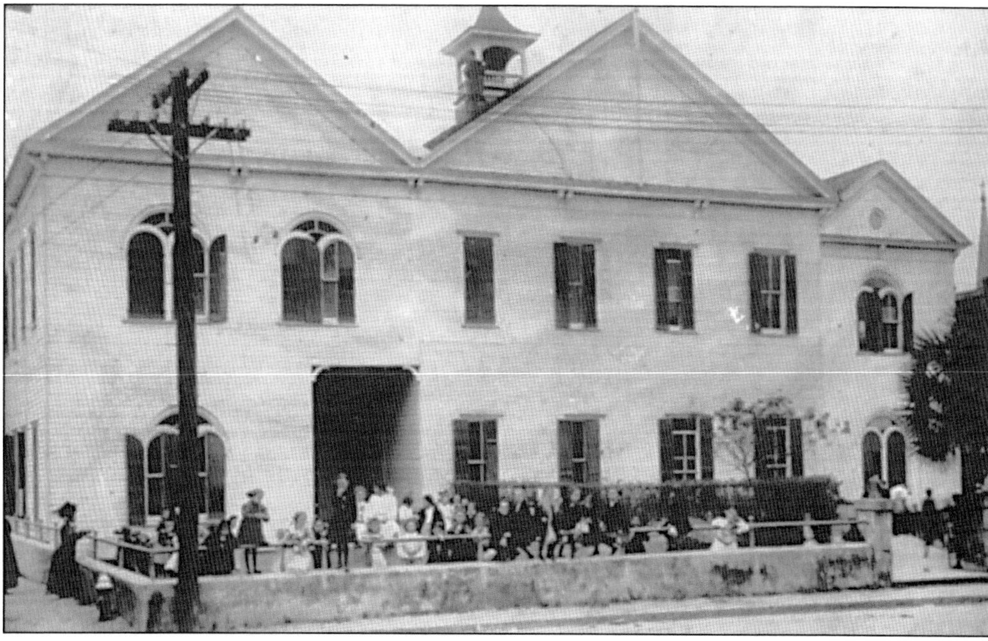

George S. Peabody, a Massachusetts philanthropist, established the Peabody Education Fund in 1867 to help the South rebuild its schools after the Civil War. School No. 1, known as the Peabody School, was located in the old city hall building on Hospital (Aviles) Street north of Artillery Lane. It opened in 1869 with 120 students and was used until 1909, when a new school building on Orange Street was completed.

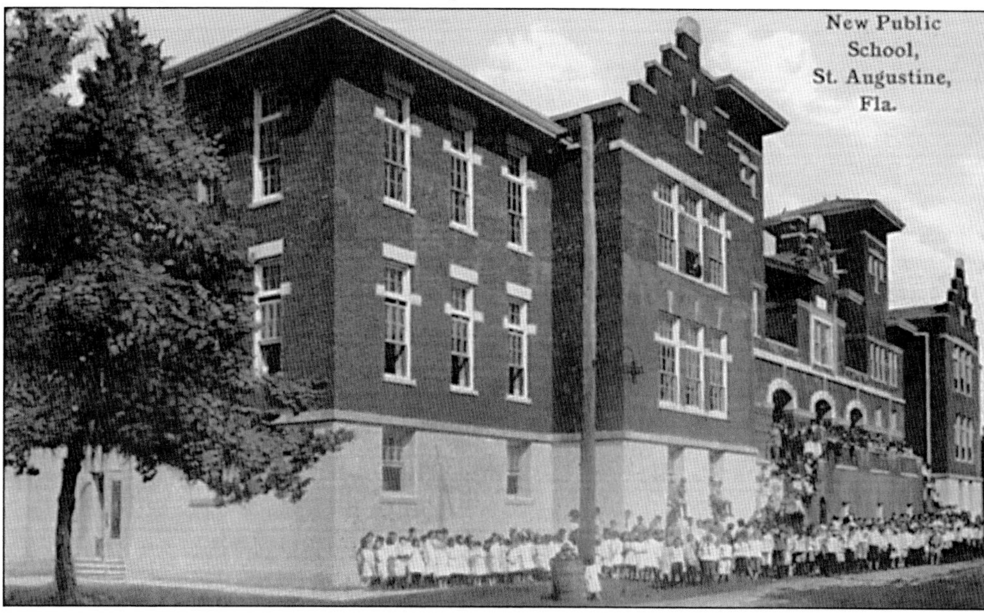

The new public school on Orange Street was built on the site of the old moat that extended west from the City Gate to the San Sebastian River. Supt. W. S. M. Pinkham was instrumental in having the property deeded over to the school board by the federal government. The red brick building was completed in 1909 and now houses the offices of the St. Johns County School Board.

Three

Public Lands and Buildings

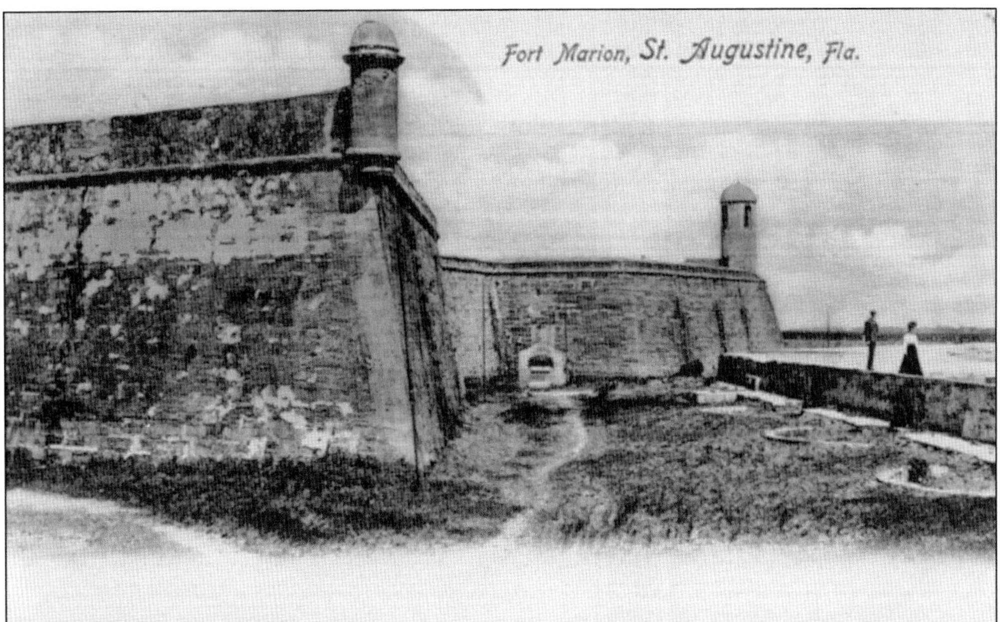

The Spanish built the Castillo de San Marcos between 1672 and 1695, using coquina stone quarried on Anastasia Island. During the British period (1763–1783), the name was changed to Fort St. Marks. When the United States purchased Florida in 1821, the name was changed once more, this time to Fort Marion, in honor of the "Swamp Fox"—Gen. Francis Marion of Revolutionary War fame. In the 1840s, army engineers turned the east moat into the water battery shown here and also improved the protective hill around the fort. The hotshot oven, shown at the center of the postcard, was used to heat cannon balls to set wooden ships ablaze.

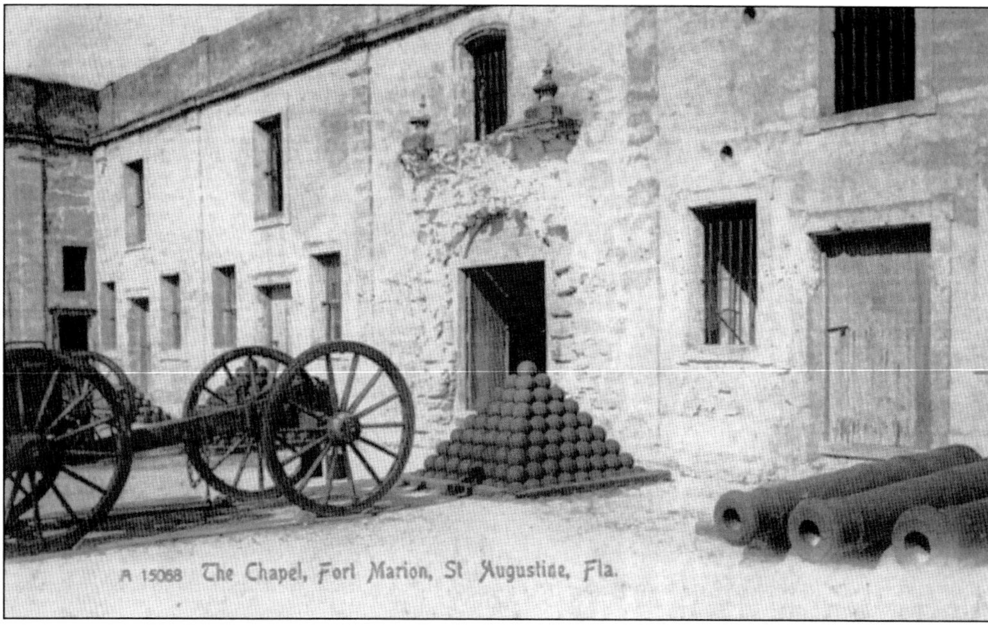

In 1884, Pres. Chester A. Arthur signed into law an appropriation of $5,000 for the restoration and preservation of Fort Marion. More appropriations were made in 1888 and 1909, and the entrance to the chapel was restored sometime after this 1905 view. Throughout its long history, the fort was never captured, as its coquina walls absorbed cannon fire and remained intact during two British sieges.

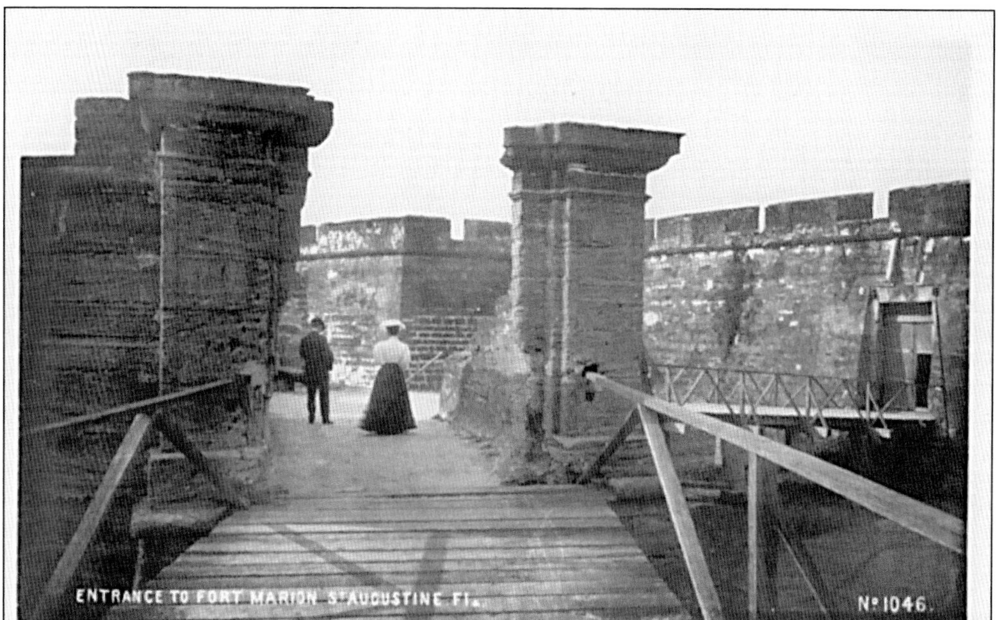

The couple is standing on the ravelin that guards the entrance to the fort. The two columns in the foreground once supported a mechanism that raised the outer drawbridge over the moat. The entrance to the fort can be seen across the bridge to the right. This postcard by Bamforth and Company is one of the few cards from this era to be published in England.

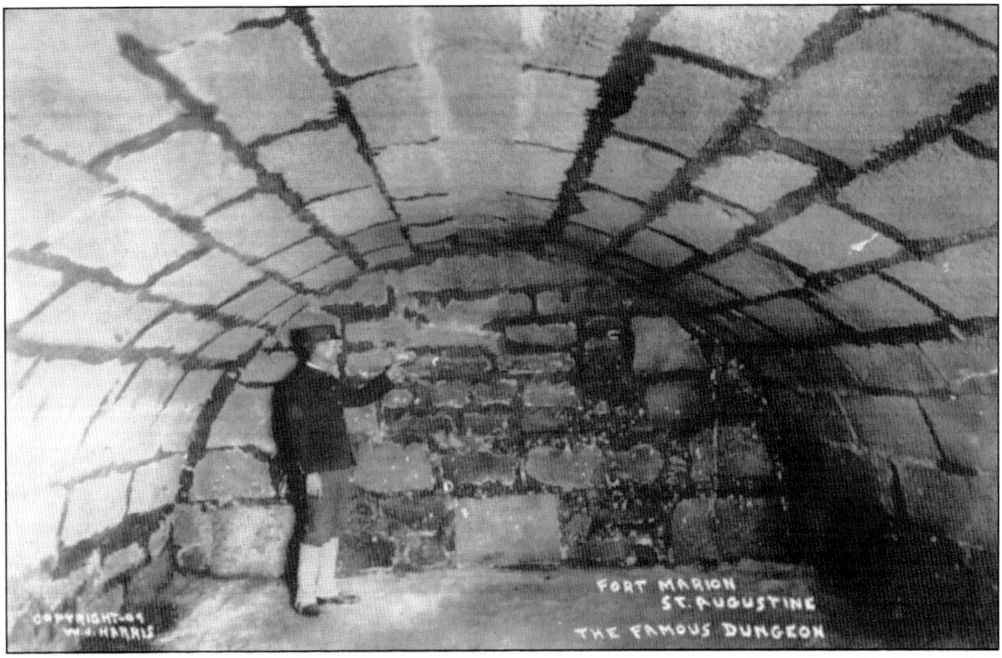

The "famous dungeon" was actually a powder magazine that proved too humid for storing gunpowder and was sealed off. It was rediscovered in 1832 when a cannon fell through from the gun deck above. Many stories developed about the bones found in the room, and in the early 1900s, tour guides concocted all kinds of tales about this so-called dungeon. This W. J. Harris view was copyrighted in 1909.

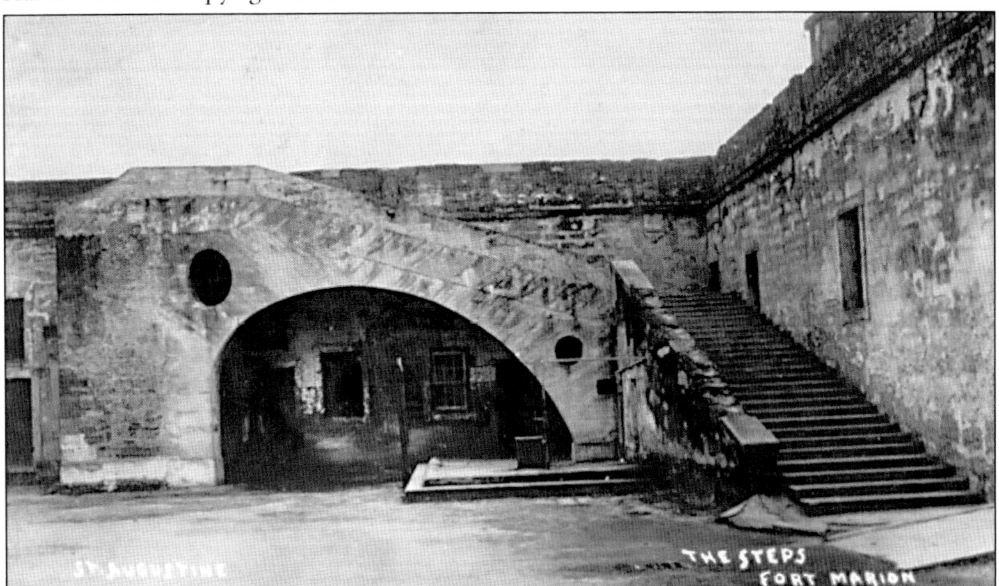

The steps at Fort Marion were originally a ramp leading to the gun deck above. Fort Marion was de-activated in 1900, and after 1914, the St. Augustine Historical Society acted as caretaker of the fort and provided guides for tourists. Declared a national monument in 1924, the fort was transferred from the War Department to the National Park Service in 1933 and the name restored to Castillo de San Marcos in 1942.

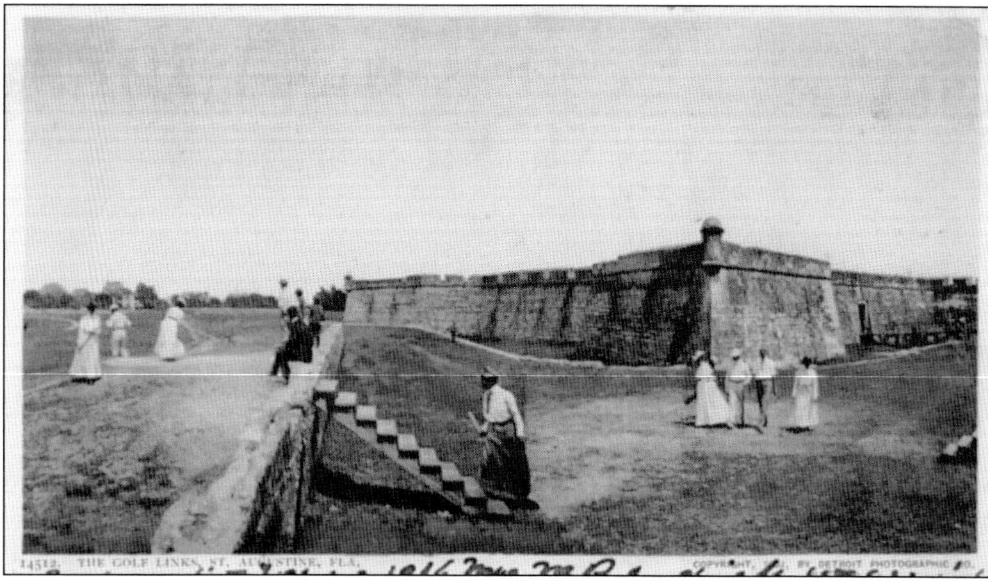

The first golf course in St. Augustine was laid out on the grounds of Fort Marion in 1895. It consisted of three links named "San Marco," "Fort Marion," and "The Palmetto"; each link was played three times to complete the 1,900 yard, nine-hole course. When it opened, the St. Augustine Country Club had 200 members, 70 of whom were women. Admission to the club was 50¢, and new players had to be introduced by a member. St. Augustine soon developed into the winter golf capital of the United States, and the club became the social center for affluent visitors. The upper postcard was copyrighted in 1902 by the Detroit Photographic Company and shows golfers near the southwest corner of Fort Marion. The bottom card shows an early aerial view of the fort; notice the sand traps along the course.

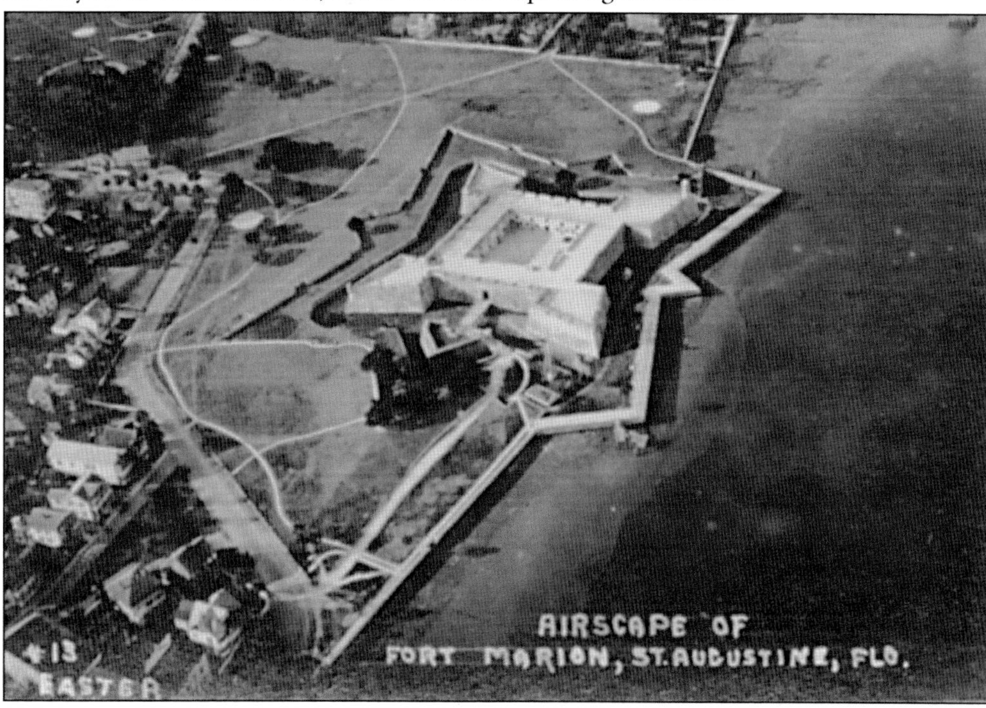

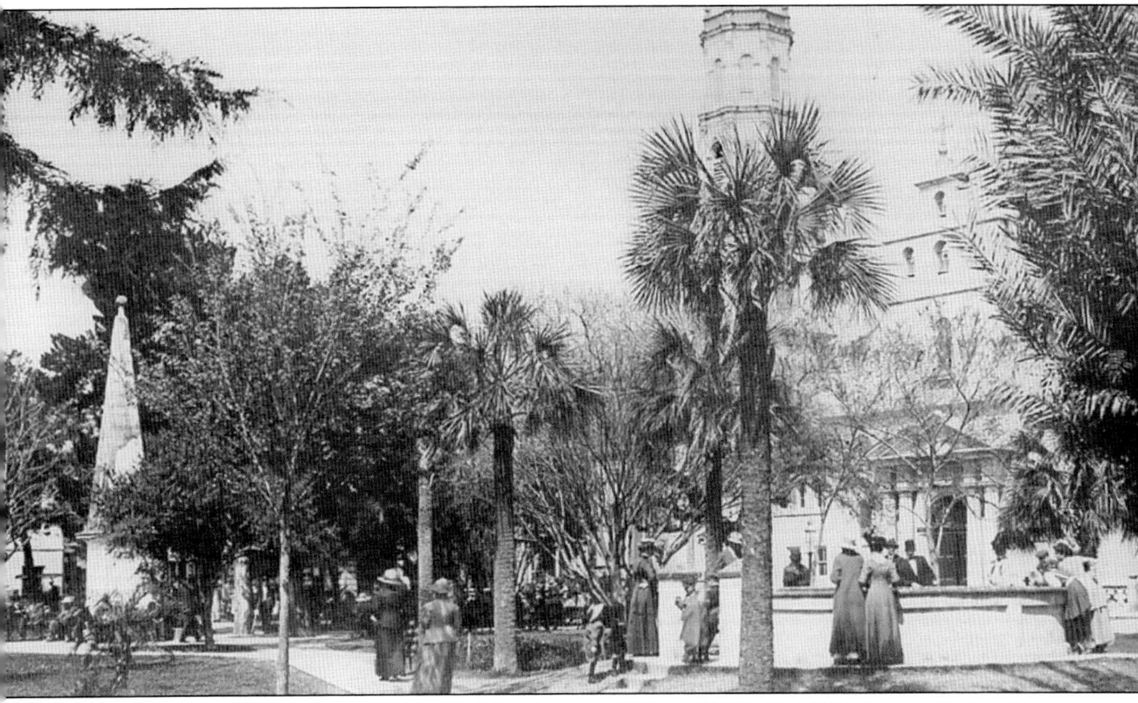

St. Augustine's plaza was laid out in 1598 by decree of King Phillip II of Spain, requiring that all Colonial towns have a central plaza with the principal streets leading from it. The layout of the streets in the downtown area has changed very little since that time. The monument at the west end of the plaza was built in 1813 to honor the Spanish Constitution of March 9, 1812. It was one of many constitution monuments erected all over Latin America, but it may be the only survivor, as Mayor Geronimo Alvarez refused to allow it to be torn down when King Ferdinand VII abolished the Spanish constitution upon his return to power in 1814. The women are seen looking into a round pool in the middle of the plaza where alligators were on display. The entrance to the cathedral can be seen in the background.

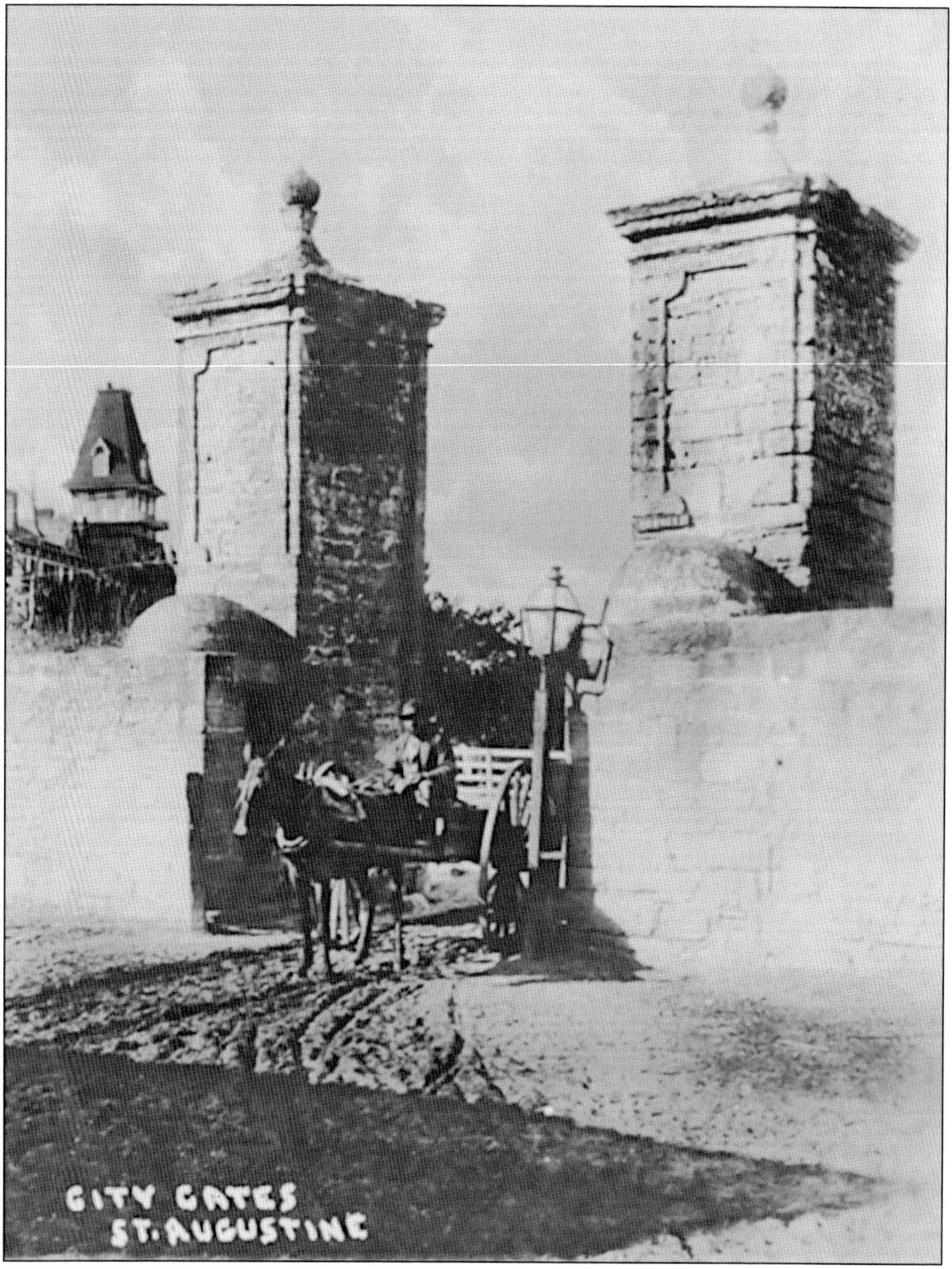

The City Gate, also known as the Land Gate, was built in 1808 during the second Spanish period to replace a wooden structure. The 12-foot opening is framed by 14-foot-high coquina pillars capped with a pomegranate, the symbol of the kingdom of Granada. The gate was originally covered in white masonry trimmed with red plaster. The structure sheltered sentries that guarded a drawbridge over a moat outside the gate. A causeway was later built to replace the bridge, and in 1879, the city appropriated funds to rebuild the crumbling sentry boxes. This 1908 postcard by W. J. Harris was made from an earlier photograph, as it shows one of the towers of the San Marco Hotel in the background. The hotel was destroyed by fire in 1897. (Connahey collection.)

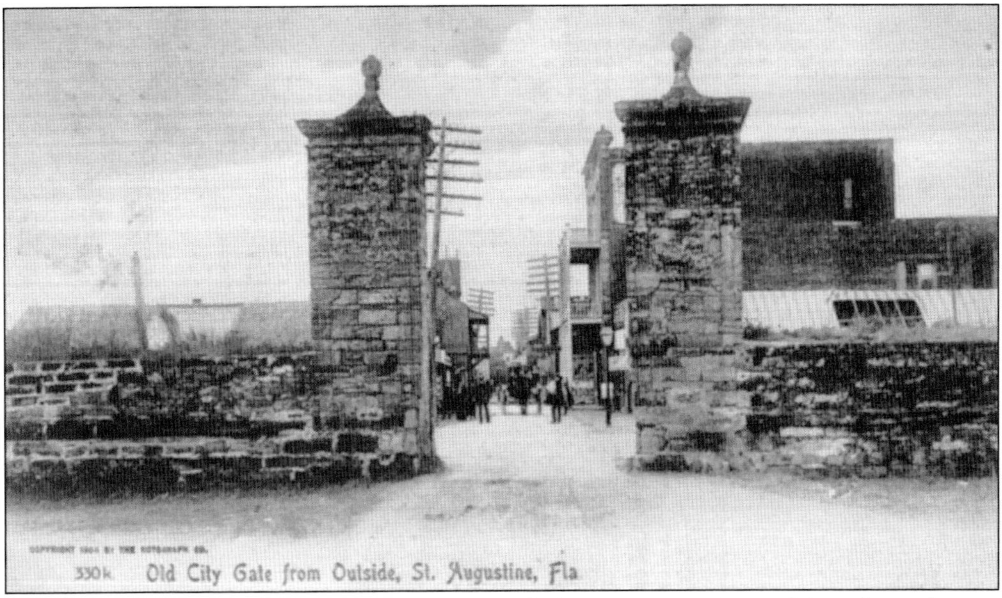

Over the years, the City Gate has come to symbolize St. Augustine and has always been a favorite spot for tourists to have their picture taken. Several photographers had studios near the gate and specialized in photo postcards for the visitors to send home. The two buildings just inside the City Gate in this 1904 postcard are both photographers' studios; notice the skylights in the roofs of each building.

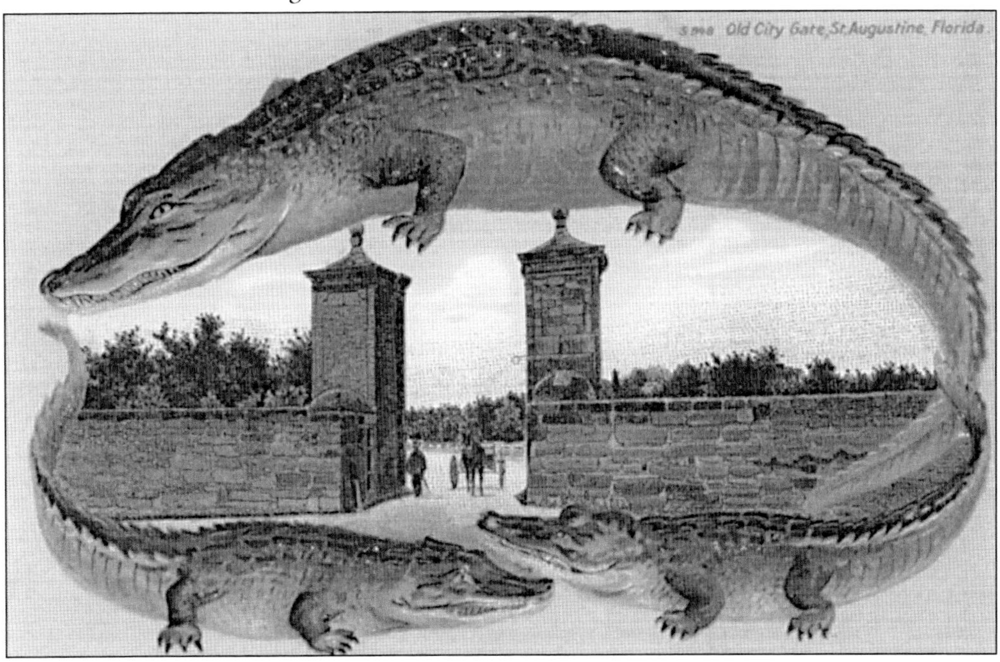

S. Langsdorff and Company of New York published a series of 165 alligator-border postcards with Florida scenes. Printed in Germany, the cards have exceptional color quality and graphics, with embossed scales on the backs of the alligators. There were 16 views from St. Augustine, including this scene of the City Gate. Today these alligator-border postcards are highly prized by collectors.

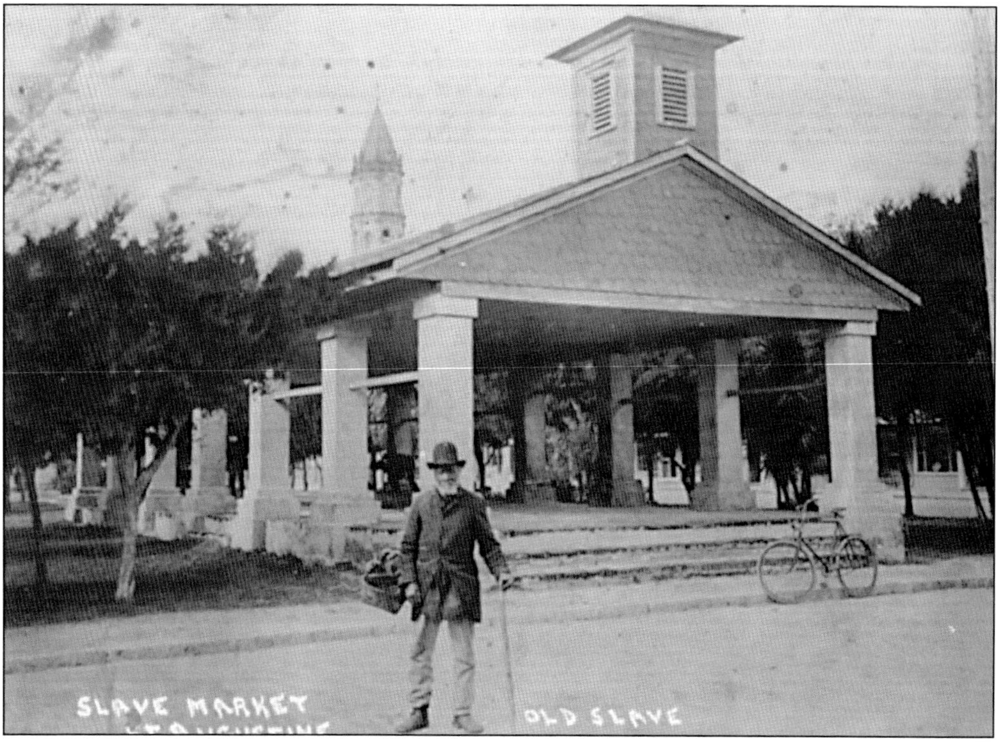

The market building at the east end of the plaza was built in 1824, shortly after Florida became a U.S. territory. This photo postcard by W. J. Harris pictures an "old slave" in front of the "Old Slave Market." There is some debate as to whether slaves were ever sold at the market, but perhaps Harris felt that the label "slave market" would sell more postcards to the tourists. (Connahey collection.)

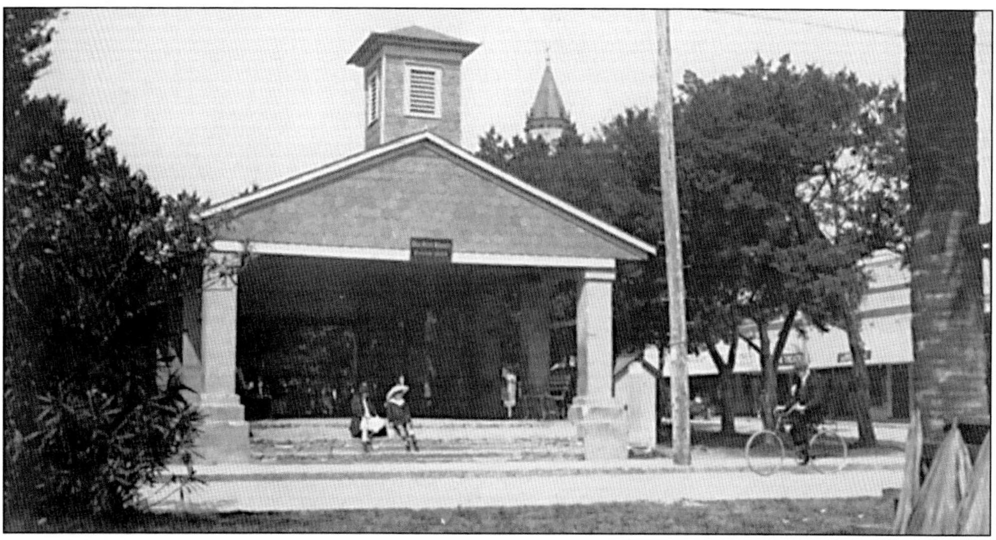

Local historian and tourist guidebook author Charles B. Reynolds had an ongoing debate with W. J. Harris over what Reynolds felt were Harris's exaggerations and historical falsifications. Notice the sign over the children's heads that reads "Old Meat Market"; perhaps it was placed there to refute Harris's claim that the market building had been used to sell slaves.

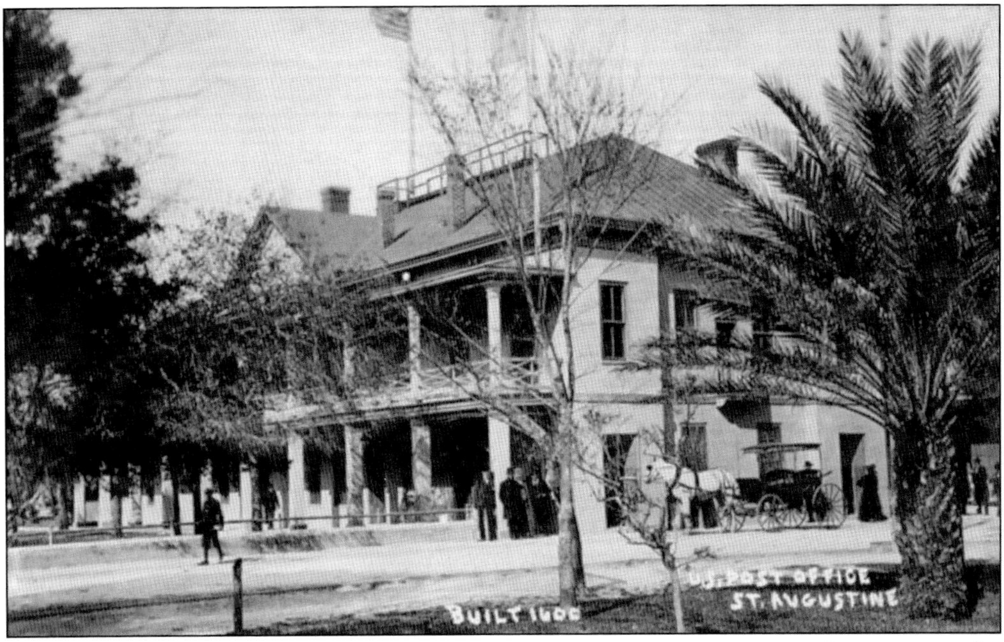

The building at the west end of the plaza has served many purposes over the years—as the residence of the governor, a courthouse, federal offices, and a customhouse. In 1873, it was again extensively remodeled and used as a post office until 1965 and now houses the Government House Museum. This view by W. J. Harris is falsely captioned "Built 1600."

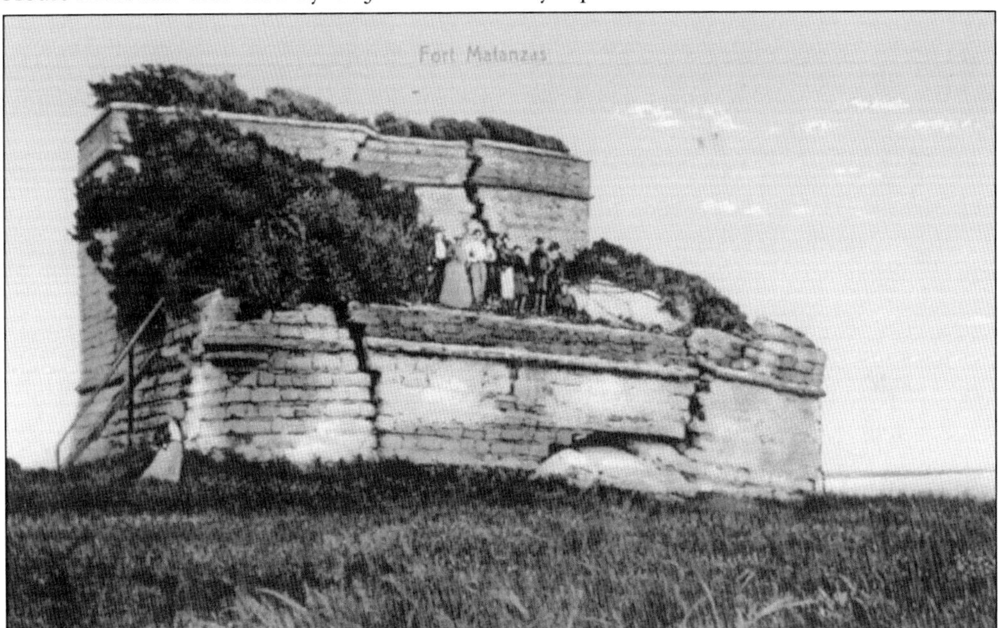

In 1740, construction began on a coquina fort to guard the southern approach to St. Augustine through Matanzas Inlet. After the United States took possession of Florida in 1821, the fort was no longer used by the military and fell victim to decay. At the urging of the St. Augustine Historical Society, it was declared a national monument in 1924 and has been restored by the National Park Service.

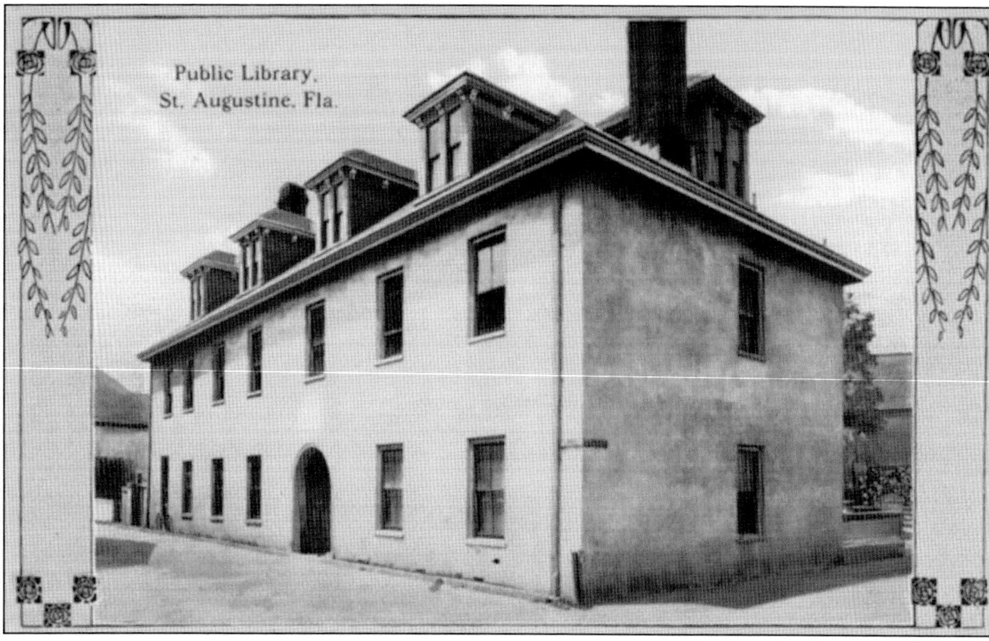

Minorcan colonist Bernardo Segui bought the property at 12 Hospital (Aviles) Street in 1786. Gen. Edmund Kirby Smith, the last Confederate general to surrender, was born in the house in 1824. John L. and Frances L. Wilson purchased the home in 1895 and donated it for use as a public library. In 1987, the library moved to larger quarters, and the building now houses the St. Augustine Historical Society's Research Library.

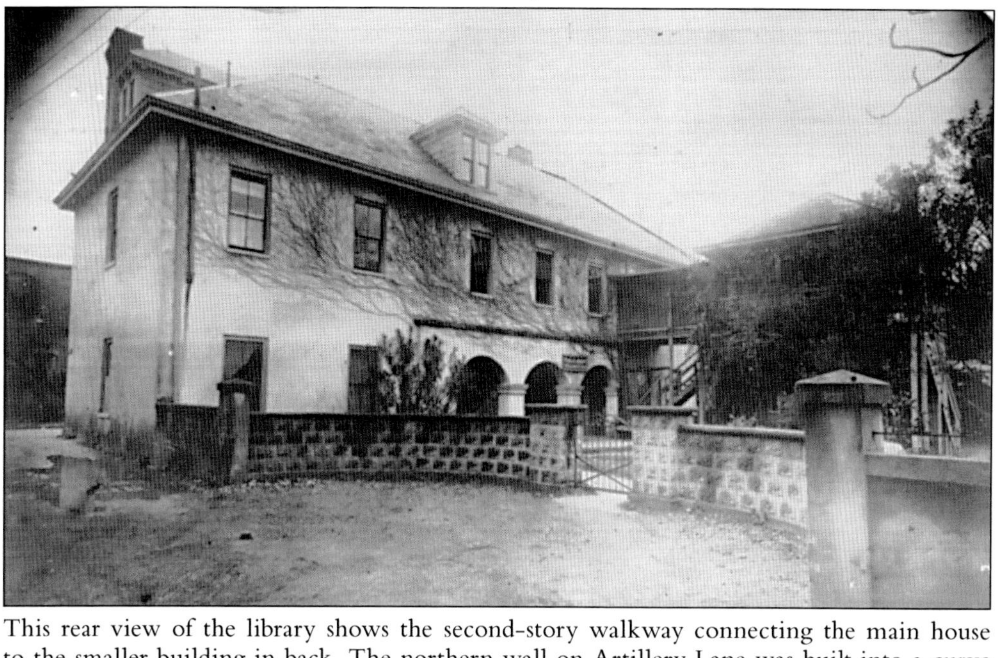

This rear view of the library shows the second-story walkway connecting the main house to the smaller building in back. The northern wall on Artillery Lane was built into a curve sometime before 1910 and rebuilt after 1930, eliminating the curve. The western boundary of the property is marked by one of the city's oldest coquina walls, which has never been rebuilt since it was first constructed.

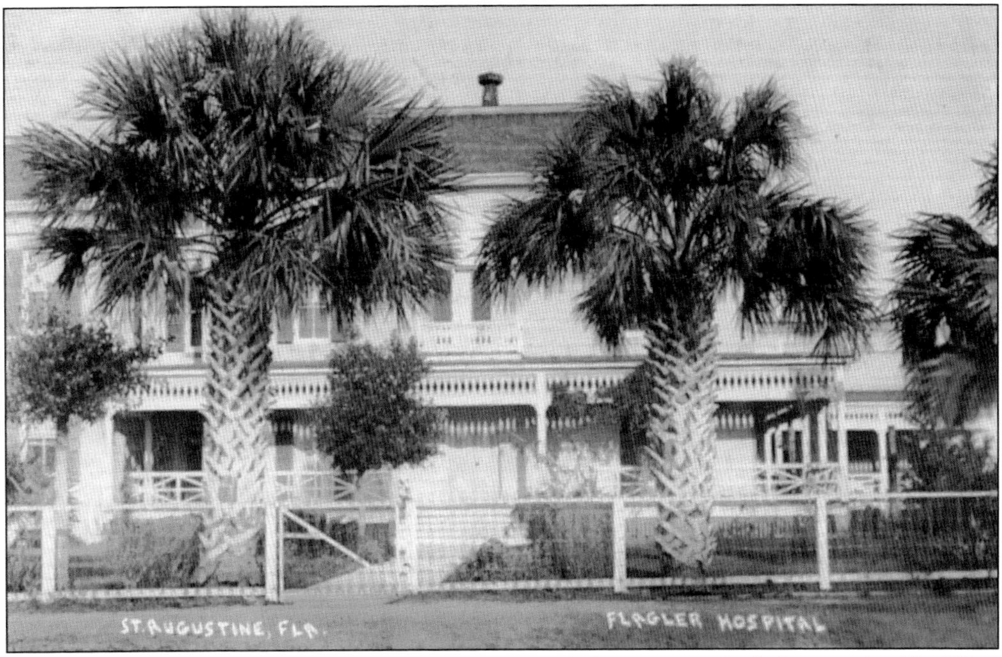

Flagler Hospital was originally named Alicia Hospital after Henry Flagler's second wife, Alice. The hospital opened in 1890 in the former home of Dr. H. C. Sloggett on Marine Street. Flagler purchased the property and deeded it to the hospital's board of trustees, chaired by Dr. Andrew Anderson Jr. The hospital, shown in this 1908 view by W. J. Harris, was destroyed by fire in 1916 and replaced by a masonry structure in 1921.

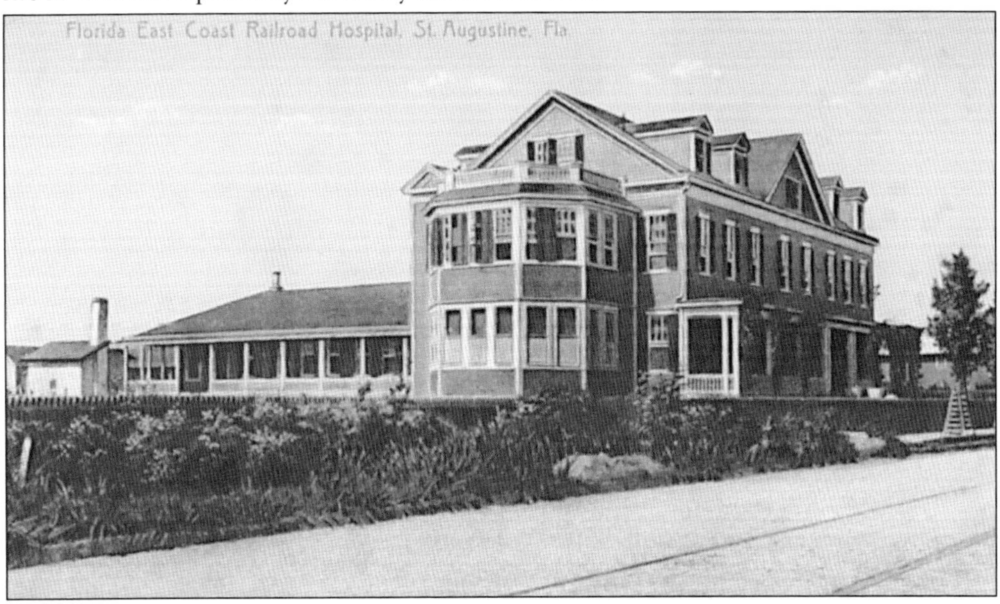

The Florida East Coast Hospital was opened in 1891 for the employees and families of Flagler's railroad. Dr. S. G. Worley was instrumental in establishing the hospital and later opened his own clinic on West King Street. The original hospital building burned in 1901 and was replaced by the building pictured here. The hospital closed in 1963, and the site is now the St. Augustine Police Department at 151 King Street.

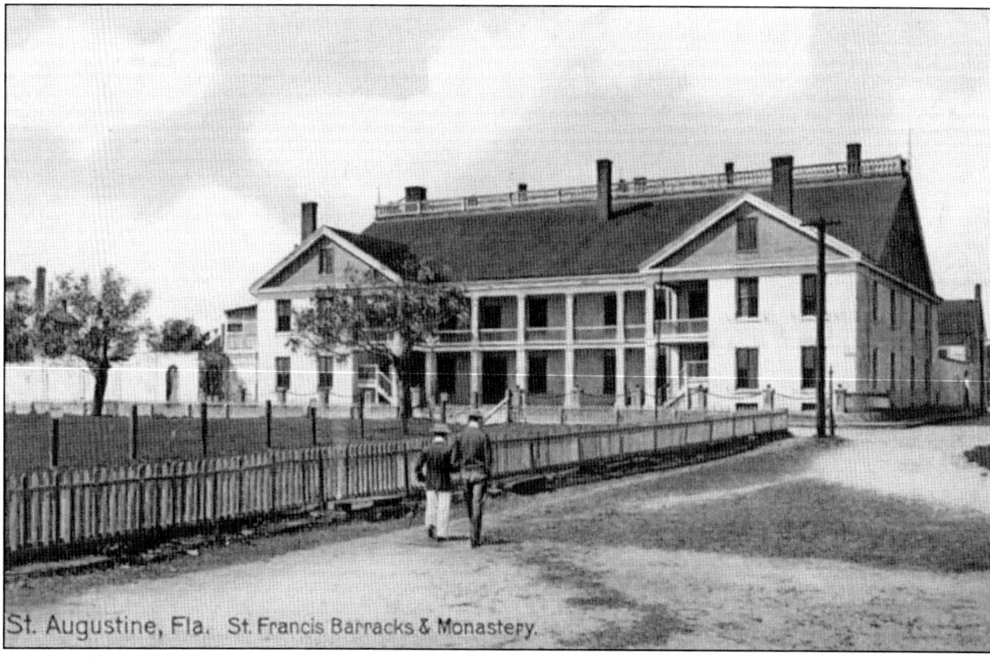

This building at the corner of St. Francis and Marine Streets was originally a Franciscan friary begun by the Spanish in 1724. The British converted the building into a military barracks after taking possession of Florida in 1763. It remained a military post after Florida became a U.S. territory in 1821 and has been the headquarters of the Florida National Guard since 1907.

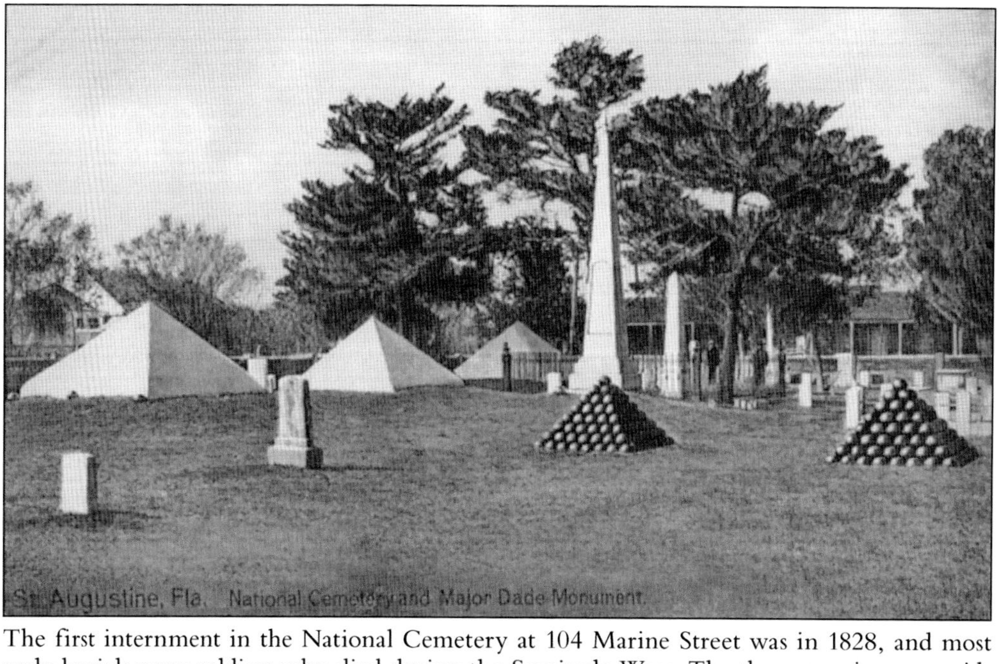

The first internment in the National Cemetery at 104 Marine Street was in 1828, and most early burials were soldiers who died during the Seminole Wars. The three coquina pyramids mark the mass graves of over 1,400 soldiers, including those of Maj. Francis L. Dade, whose troops were attacked by Seminoles in 1835 near Bushnell. The tall obelisk near the pyramids also honors those who died in the Florida Wars.

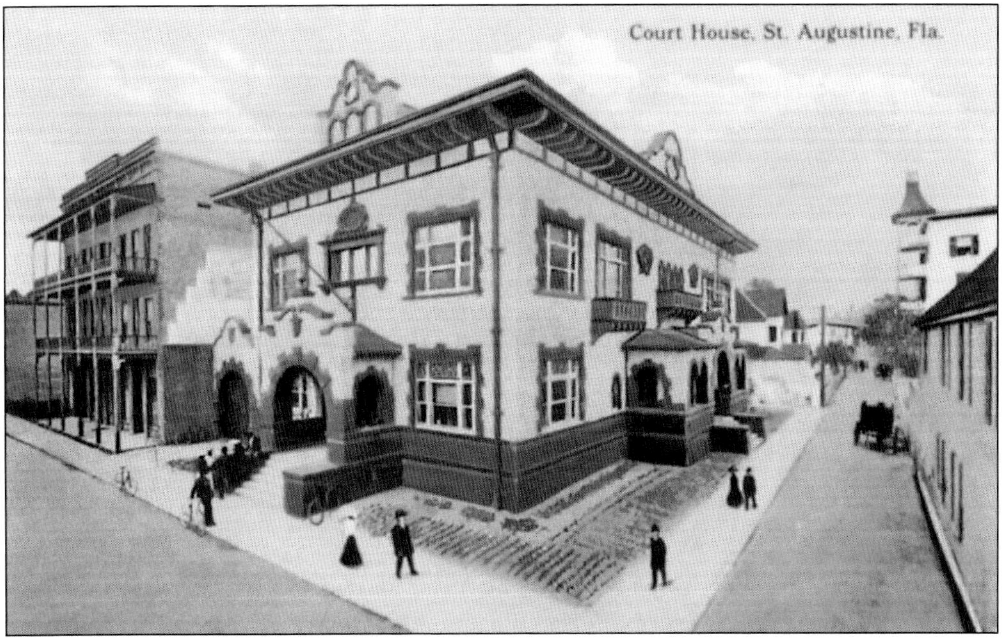

Erected in 1907 at a cost of $55,000, the St. Johns County Courthouse was located on the southwest corner of Charlotte and Treasury Streets. It would fall victim to the April 1914 fire and be rebuilt on the same site. This new courthouse remained in use until 1968, when the county government moved into the former Cordova Hotel.

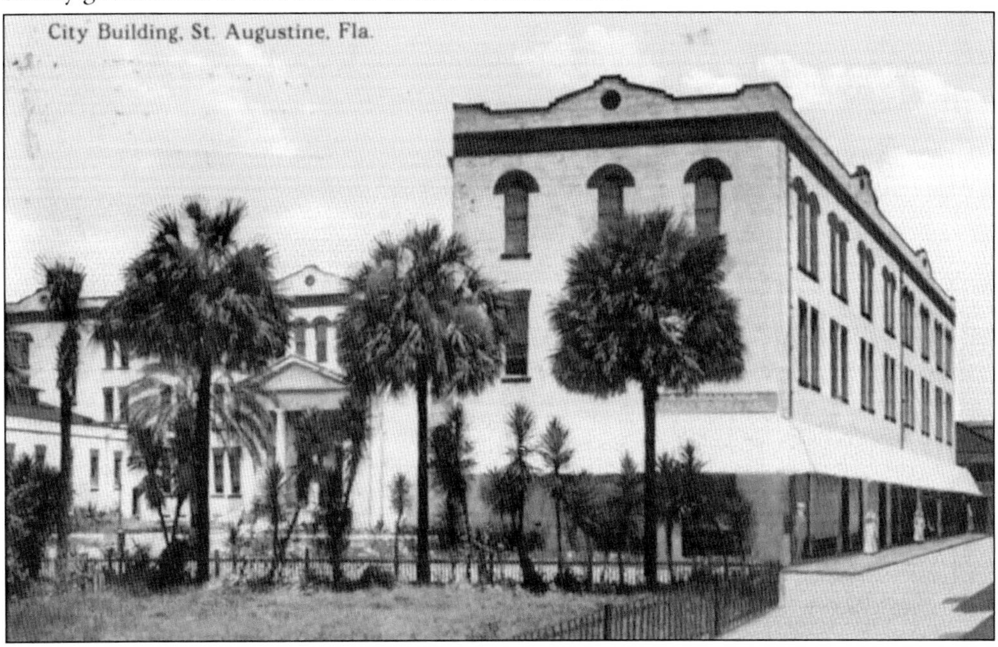

The City Building was constructed by Henry Flagler in 1890–1891 and leased to the city through his Model Land Company. The building faced Hypolita Street and occupied the entire block from St. George to Spanish Streets. It housed city offices, a city commission meeting room, courtroom, judges' chambers, fire department, and the city jail. Demolished in 1973, it is now the site of the Columbia Restaurant.

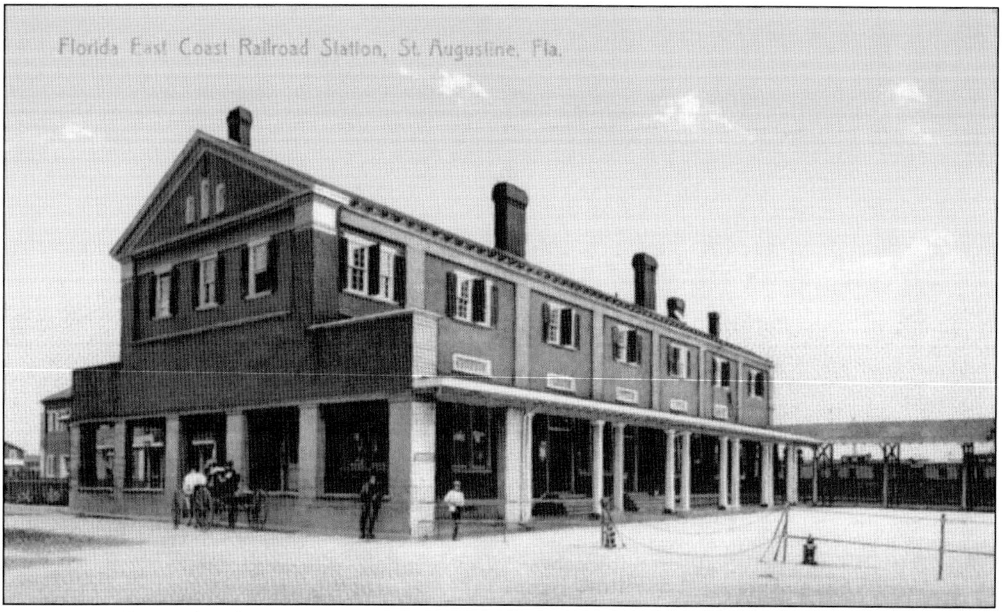

Henry Flagler realized that the key to developing Florida as a tourist destination was a good transportation system. He purchased the Jacksonville, St. Augustine, and Halifax River Railroad in 1885 and converted the line to standard gauge. Other lines were added to Flagler's railroad empire, and he built the Union Station on Malaga Street to serve his railroads, replacing the old depot on Orange Street.

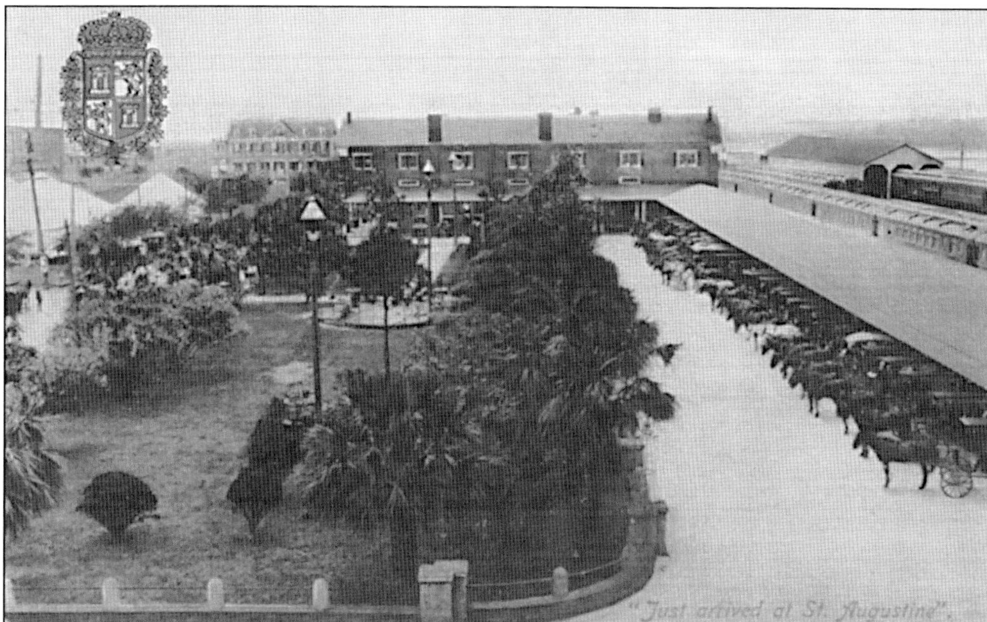

In 1895, Flagler incorporated his railroad empire as the Florida East Coast Railway, with headquarters in St. Augustine. In 1959, a new FEC terminal was built north of town, as plans were underway to construct Ponce de Leon Boulevard (U.S. 1) through the site of the old depot. The small park next to the fire station on Malaga Street is the only remnant of the FEC Union Depot.

Construction of the brick lighthouse began in 1871, to replace the old coquina tower that was being undermined by the encroaching sea. The first-order Fresnel lens was first lit on October 15, 1874, atop the 165-foot tower with its distinctive black-and-white spiral and red top. The Junior Service League of St. Augustine has restored the light keeper's house and operates the lighthouse as a museum.

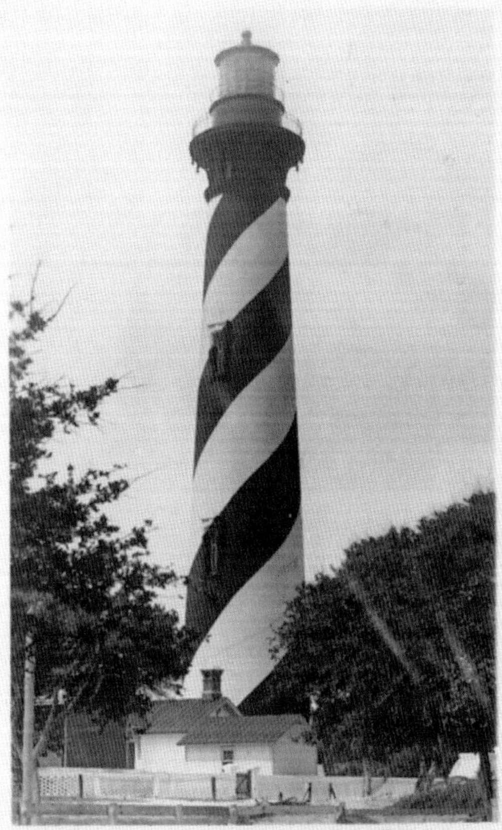

Photo by Blair's Studio,
P1322 Light House near St. Augustine, Florida.

The wireless station is seen in this view from the top of the St. Augustine Lighthouse, looking northeastward. The station was part of a system established by the U.S. Navy to provide radio communication with its ships. Completed around 1904, it served as a government telegraph station until after World War II. The house is now a private residence at 106 Carver Street, East.

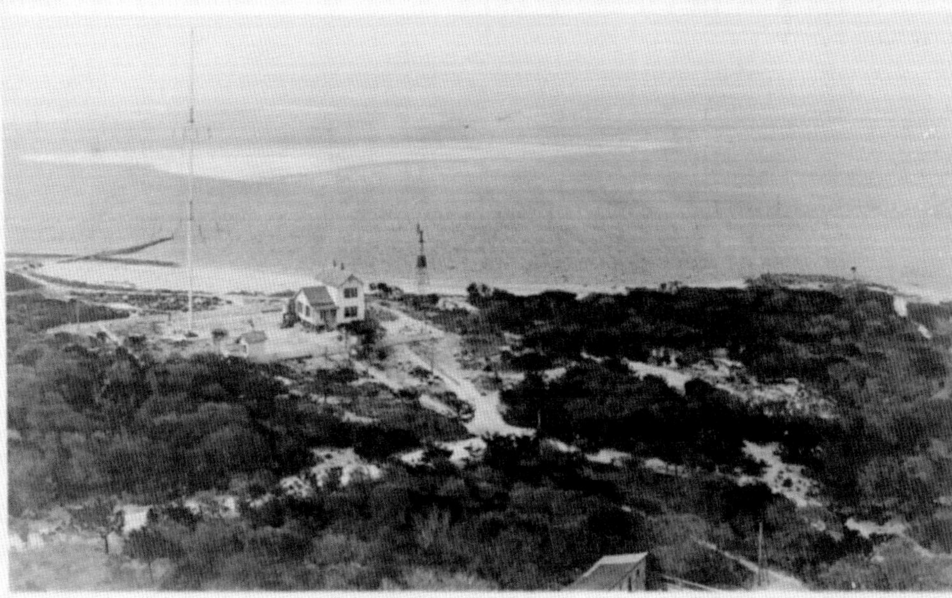

P1313 Wireless Station near St. Augustine, Florida. Photo by Blair's Studio

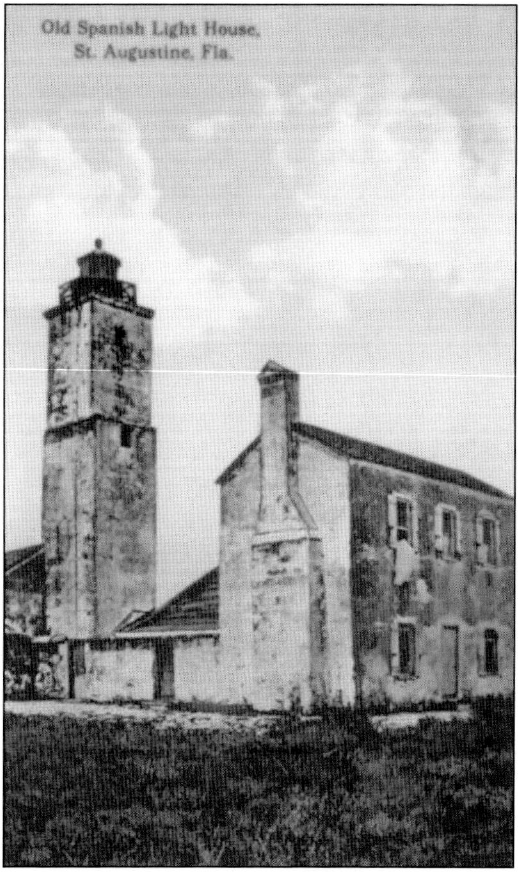

This 1910 W. J. Harris postcard of the old Spanish lighthouse was made from a much earlier photograph of the structure. The Spanish had built a stone lookout tower northeast of the present lighthouse, and in 1824, the U.S. government replaced it with a coquina tower. Erosion from the sea caused the keeper's house to collapse in 1878, and the tower fell over two years later in 1880.

The Spanish-American War began on April 25, 1898. One week later, this eight-inch muzzle-loading gun was moved from Fort Marion to a battery in front of the lighthouse to guard the approach to the harbor. The ruins of the water battery became a popular tourist spot in the early 1900s.

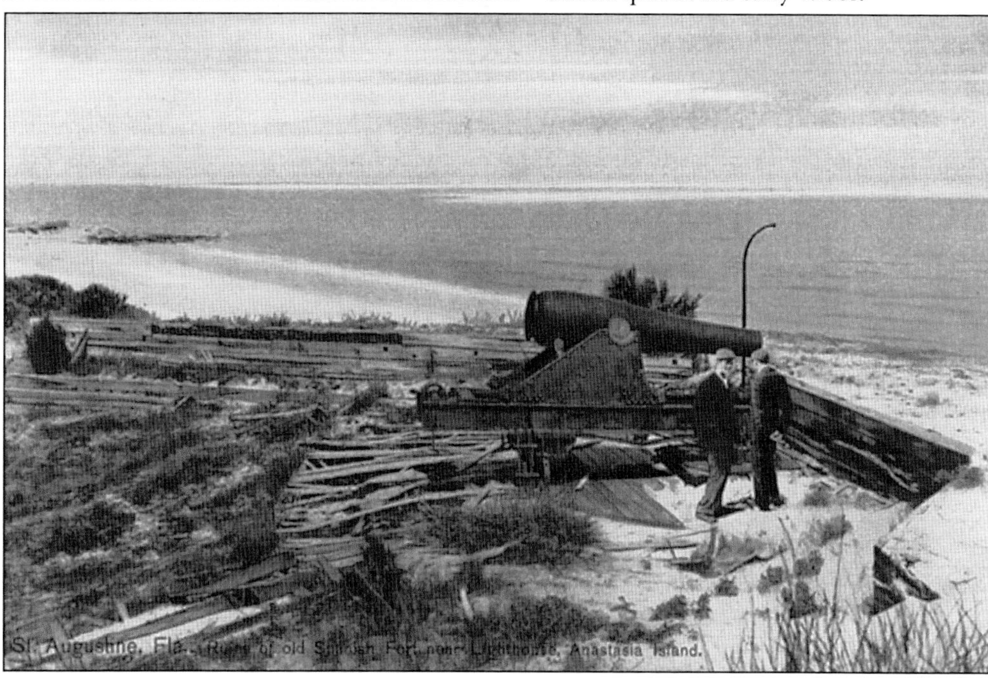

Four

Notable Buildings and Homes

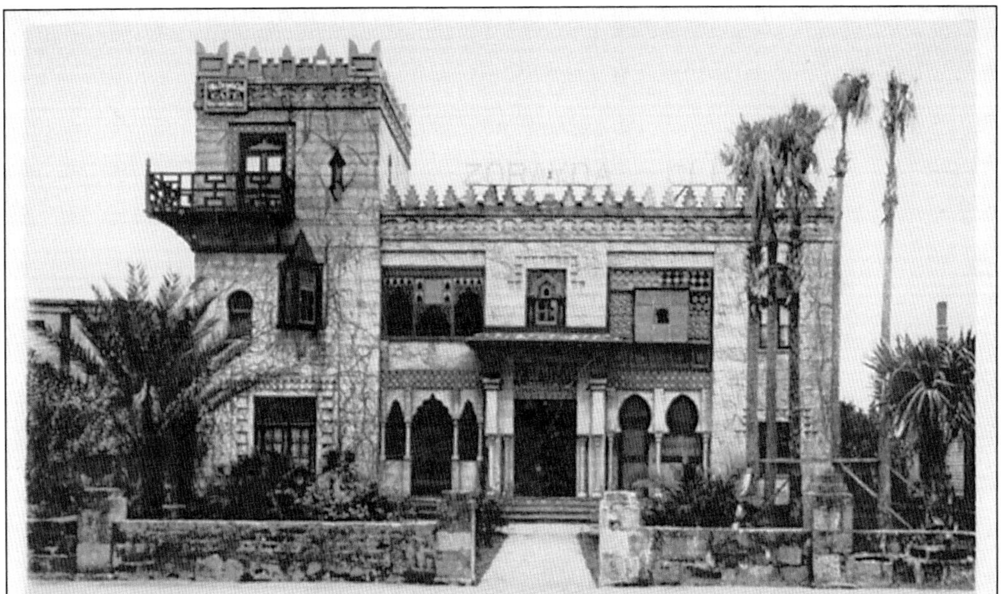

Bostonian Franklin W. Smith built the Villa Zorayda in 1883 and modeled it after the Alhambra Castle in Spain. It is the second building in the United States to be built of poured concrete, a technique later employed in the construction of the Ponce de Leon, Casa Monica, and Alcazar Hotels. Smith named it Villa Zorayda in honor of the second of the three princesses in Washington Irving's *The Alhambra.* Over the entrance, he inscribed in Arabic "There is no conqueror but God." During the early 1900s, it operated as the Zorayda Club, as indicated by the sign on the roof in this 1904 postcard by the Detroit Photographic Company. It would later become a tourist attraction, the Zorayda Castle.

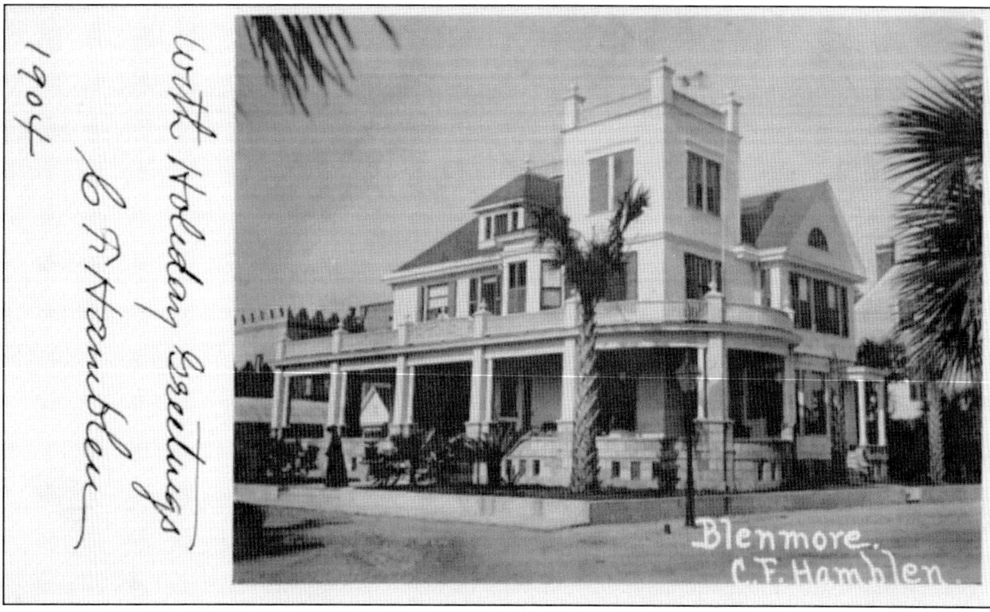

Blenmore was the home of Charles F. Hamblen, located at what is now 1 Anderson Circle. The residence later became the Blenmore Hotel and was remodeled in the Mediterranean Revival style during the 1920s as a sales office for D. P. Davis, the developer of Davis Shores. It is now the home of the American Legion Post 37. This postcard "With Holiday Greetings" was sent by Hamblen in 1904.

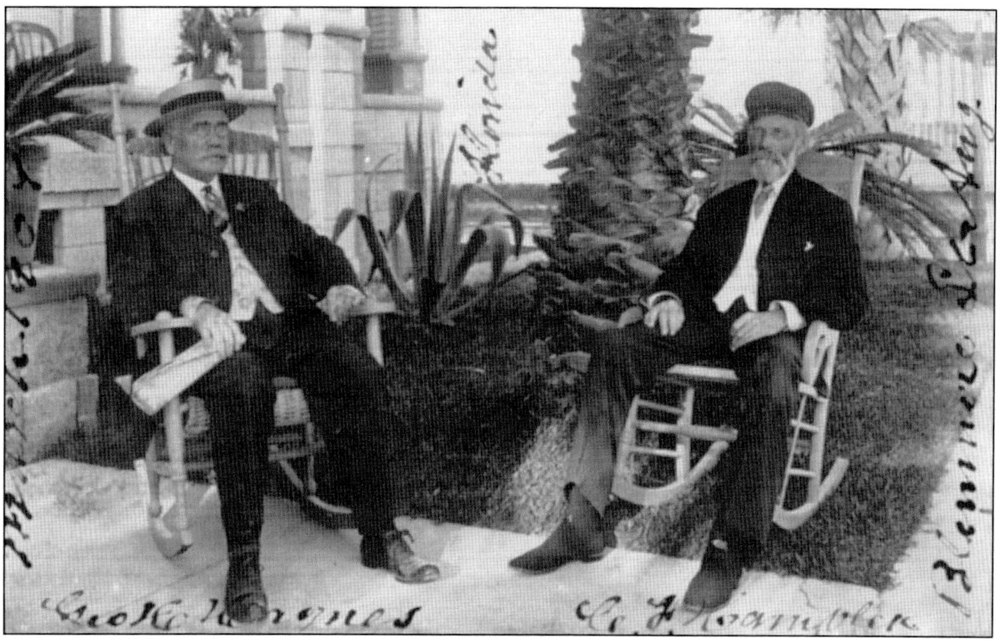

Charles F. Hamblen was a Maine native who ran a successful hardware business at 11 Hospital (Aviles) Street. He is pictured here on the right in front of Blenmore with George G. Haynes in this March 1909 view. Hamblen moved his operations into a warehouse at 4 Artillery Lane that later became a tourist attraction known as the Oldest Store. Hamblen Hardware is still in operation today at 111 King Street.

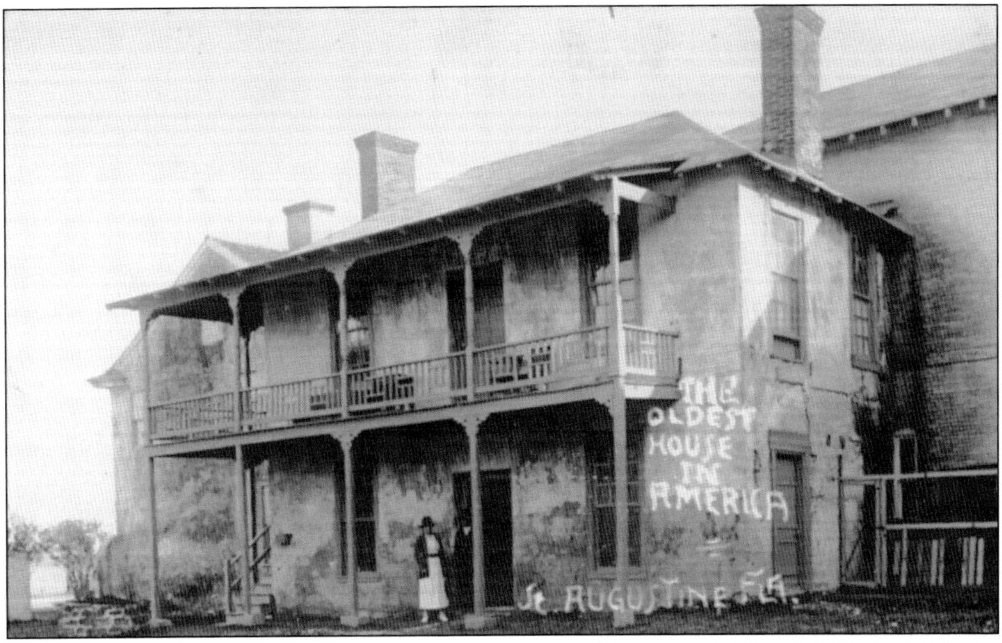

The coquina house at 16 Marine Street was constructed between 1791and 1799. In 1868, the home was sold to Margaret Stafford Worth, widow of Gen. William J. Worth (1794–1849), one of the most important military figures of the 1830s and 1840s. Lake Worth, Florida, and Fort Worth, Texas, are both named for him. Margaret Worth died in 1869 and is buried in the National Cemetery on Marine Street. Daughter Margaret Worth owned the house until 1904, when it was sold to P. F. Carcaba, a local cigar manufacturer. The house later became the home of the Elks Club from 1907 until 1913. By the late 1950s, the building had fallen into disrepair and was torn down in 1961. The Worth House was reconstructed at 118 Marine Street using the original coquina blocks and now houses a restaurant.

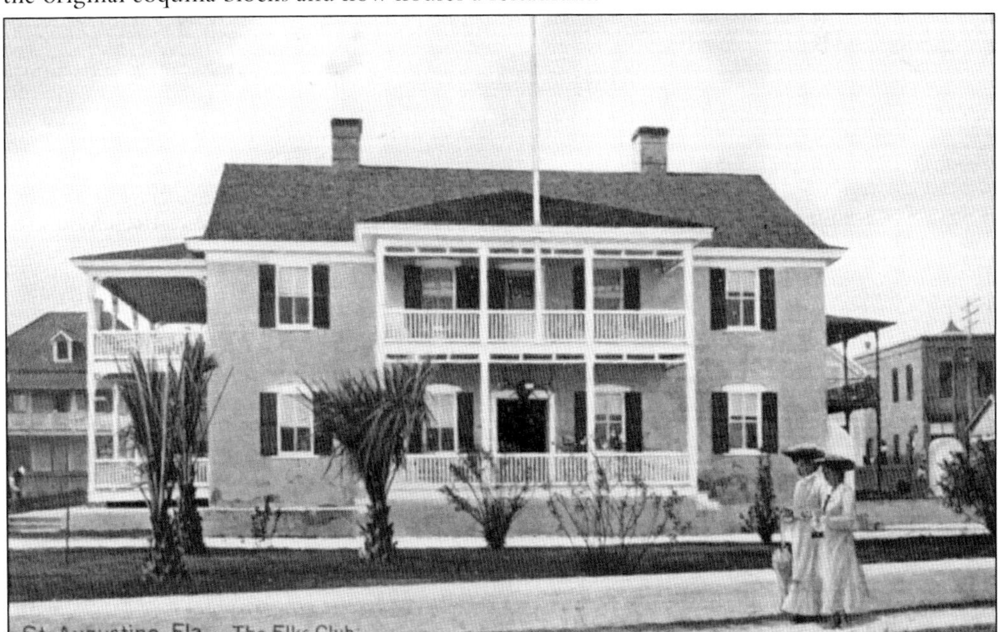

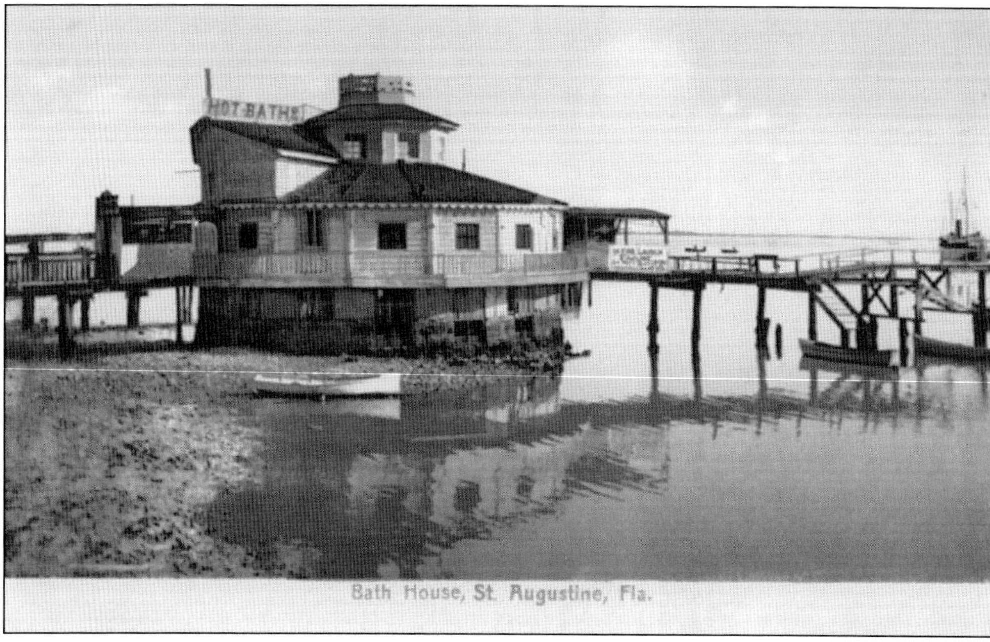

Capo's Bath House was an octagonal wooden building with stone foundations located on the bay at the foot of Treasury Street. It was built in the 1870s by Philip V. Capo, a native of St. Augustine, and offered hot and cold seawater and sulfur baths. Capo died in 1901, and the bathhouse was later owned by A. W. Pacetti. It was destroyed in the 1914 fire.

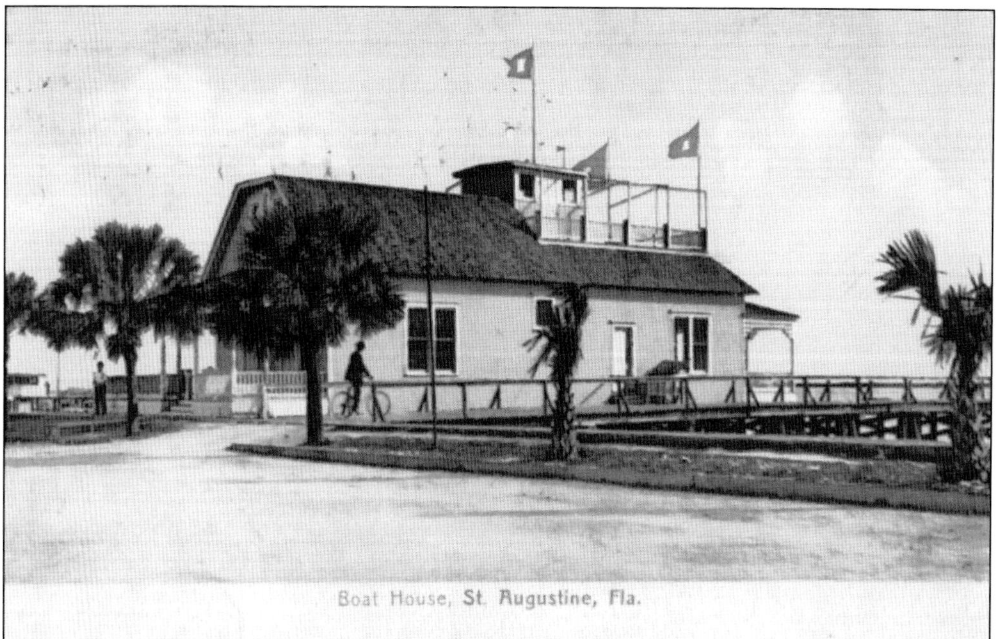

The St. Augustine Yacht Club was founded in 1873 as the second chartered yacht club in the state of Florida. In its earliest years, the yacht club was commissioned by the War Department, under Pres. Ulysses S. Grant, to defend St. Augustine by blockading the inlet in times of war. The clubhouse and dock were located in front of 46 Avenida Menendez.

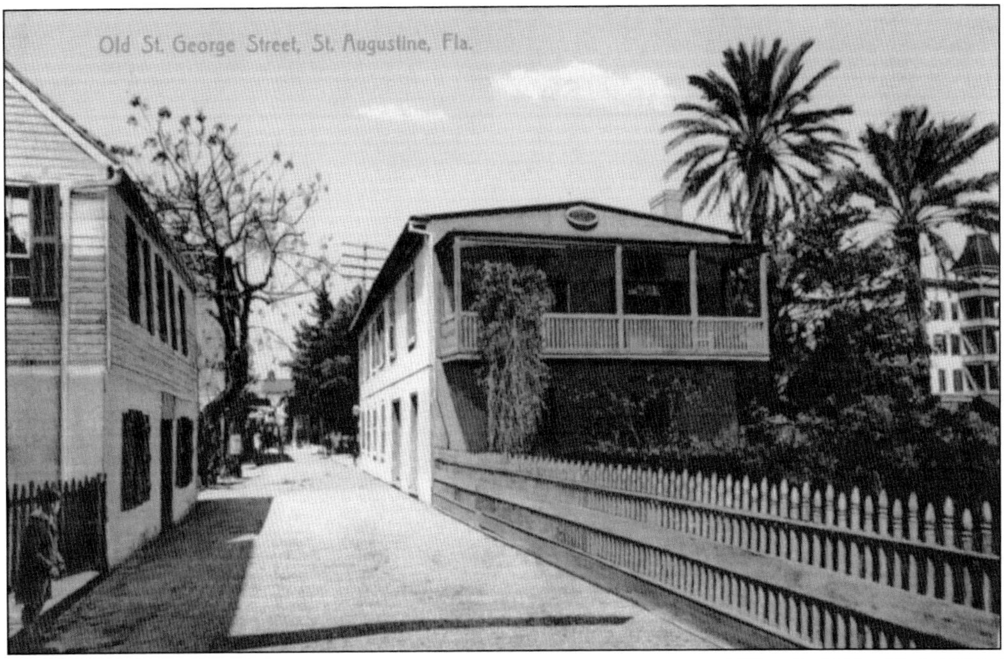

The house on the southeast corner of St. George and Treasury Streets was constructed around 1750 as the residence of the royal treasurer, Juan Esteban de Peña. Dr. Seth Peck purchased the home in 1837 and remodeled it, adding a second story. The Peck family lived in the house until 1931, when Anna Gardner Burt willed the property to the city as a house museum.

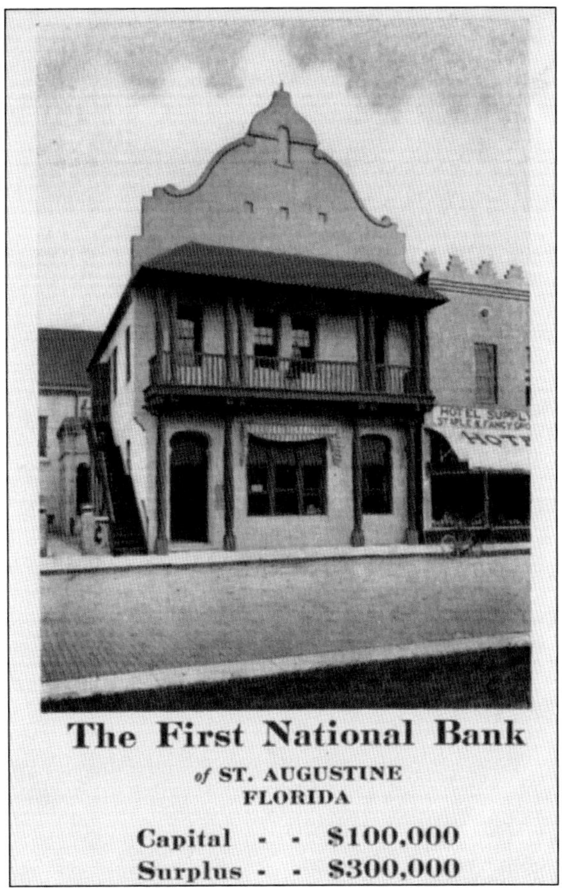

This 1910 postcard of the First National Bank advertises "$100,000 in Capital and $300,000 in Reserves." Located at 30 Cathedral Place, it was listed in the 1911–1912 City Directory as "Florida's Oldest National Bank," with John T. Dismukes as president and G. B. Lamar as vice president. The building would later house the offices of the St. Augustine Gas Company and was demolished in 1965 during the renovation of the cathedral.

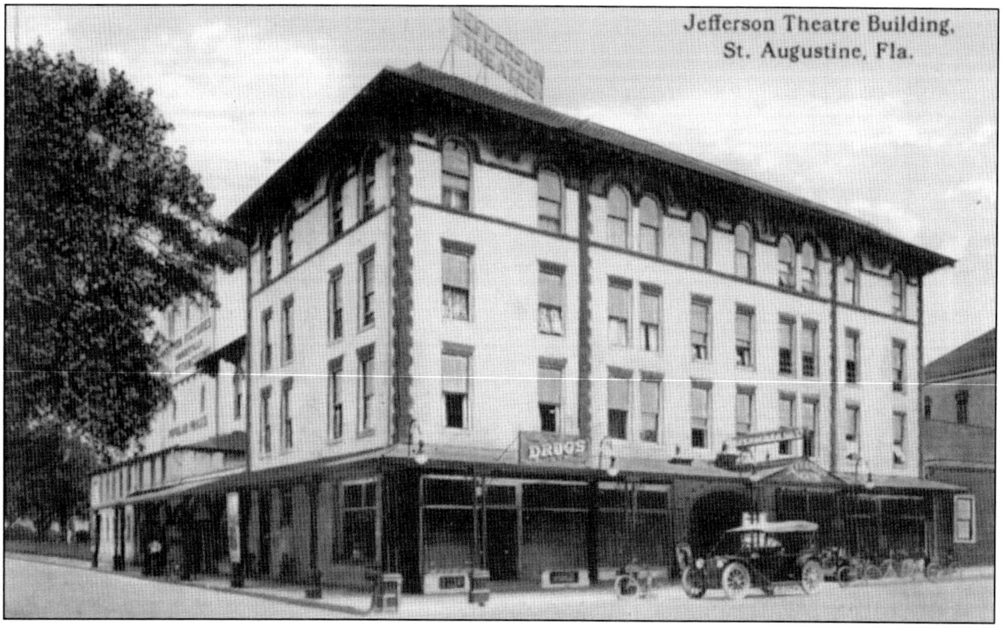

The Jefferson Theatre was built in 1909 on the corner of Cathedral Place and Cordova Street. The theater was named for brothers Joseph and William Jefferson, noted thespians of the day. The ground floor contained shops, with an arcade in the center of the building and the theater at the rear. The building was razed in the 1960s and is now the site of the downtown branch of the Bank of America.

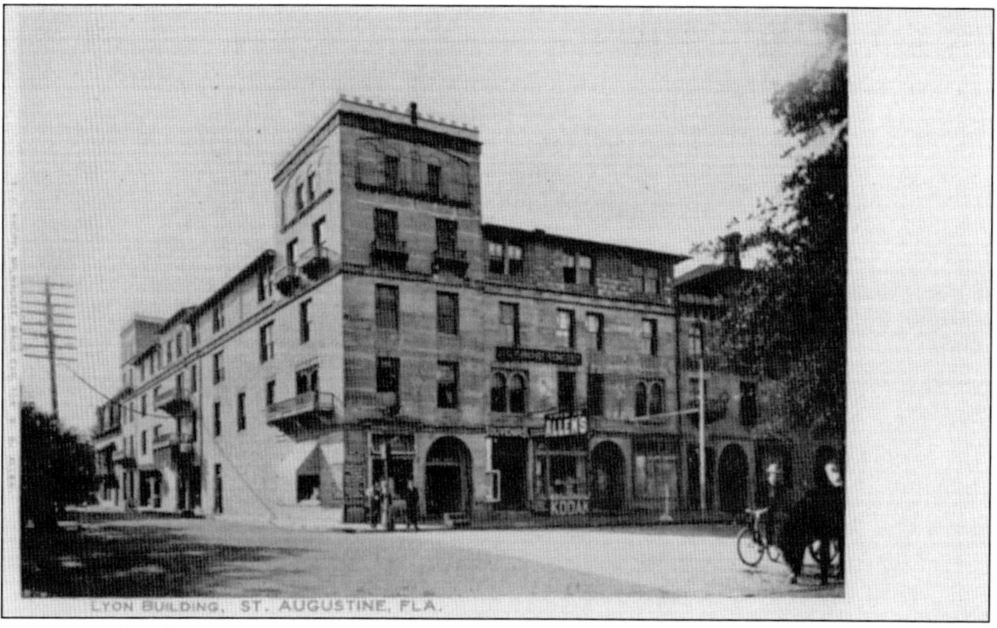

Oscar B. Bliss built the Moorish Revival Lyon Building on the southwest corner of King and St. George Streets in 1886–1887. Bliss's wife was the daughter of Walter Lyon, who had operated the Lyon Grocery Company at this location. The grocery business closed in 1908, and the upper floors rented as furnished rooms. The Lyon Building was renovated in 2000 into condominiums and retail shops.

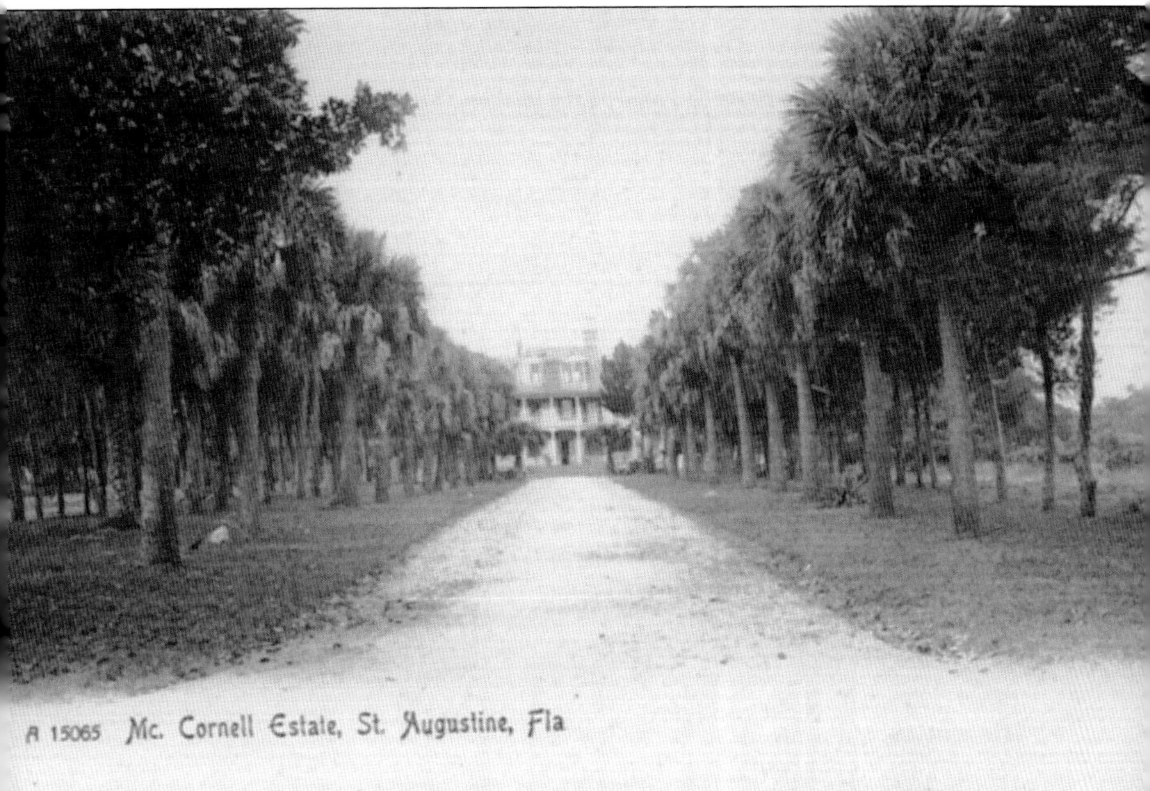

The McConnell estate was originally the home of Henry H. Williams, who purchased 225 acres in North City in 1868. His Paradise Grove estate extended from the Shell Road (San Marco Avenue) to Macaris Creek and included an orange grove and famous rose garden. In 1900, the property was sold to Eward and Louella McConnell of the Yukon Territory and later developed into the Fountain of Youth. The Williams house was moved twice and last located on the southeast corner of Magnolia Avenue and Dufferin Street. After World War II, it became the home of the Florida Naval Academy and was demolished in 1959. Four Victorian-style residences now occupy the site.

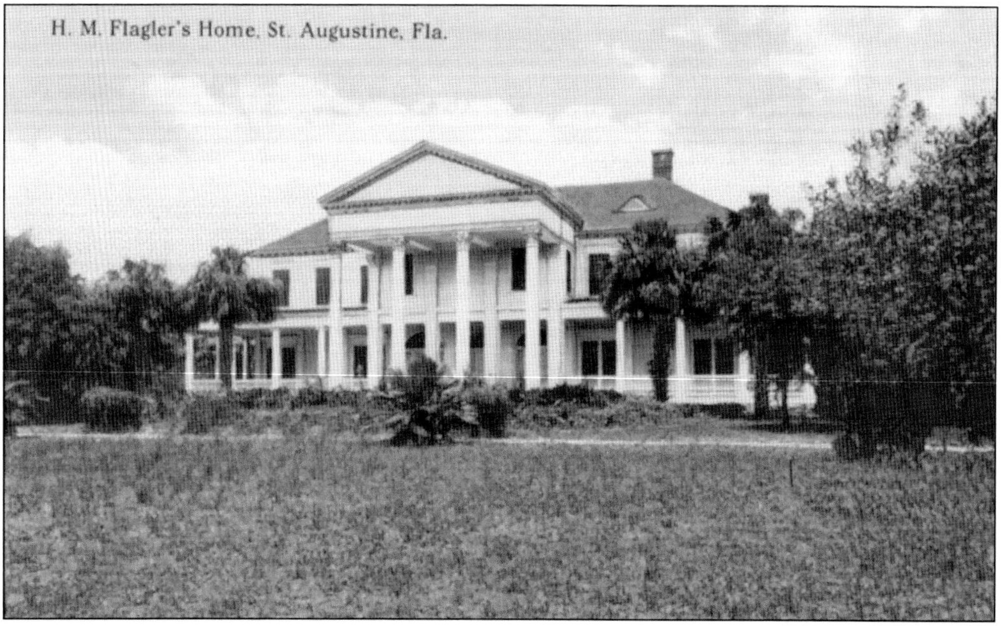

Constructed in 1892–1893 by J. A. MacDonald, Kirkside was the home of Henry Flagler. The southern Colonial mansion was situated on five acres west of the Memorial Presbyterian Church, bounded by Valencia, Riberia, and Carrera Streets. The house was torn down in 1950 and the property divided into 13 residential lots. Architect F. A. Hollingsworth built the Kirkside Apartments at 55 Riberia Street, using the elegant columns salvaged from the mansion.

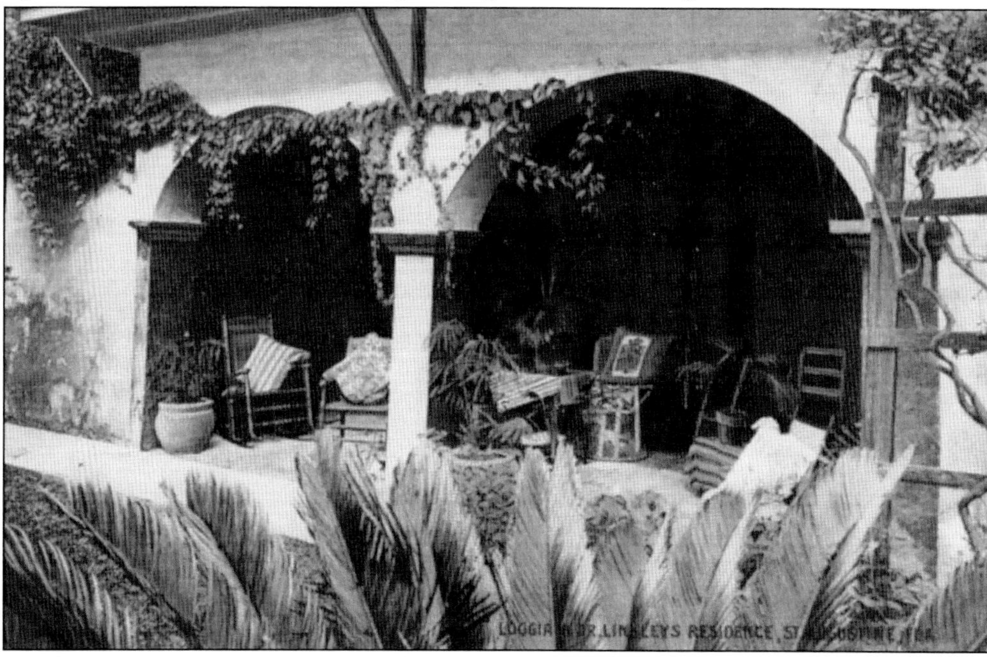

This house at 214 St. George Street is one of the oldest in the city, dating from the first Spanish period prior to 1763. In 1896, it was sold to Dr. Horace Lindsley, a homeopathic physician and nephew of Pennsylvania lumber baron Albert Lewis, a prominent winter resident of St. Augustine. This view shows the loggia on the south side of the house.

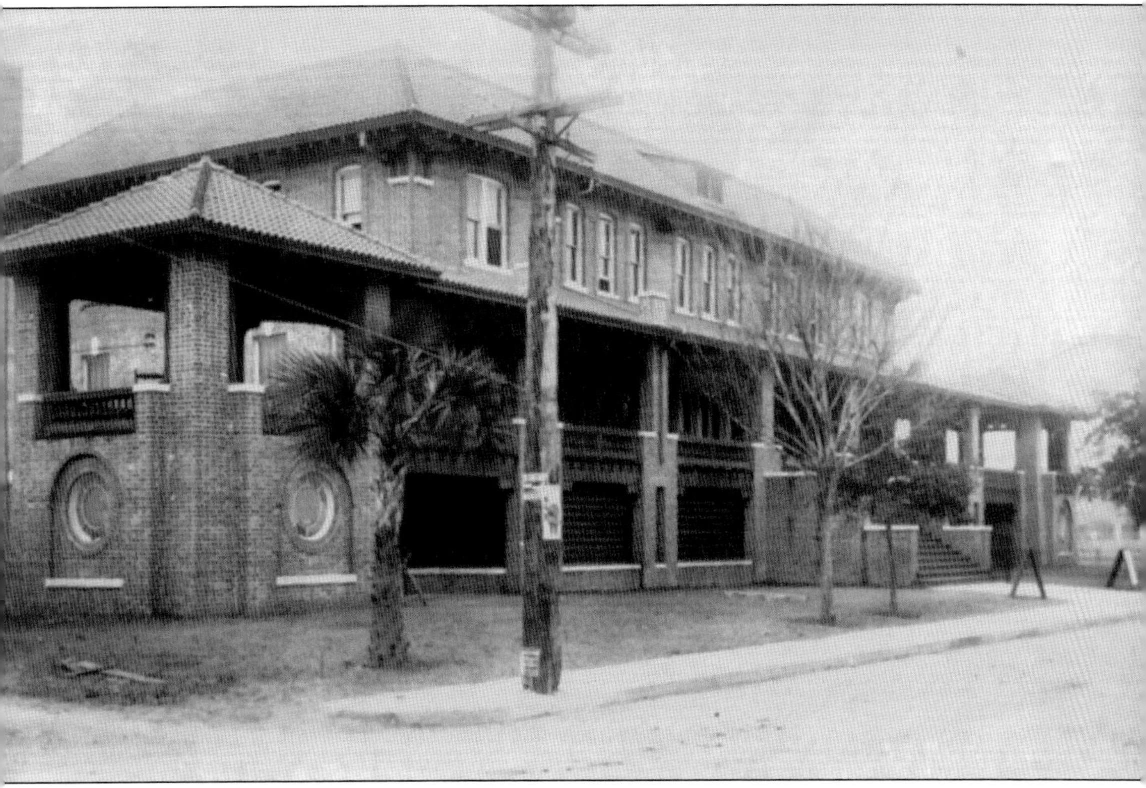

Henry Flagler built the YMCA in 1907 as a place for Christian fellowship and recreation for the employees of his Florida East Coast Railway. The architect was John W. Ingle, and the two-story red brick building featured an above-ground basement on the bottom level. Constructed by W. P. Richardson of Jacksonville at a cost of $85,000, the Y had bowling alleys, a gym, an indoor swimming pool, and sleeping rooms for railroad men. A separate wooden gymnasium was added at the rear of the building in 1928. Located at the corner of Valencia and Riberia Streets, the YMCA was torn down in 1983, and the site is now the Flagler College Tennis Complex. This 1912 view is by W. J. Harris.

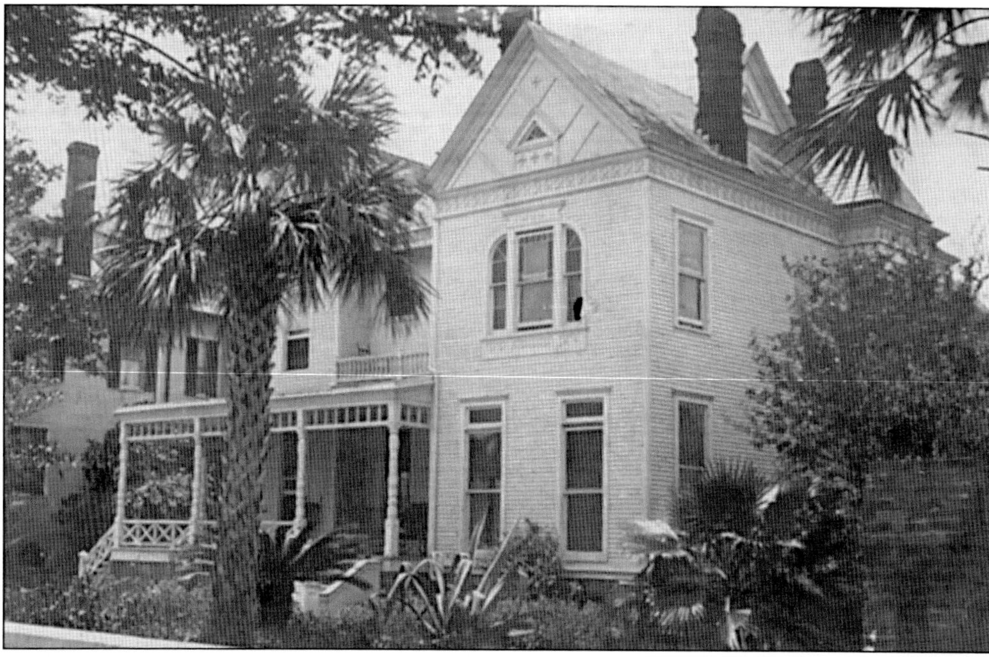

The home at 272 St. George Street was built in 1888 for Curtis A. Hibbard of Vermont. In 1904, it became the residence of Reginald White, a prominent St. Augustinian who was vice president of the First National Bank. White's mother-in-law, Mary Frazer, ran the Valencia Hotel next door at 276 St. George Street. The house was renovated in 1999 and is an outstanding example of St. Augustine's Victorian architecture.

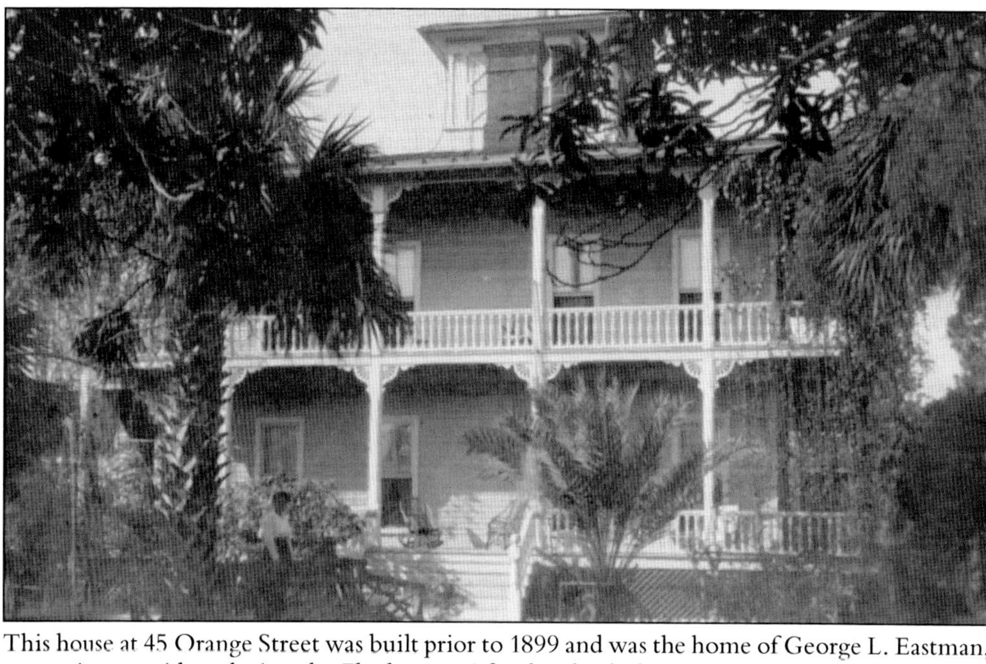

This house at 45 Orange Street was built prior to 1899 and was the home of George L. Eastman, a prominent resident during the Flagler era. After his death, his widow, Margaret B. Eastman, continued to live in the home for many years. The house was razed, and the site is now the parking lot east of the Anita Yates Center at 47 Orange Street.

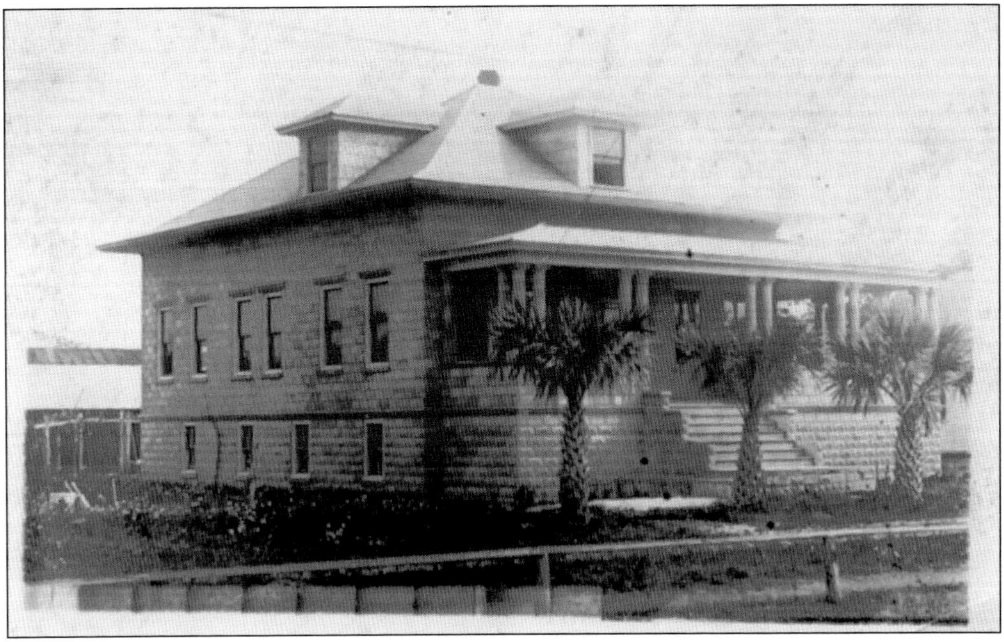

Frederick A. Capo, who worked as a blacksmith at the Florida East Coast Railway, constructed this house at 24 Cincinnati Avenue around 1910. It is the finest example of construction using locally produced coquina concrete and features decorative block and cast concrete columns. Insurance maps show a stone casting factory in the backyard before the house was erected.

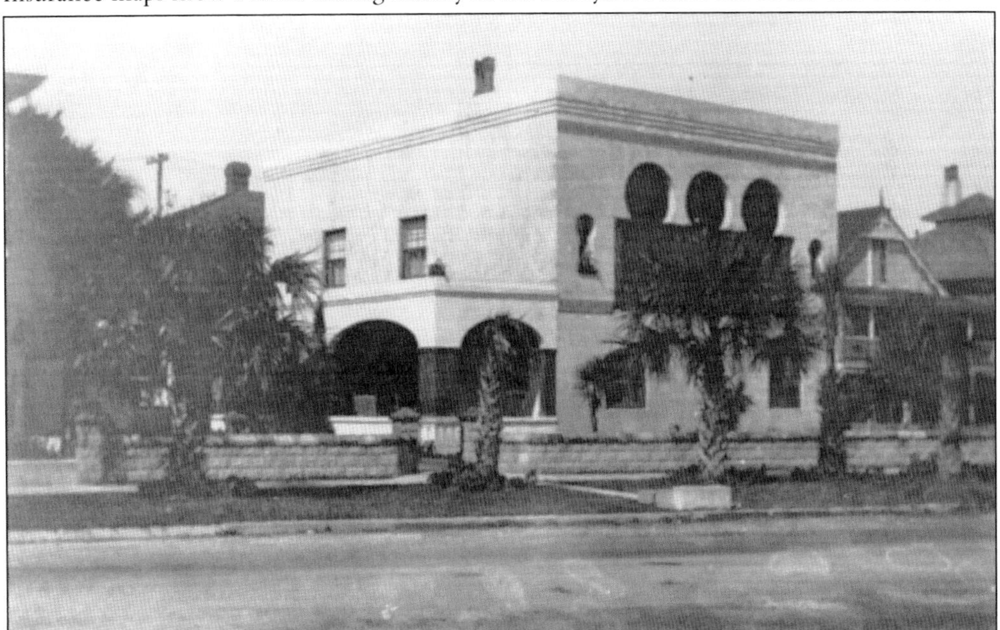

Originally known as the Brooks Villa, this Moorish Revival home was built in 1891 for brothers Charles S. and Tracy Brooks. It lacks the ornamental parapet of other Moorish Revival buildings constructed in St. Augustine at that time but has the classic horseshoe arches on the second-story loggia. A one-story open porch was later added to the south side of the home at 174 Bay Street (Avenida Menendez).

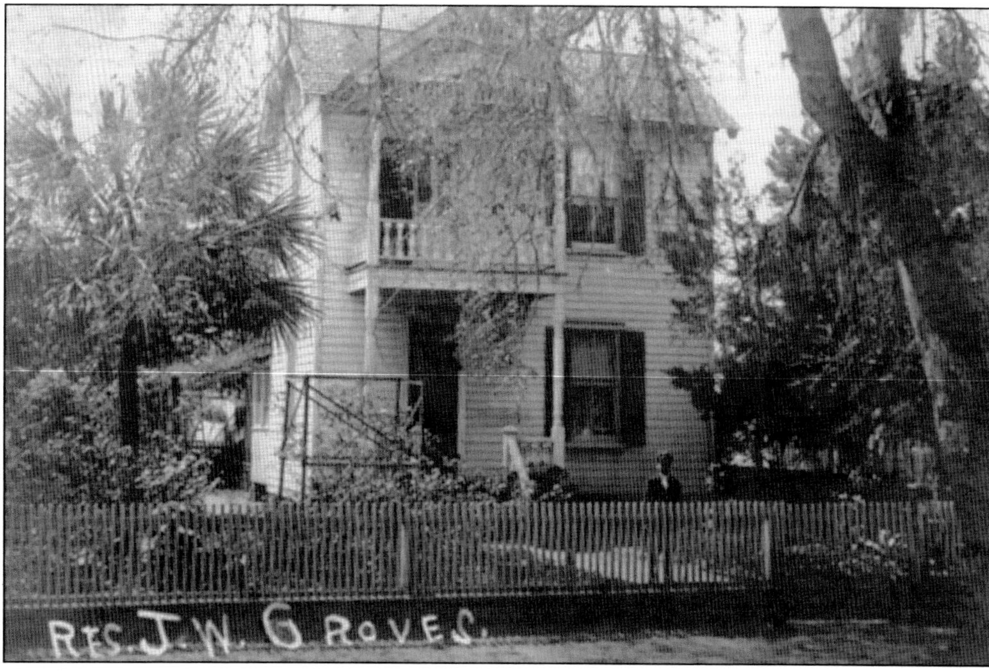

The house at 11 Rohde Avenue was built between 1885 and 1894 by Henry Rohde, who developed a former orange grove into a subdivision in the 1880s. It is one of four identical houses built by Rohde, and the street and subdivision are both named for him. In the early 1900s, the home was the residence of J. W. Groves; it was later enlarged with an addition on the east side.

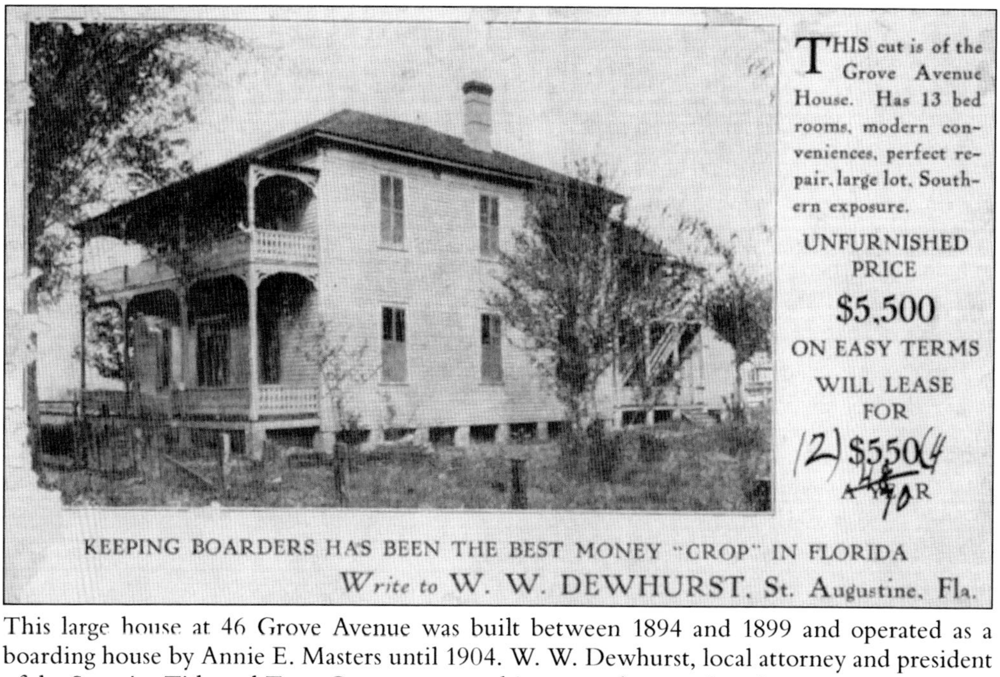

This large house at 46 Grove Avenue was built between 1894 and 1899 and operated as a boarding house by Annie E. Masters until 1904. W. W. Dewhurst, local attorney and president of the Security Title and Trust Company, sent this postcard as an advertisement to prospective buyers. The house later became an inn, the Riverside House, and is now a private residence.

Five

Attractions

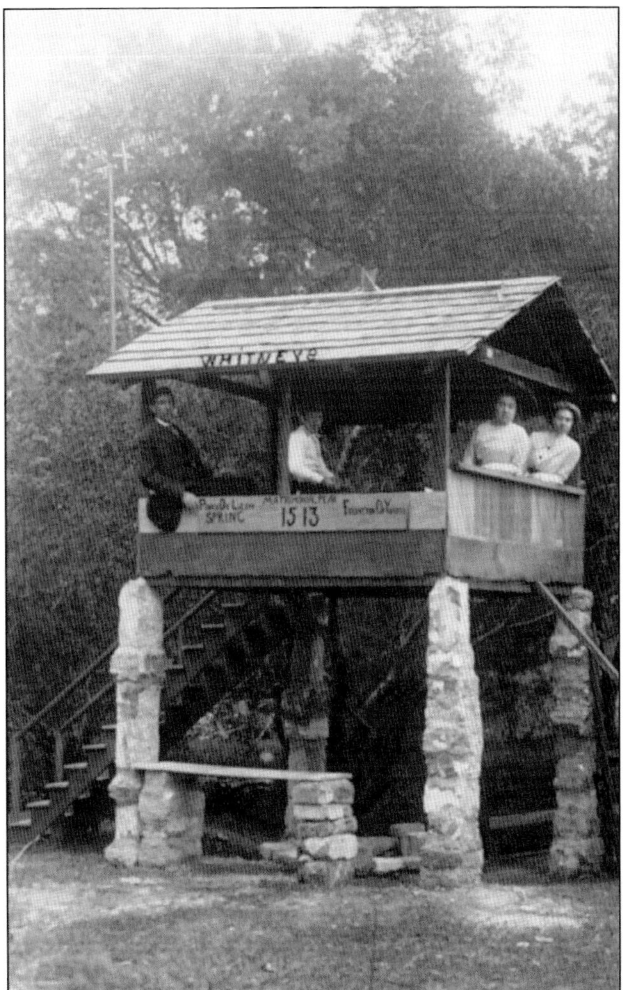

Whitney's Ponce de Leon Spring was located in West Augustine, near present-day Spring Street. Owner John Whitney, a former newspaper publisher in Boston and New York who came to St. Augustine after the Civil War, promoted it as the original Fountain of Youth. Whitney, a grandson of cotton gin inventor Eli Whitney, was a "tourist entrepreneur" and operated several attractions for winter visitors. Whitney's Alligator Farm was originally located on the Horn Road (today's Masters Drive) near his Ponce de Leon Spring. He developed land in the North Beach and Ravenswood areas, and Whitney Street in West Augustine is named for him. After his death in 1902, his son, Everett C. Whitney, took over his tourist operations and real estate business.

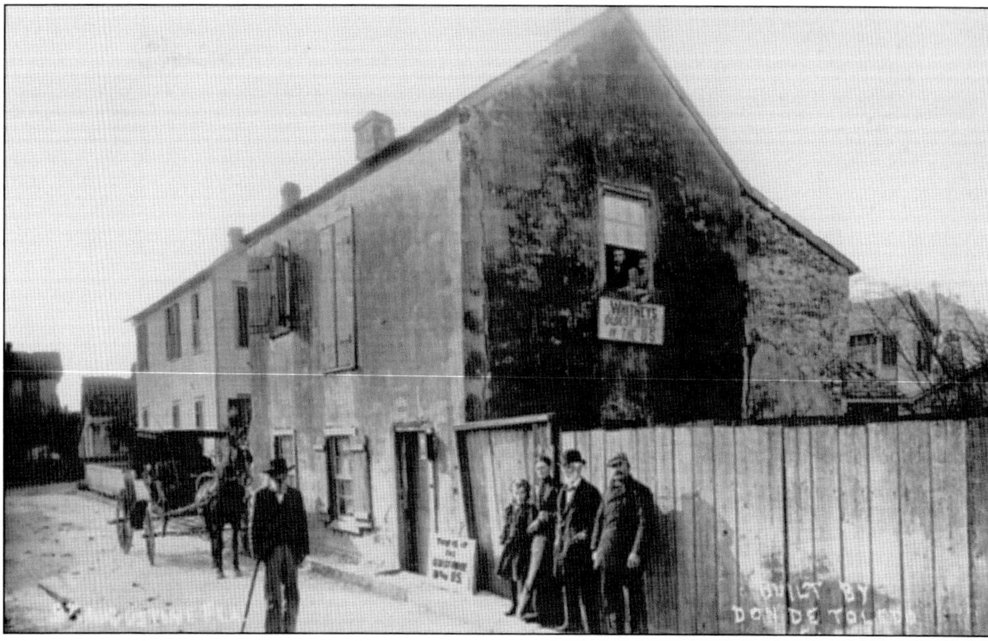

The coquina house at 36 Hospital (Aviles) Street was built between 1803 and 1817 by Gaspar Papy, a Greek who had emigrated with the Minorcan colonists. In 1903, it was leased to Everett C. Whitney and became a tourist attraction known as Whitney's Oldest House. This view by W. J. Harris is captioned "Built by Don Toledo in 1516," which is sheer exaggeration, as St. Augustine was not founded until 1565.

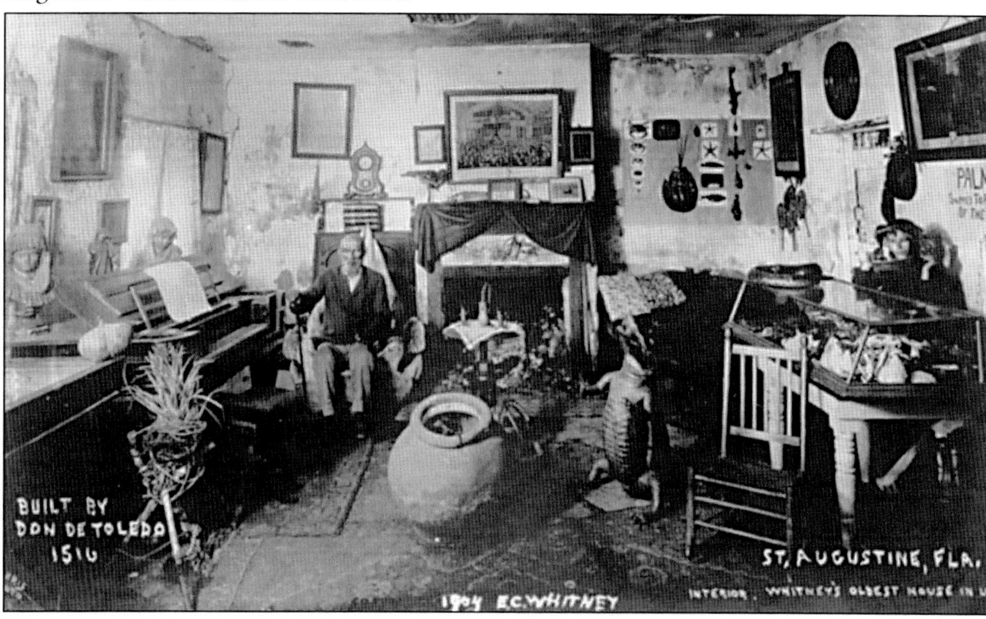

This interior view of Whitney's Oldest House shows the eclectic collection of artifacts on display. Whitney operated the attraction until 1912, and it later became known as the Don Toledo House. The Sisters of St. Joseph purchased the property in 1928 and later remodeled the house; today it retains little of its original appearance. The St. Augustine Historical Society purchased the collections and contents of the house.

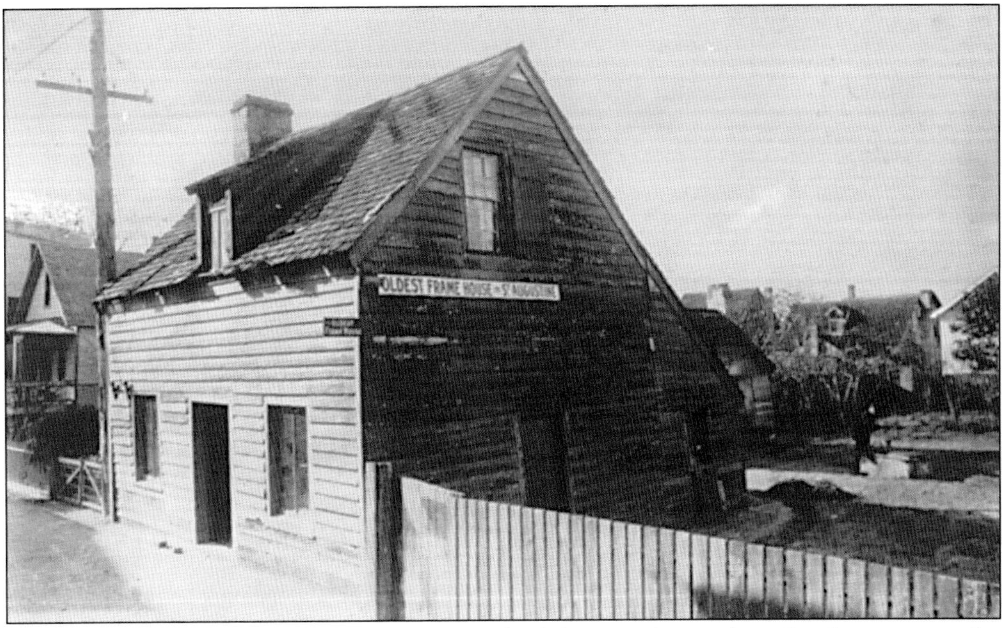

The wooden house at 14 St. George Street was built by Juan Genopoly, a Greek carpenter who came to St. Augustine with the Minorcans, and is the only known surviving second Spanish period frame building in the city. In the early 1900s, occupants Thomas and Cora Kearns sold novelties and souvenirs to tourists and began to advertise their business location as the "Oldest Frame House."

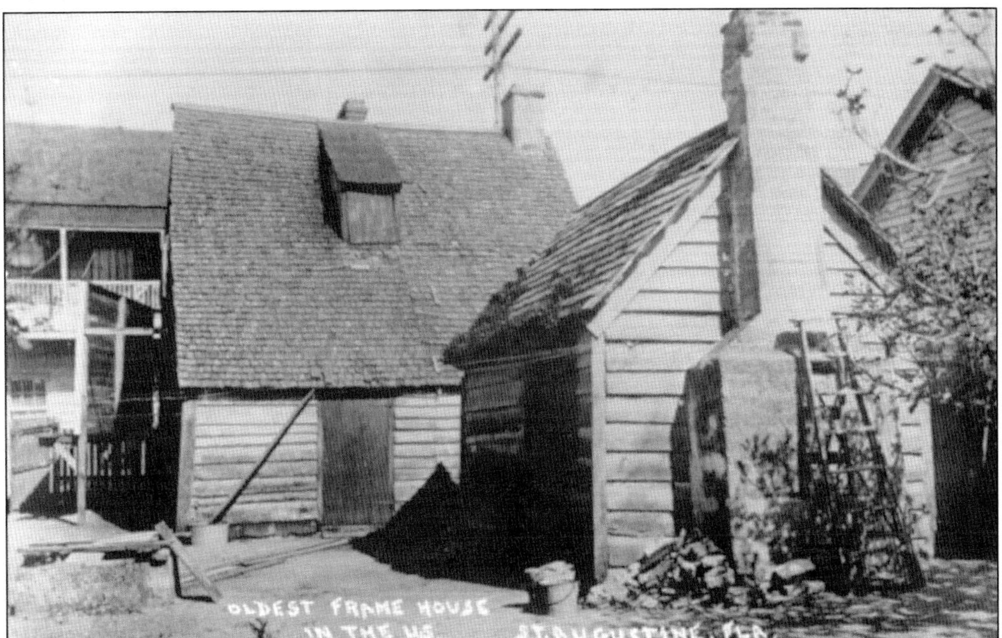

The rear view of the "Oldest Frame House" shows the detached kitchen on the right. The house is constructed of pest-resistant red cedar and cypress timbers secured with wooden pegs. In 1931, W. J. Harris purchased the property, renamed it the Oldest Wooden Schoolhouse, and began its operation as a tourist attraction.

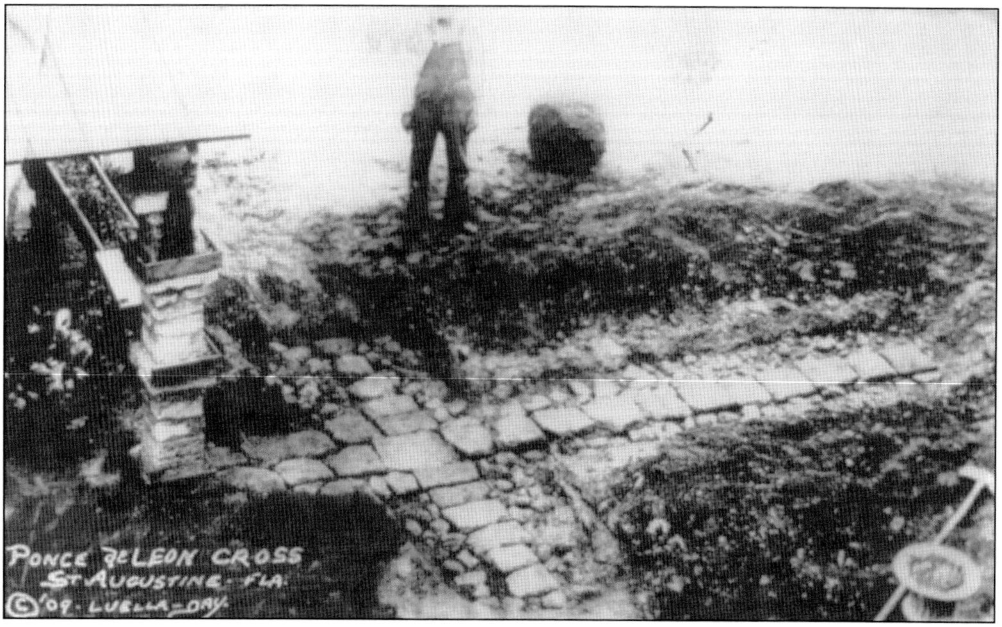

Edward and Louella Day McConnell made their fortune in the Klondike gold rush and purchased the Williams estate in North City in 1900. After her husband's death, Louella became involved in historical research and became convinced that her property was the site of Ponce de Leon's landing. On April 19, 1909, her workman, John Henry Lee, uncovered a coquina cross while digging out a palmetto stump. The cross contained 15 stones vertically and 13 stones on the horizontal, thus signifying the date "1513." Photographer W. J. Harris was sent for and took this photograph shortly after the discovery. Louella built this enclosure around her nearby "spring"—some said it was a dug well—and began charging for glasses of water from the Fountain of Youth. She later built a gate and archway at the entrance and charged admission to the grounds.

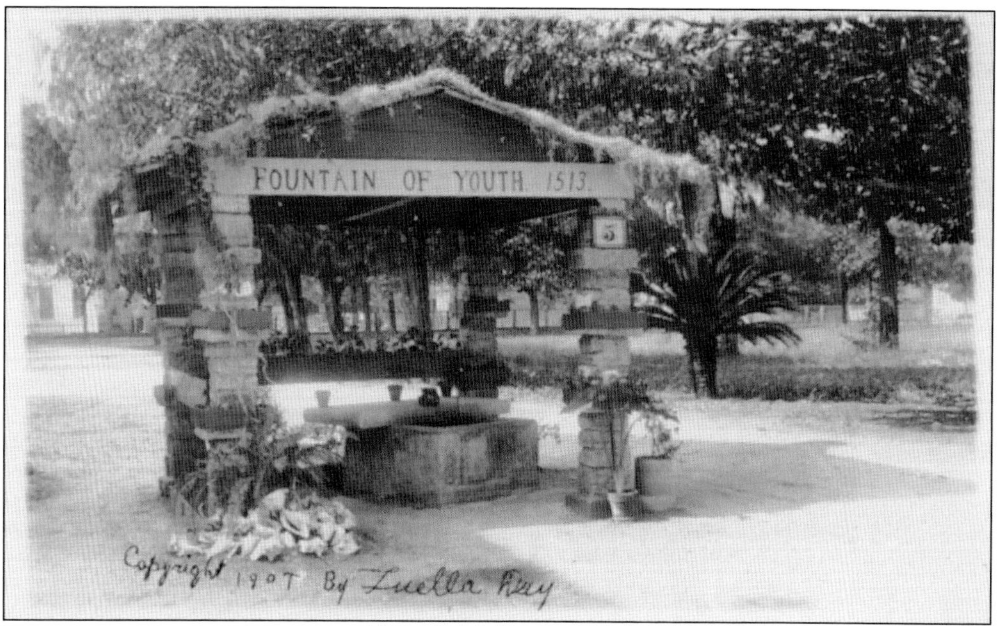

Also unearthed with the cross was a silver casque containing an affidavit of the sealing of the image by Ponce de Leon. Louella had this representation of the casque made for her historical displays. During World War I, a secret German wireless was found on her property, and Louella was arrested and sent to an internment camp until the war's end in 1918.

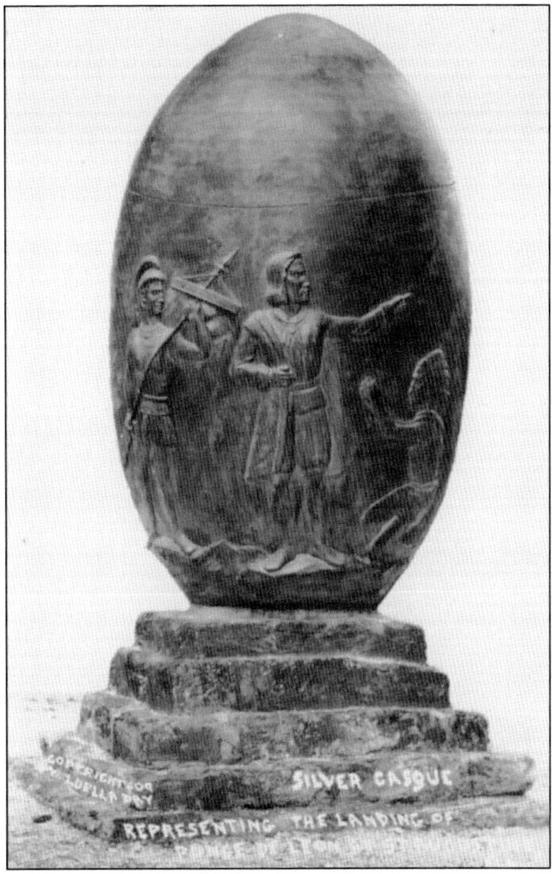

Louella McConnell built this corrugated-iron chapel to house her historical exhibits at the Fountain of Youth. She later sold the property but stayed on in her house and refused to leave, resulting in many lawsuits between her and the new owners. Louella died in a car crash on the Hastings Road on June 24, 1927, ending the era of one of St. Augustine's most colorful characters.

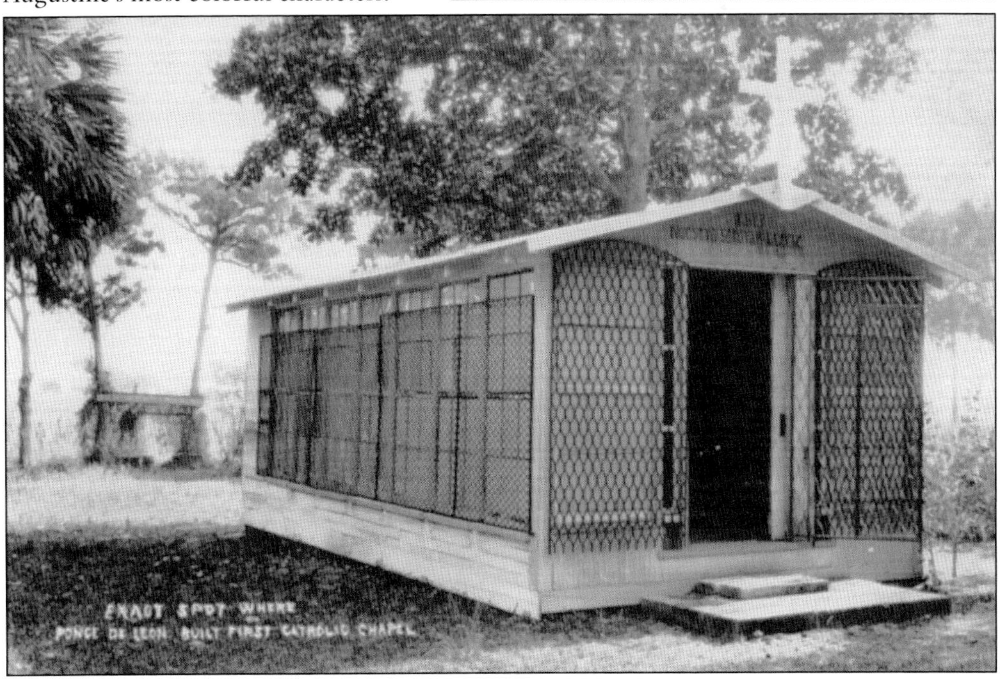

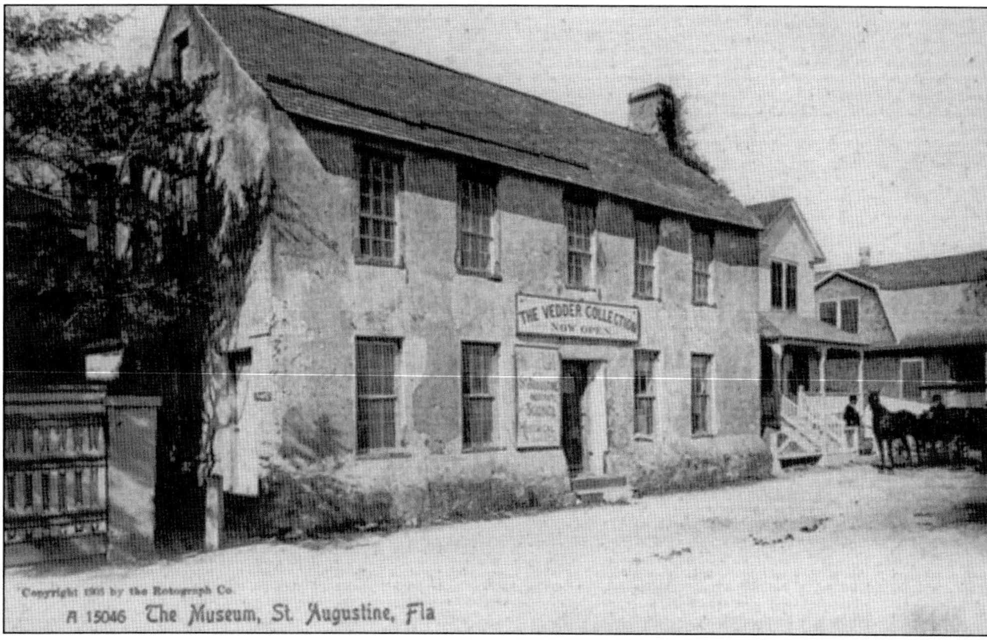

The coquina house at the corner of Treasury and Bay Streets (Avenida Menendez) dates from the first Spanish period prior to 1763. In the late 1880s, Dr. John Vedder operated a natural history museum and menagerie in the building. After Vedder's death in 1899, the St. Augustine Institute of Science (predecessor of today's St. Augustine Historical Society) purchased his collection and continued to operate the museum as the House of History.

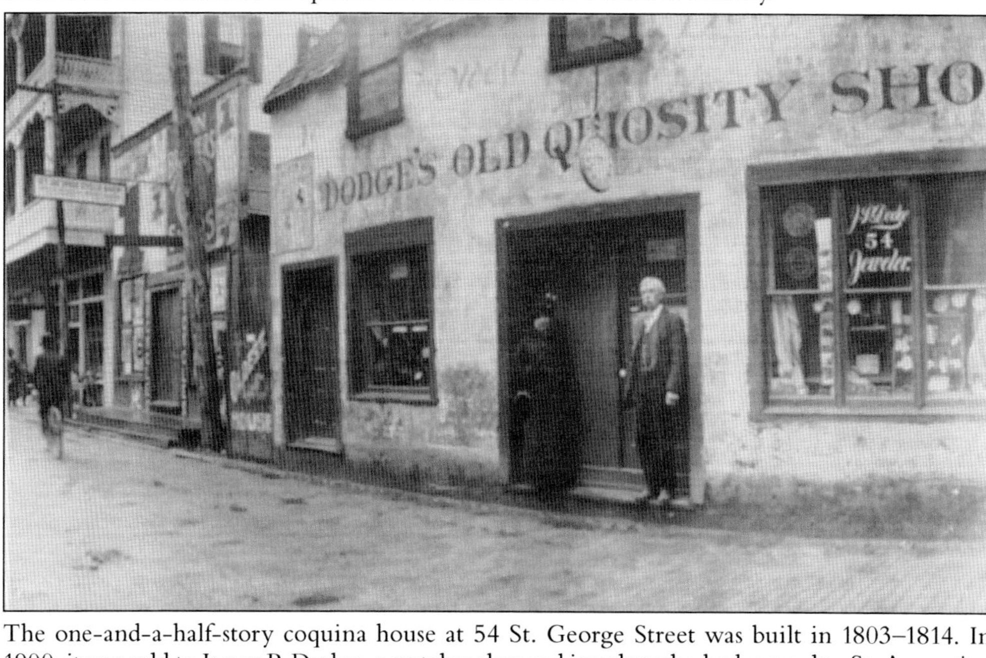

The one-and-a-half-story coquina house at 54 St. George Street was built in 1803–1814. In 1900, it was sold to James P. Dodge, a watchmaker and jeweler who had moved to St. Augustine in 1885. Dodge is pictured here in front of his Old Curiosity Shop, which he claimed was constructed in 1565. The building is now known as the Paredes-Dodge House and currently houses a gift shop.

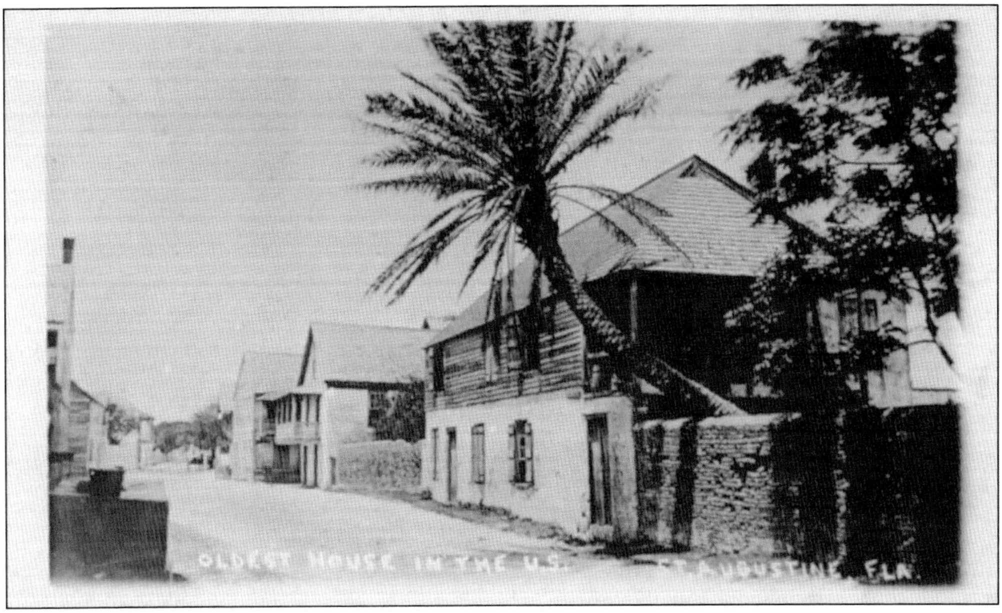

This W. J. Harris postcard from the early 1900s was made from a much earlier photograph of the Oldest House, with its famous date palm tree curving over the wall. Known today as the González-Alvarez House, it is the oldest surviving Spanish Colonial dwelling in Florida. The site at 14 St. Francis Street has been occupied since the 1600s, and the present house dates to the early 1700s.

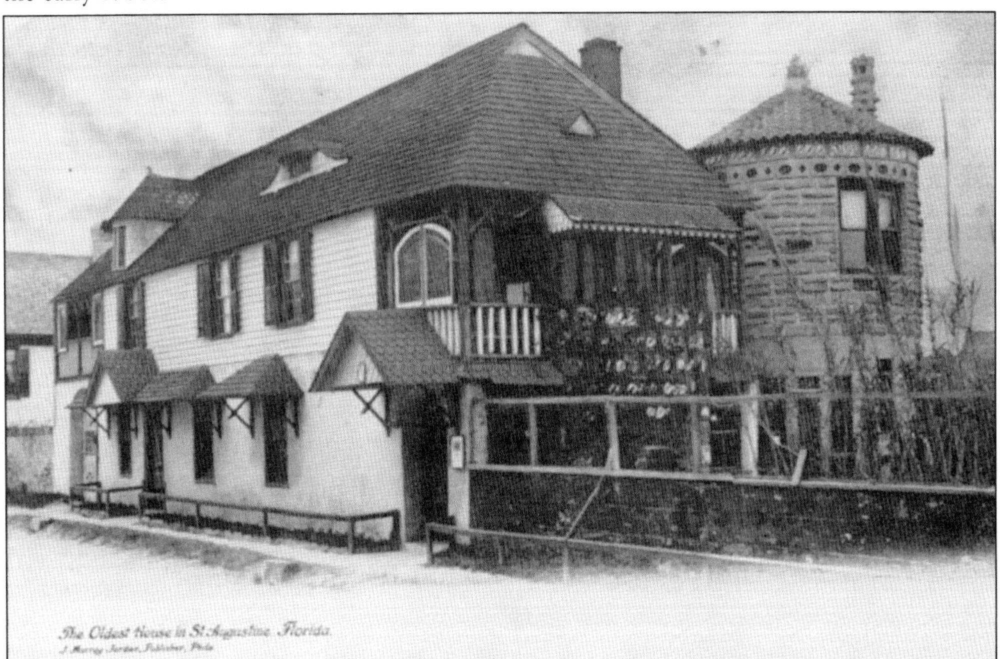

Dr. Charles Carver, a local dentist, purchased the house in 1884 and began promoting his home as "The Oldest House" in the 1890s. In 1918, the St. Augustine Historical Society purchased the house. They restored the structure to its Colonial appearance in 1960 with the removal of the masonry tower, dormers, and other Victorian-era additions seen in this early-1900s postcard.

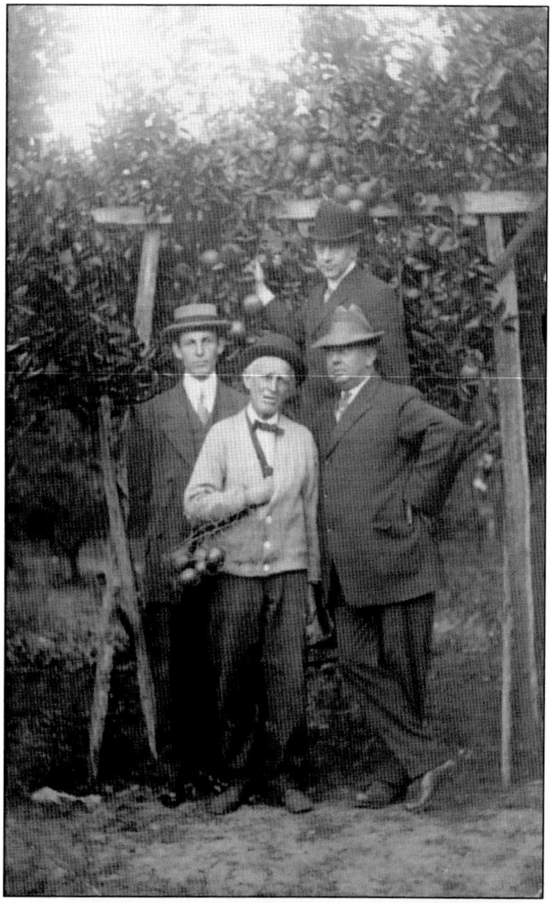

Dr. Reuben B. Garnett was a retired physician who had a large estate and citrus grove west of the Shell Road (San Marco Avenue) and north of St. Louis (Old Mission) Avenue. In 1891, Dr. Garnett donated land on Sebastian Avenue to the Catholic Church for St. Agnes School and Church. In this photo postcard, Dr. Garnett is in front holding a basket of fruit from his grove.

With its beautiful live oak drive, Dr. Garnett's Orange Grove became a popular tourist destination in the early 1900s. After Dr. Garnett's death in 1922, his daughter, Katherine E. Murphy, operated it as the Oldest Orange Grove, with a riding stable on the grounds. Garnett's granddaughter, M. K. Murphy, became an accomplished horsewoman and has led St. Augustine's Easter Parade for over 50 years.

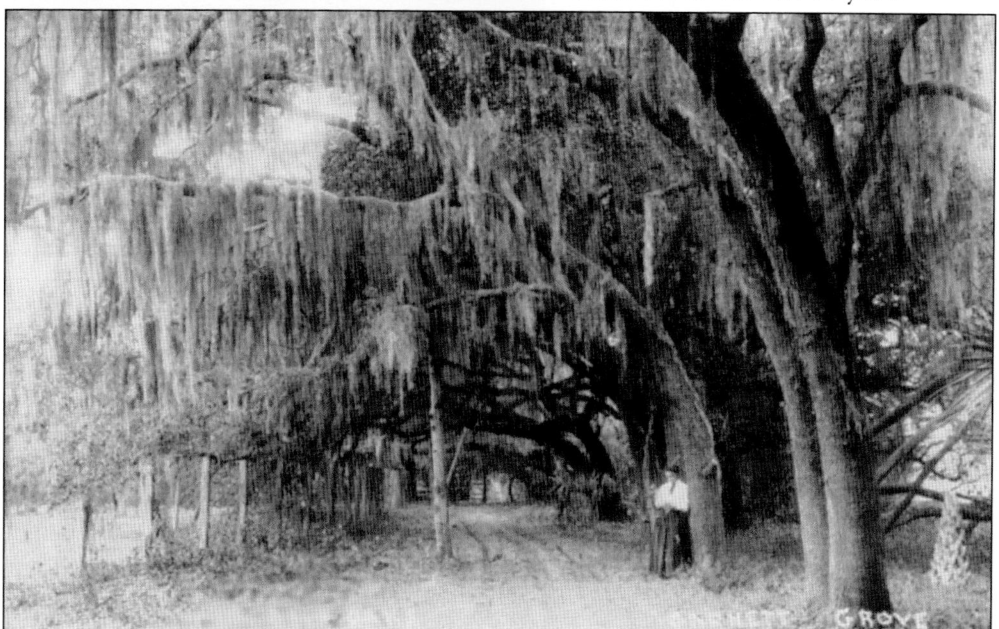

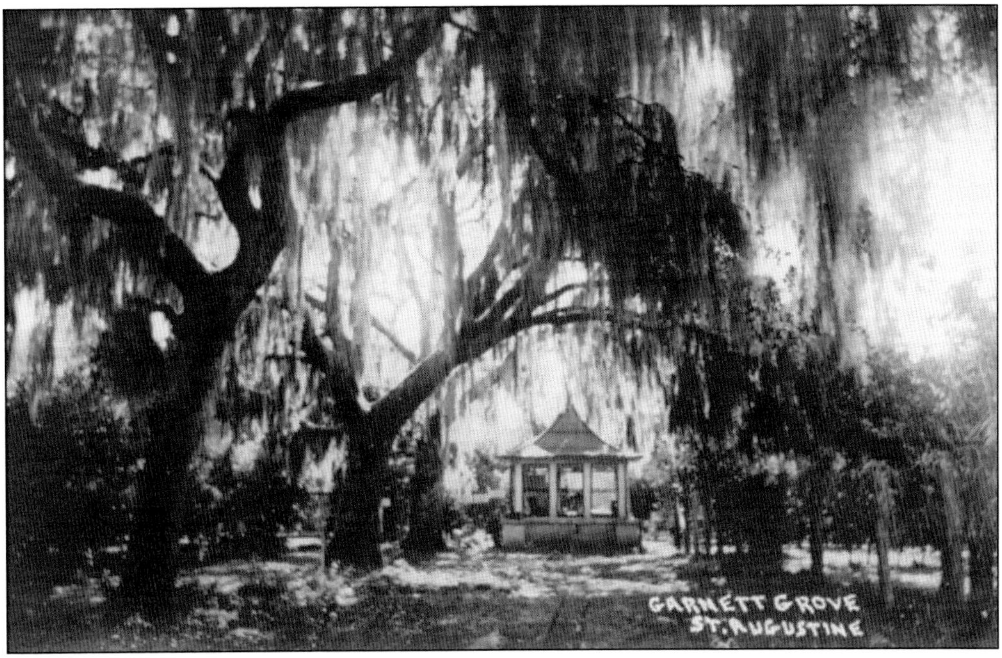

This photo postcard by W. J. Harris depicts a portion of Garnett's live oak drive known as "Lovers Lane." Dr. Garnett's house at 114 San Marco Avenue was razed in 1954. In the 1960s, Ponce de Leon Boulevard (U.S. 1) was built across the western portion of Garnett's property, and the ancient live oaks were cut down and replaced by a supermarket and motels.

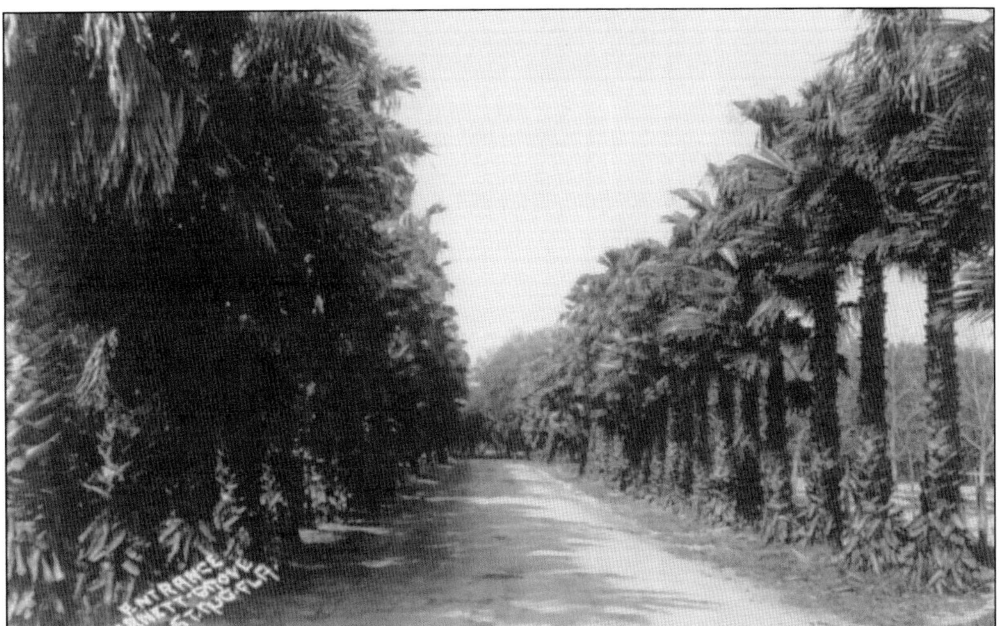

This avenue of *Washingtonia robusta* palms was a popular vista at Dr. Garnett's Grove. The only vestige of the estate that remains today is a group of live oak trees just west of Ponce de Leon Boulevard between Old Mission and Sebastian Avenues. Two blocks farther north is Garnett Avenue, named for him.

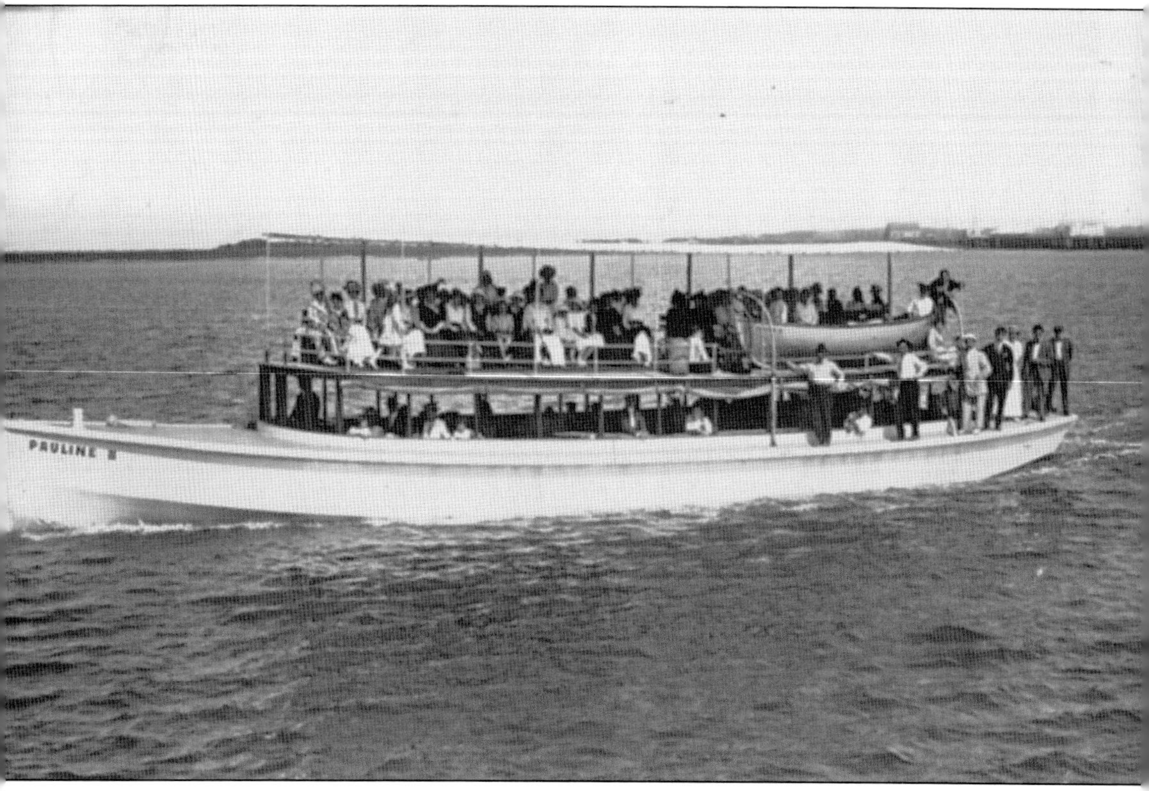

This view by W. A. Kugler shows the *Pauline II* on Matanzas Bay taking a load of passengers to Capo's North Beach. Anastasia Island and the lighthouse can be seen in the distance behind the stern of the boat. In 1904, Paul and Helen ("Ellen") Walton Capo moved to what is now Surfside Avenue in Vilano Beach. They erected a boat landing and pavilion on the east side of the Tolomato River (also called North River) and served seafood dinners to their visitors. A July 23, 1910, article in the *Evening Record* described a typical outing: "A large crowd enjoyed Sunday at North Beach and many indulged in a dip in the surf. Schools of mullet were noticed by the bathers and a net was secured and a quantity of fish caught."

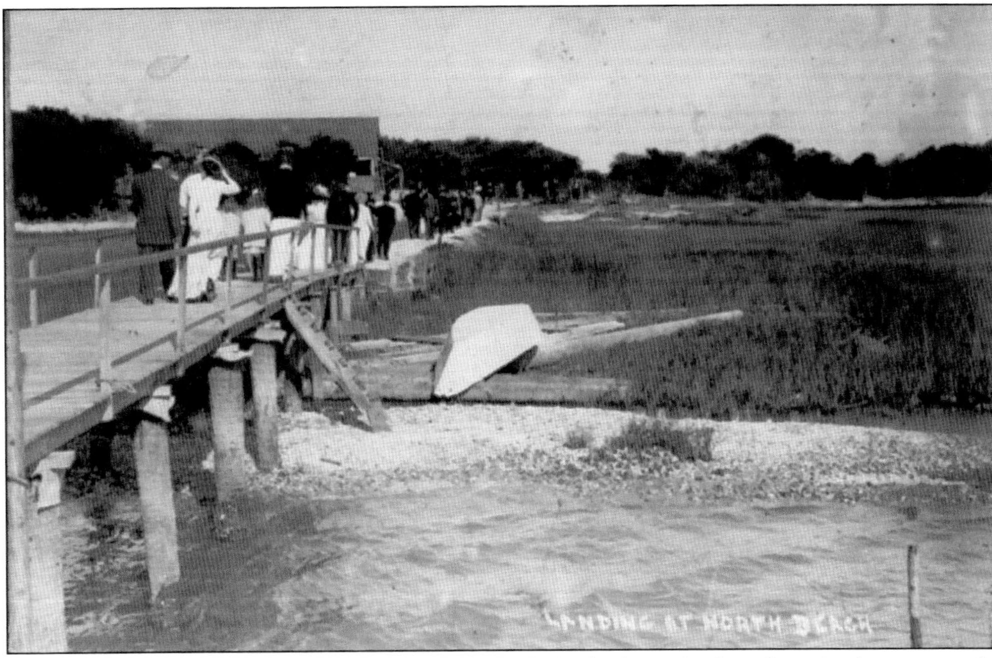

Passengers departed for North Beach from Capo's dock along the bay front in downtown St. Augustine. They then rode up the Tolomato River to Capo's Landing at the western end of what is now Surfside Avenue. This photo postcard by W. J. Harris shows passengers walking up the Tolomato River dock toward the pavilion.

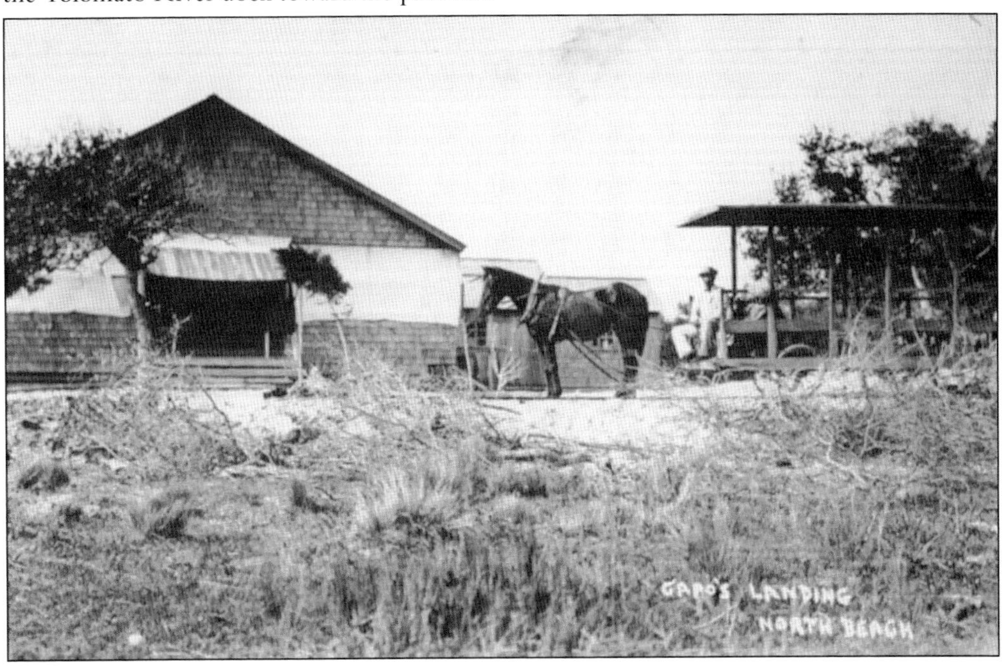

The Capos built a horse-drawn trolley to carry guests over the dunes to the beach. This Harris view shows the horse cart stopped in front of the pavilion, which seated 120 guests and offered a five-course meal, including roasted oysters, pilau, clam chowder, and fish, for 25¢. A small hotel was later built next to the pavilion.

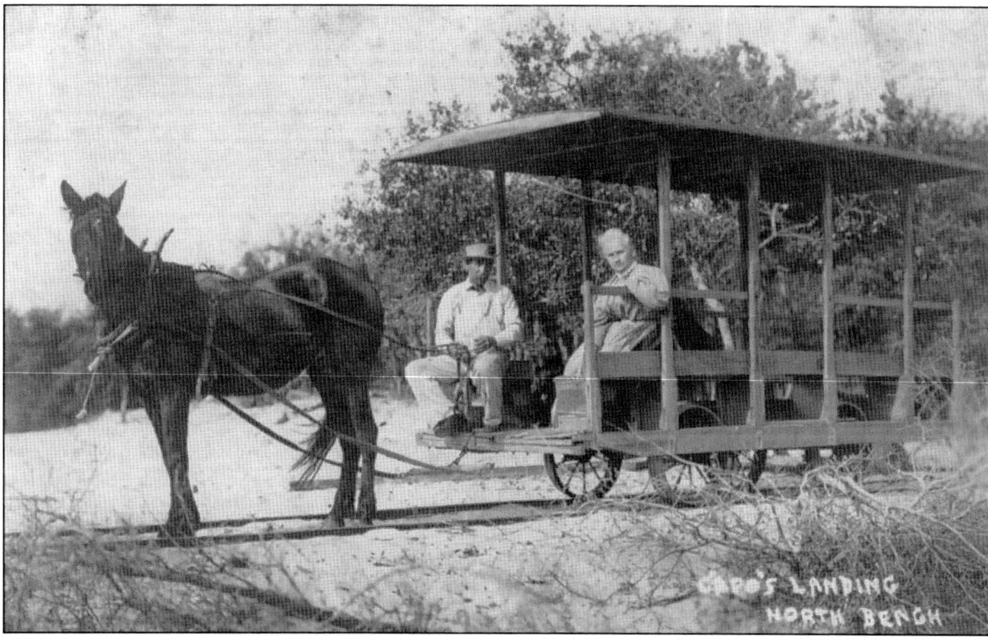

Ellen Capo sits on the right in the horse-drawn trolley stopped by the landing on the Tolomato River. The trolley was originally pulled from the front, as shown here. Later a larger trolley was constructed, with the horse hitched to a platform on the side. The platform would pivot, making it easier to change directions at each end of the trip.

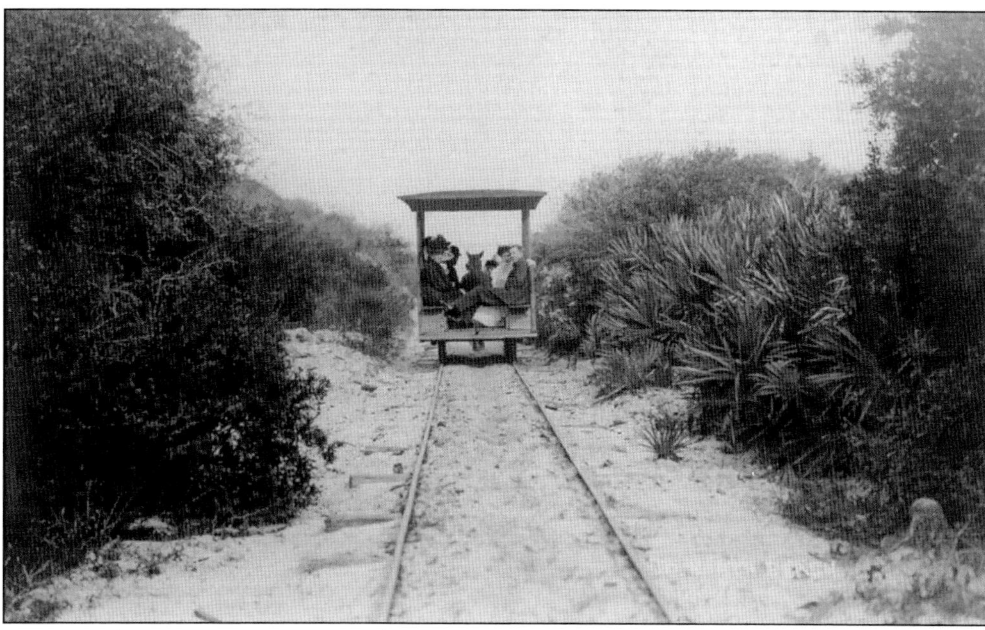

This view by W. J. Harris shows Capo's horse-drawn trolley heading east across the sand dunes to the beach. The trolley line ran along what is now Surfside Avenue in Vilano Beach and ended at a bathhouse at the beach. The site of the bathhouse would later be developed into the Surfside Casino, which was razed in the 1970s and is now a beachfront park.

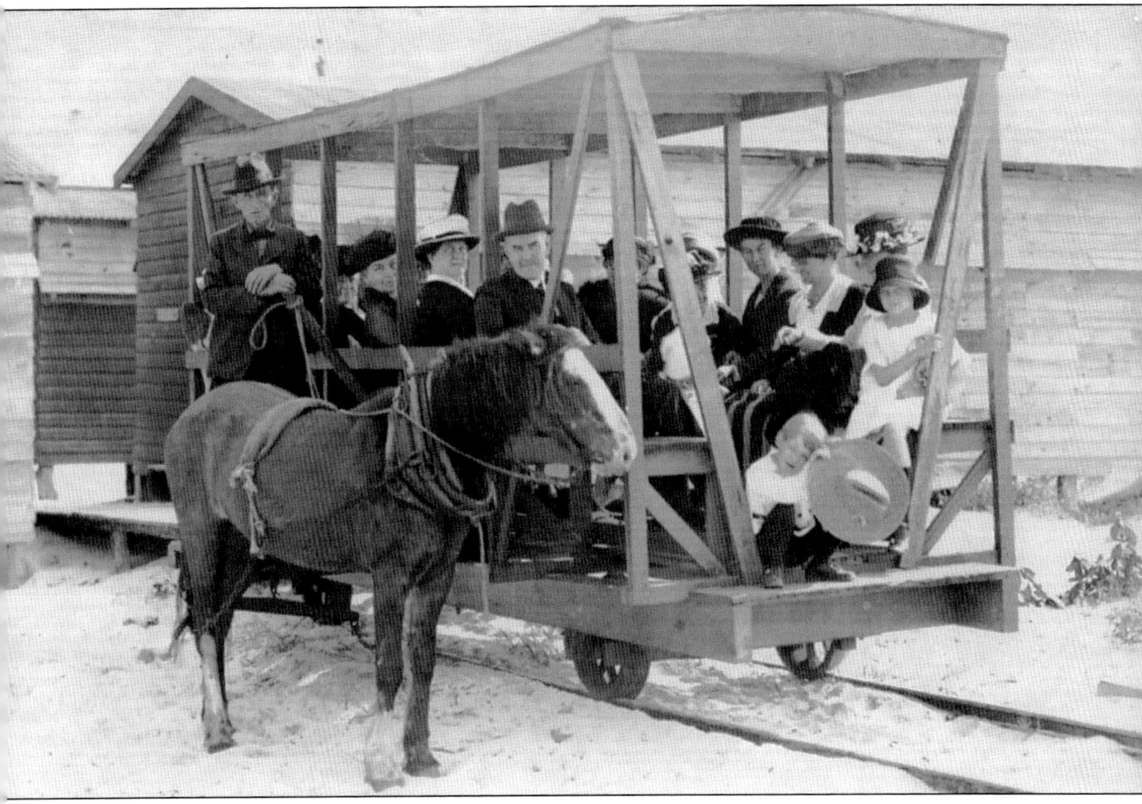

In 1900, Frank and Catherine ("Kate") Evans Usina settled in North Beach after a yellow fever epidemic in Miami forced them to return to St. Augustine. Henry Flagler persuaded the Usinas to host oyster roasts for his hotel's winter guests. They purchased a used boat they named the *Victory I* to bring passengers from the downtown waterfront and erected a pavilion on the Tolomato River in 1909. A horse-car railway was built to carry guests to the beach and remained in operation until 1931. The route of the tram was through what is now Usina's North Beach Campground. This postcard shows the horse cart at the Usinas' beach pavilion near the present-day site of an oceanfront restaurant. In 1918, Warren Sanchez built a new boat, *Victory II*, for the Usinas; the family now operates the *Victory III* on daily sightseeing tours of Matanzas Bay.

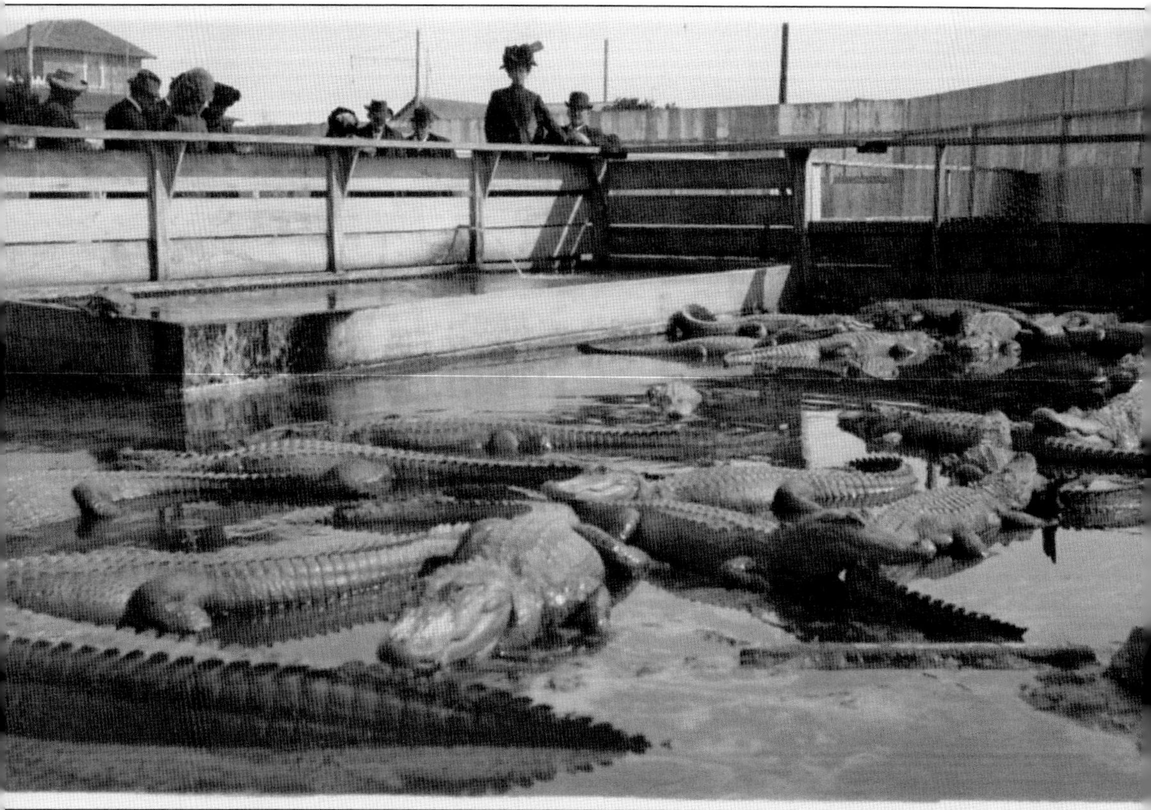

To draw visitors to South Beach, an attraction was needed for the end of the tram line that ran across Matanzas Bay to Anastasia Island. Everett C. Whitney's Burning Spring Museum featured a collection of marine curiosities and an artesian well whose sulfuric water was mixed with gasoline and ignited. The museum also displayed live alligators that had been collected on the island. The attraction was sold to Felix Fire and George Reddington, who renamed it the South Beach Alligator Farm and added live ostriches and their collections of stuffed birds to the museum. During the 1920s, beach erosion forced the Alligator Farm to move inland to its present location on Anastasia Boulevard. The original location of the South Beach Alligator Farm is now several hundred yards into the Atlantic Ocean, just north of Pope Road.

Albert Lewis, a wealthy lumber baron from Bear Creek, Pennsylvania, was a winter resident who was very active in promoting St. Augustine. In 1902, he purchased 500 acres on the north side of Moultrie Creek (today's St. Augustine South) and constructed a shell roadway from the Moultrie Road eastward to his property. A short section of this road west of U.S. 1 still retains the name Lewis Point Road.

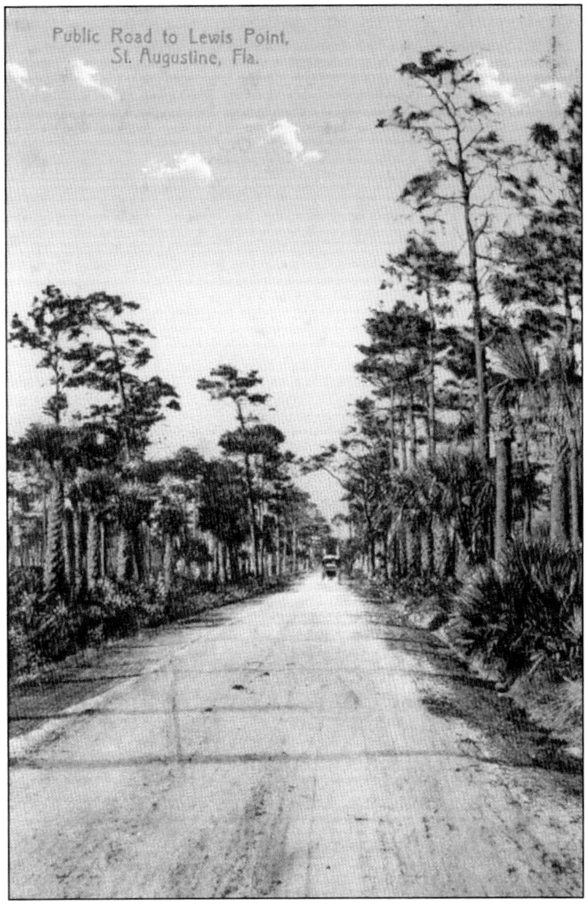

With the advent of automobiles, Lewis Point became a popular driving destination for winter visitors. Albert Lewis built a palm-thatched cabin for picnickers, shown in this view by W. J. Harris. Lewis was president of the East Florida Good Roads Association, and Lewis Speedway, Lewis Boulevard, and Lewis Park (the ball field that once stood at the south end of Marine Street) all bear his name.

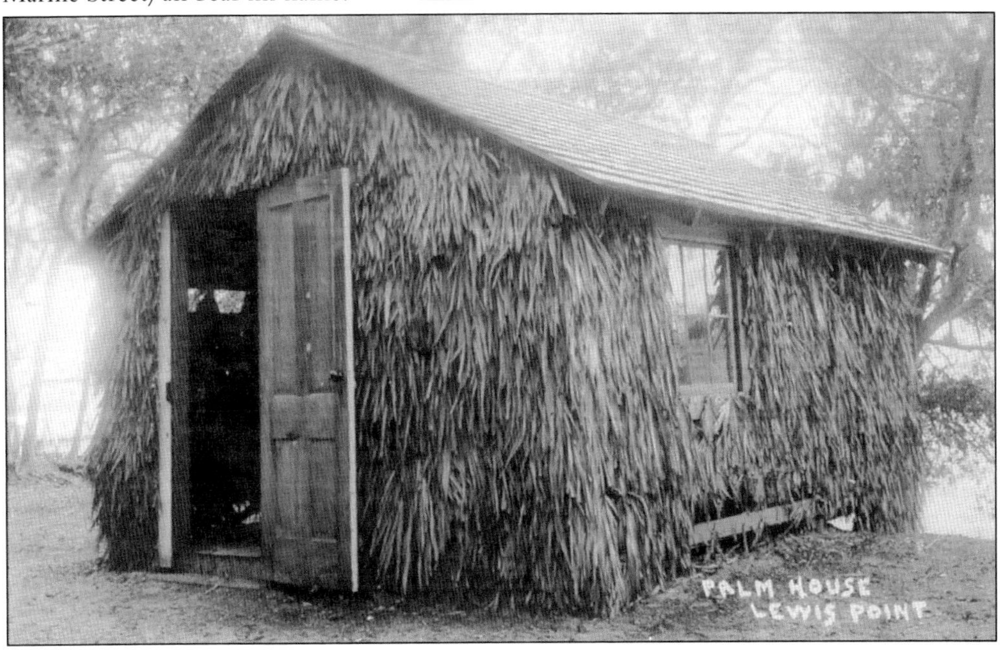

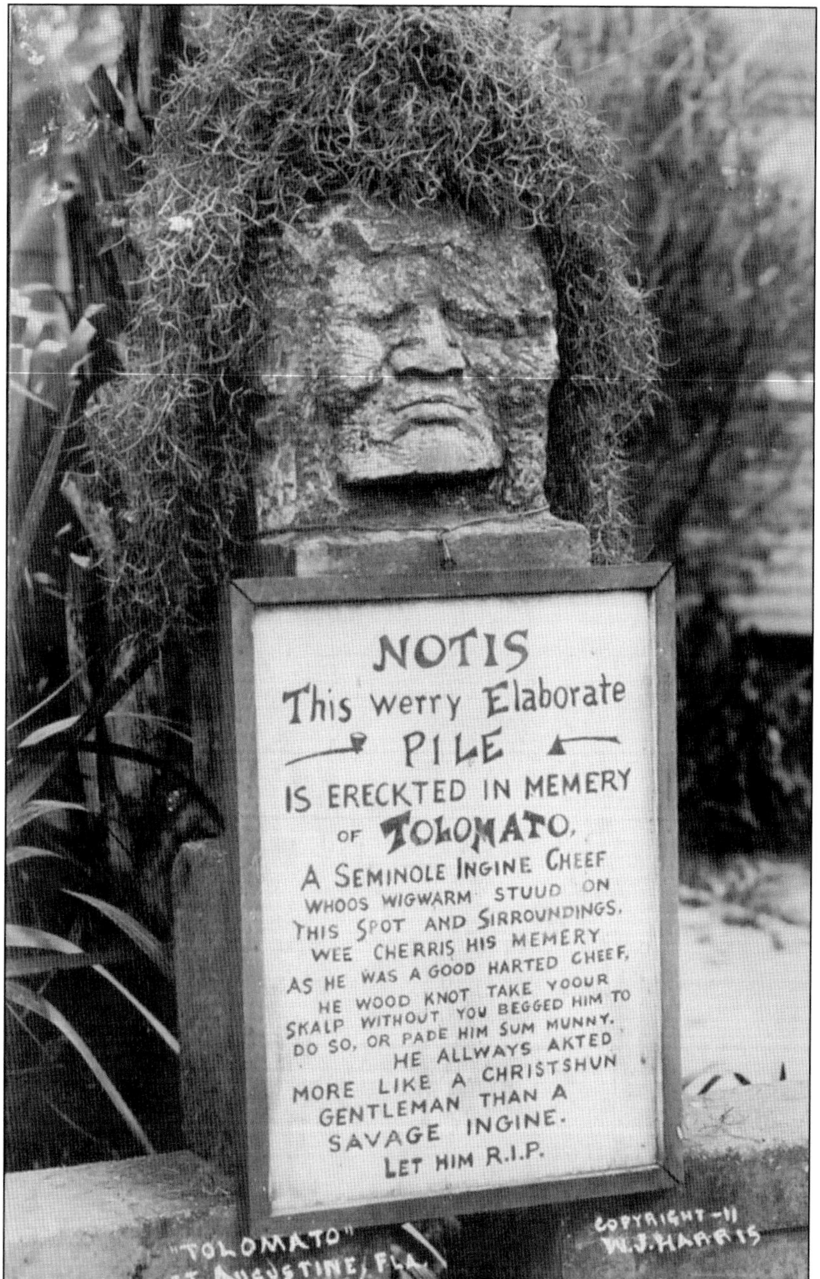

Dr. Thomas W. Speissegger erected this monument on April 1, 1893, at the corner of Cordova and Orange Streets. It marked the name change, at the request of Henry Flagler, of Tolomato Street to Cordova Street. The Tolomato Indians had come to St. Augustine from Georgia, and their mission village was near this site. Speissegger was a Confederate veteran who moved to St. Augustine in 1868 from Charleston, South Carolina. He operated a pharmacy on Bay Street (Avenida Menendez) and moved his building to its present location at 31 Orange Street after the 1887 fire. His grandsons, Richard A. and Milton S. Speissegger, continued to operate the business for many years, and it is now a tourist attraction, the Authentic Old Drug Store.

Six

STREET SCENES

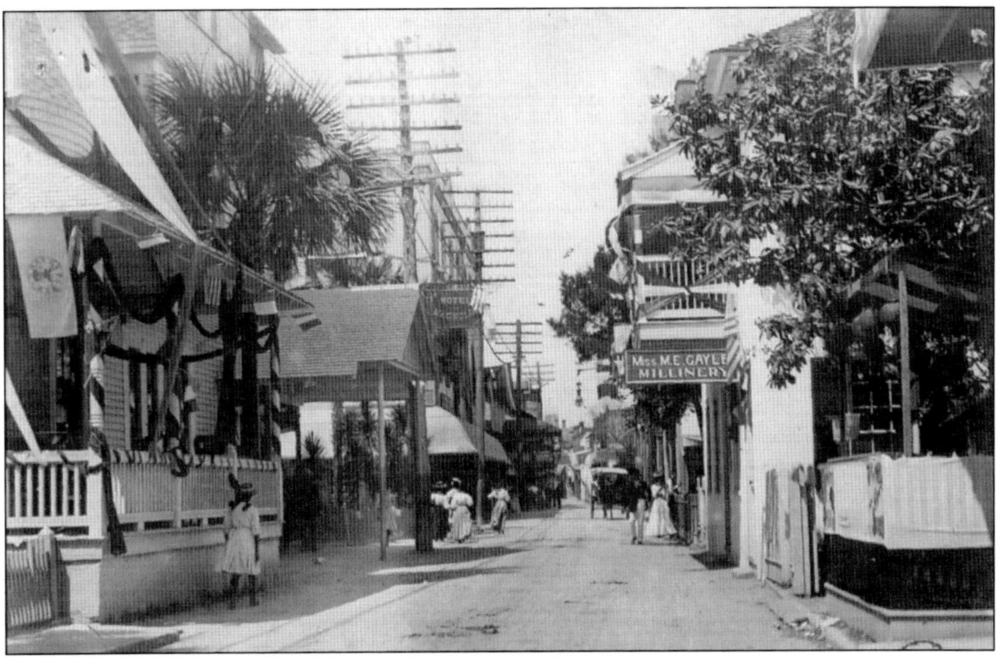

This W. J. Harris postcard shows St. George Street, looking north from the middle of the block between Treasury and Hypolita Streets. The festooned porch of the Hotel Magnolia is on the left, very likely decorated for the Ponce de Leon Celebration. Just beyond the hotel is the City Building at the corner of Hypolita and St. George Streets. The balcony at the right with the sign "Miss M. E. Gayle Millinery" marks the Sanchez House at 105 St. George Street. This coquina house was built around 1809 by Francisco Xavier Sanchez and has served as both a residence and business throughout its long history. The home was restored in 1968–1969 by the Independent Life Insurance Company and now houses a retail business.

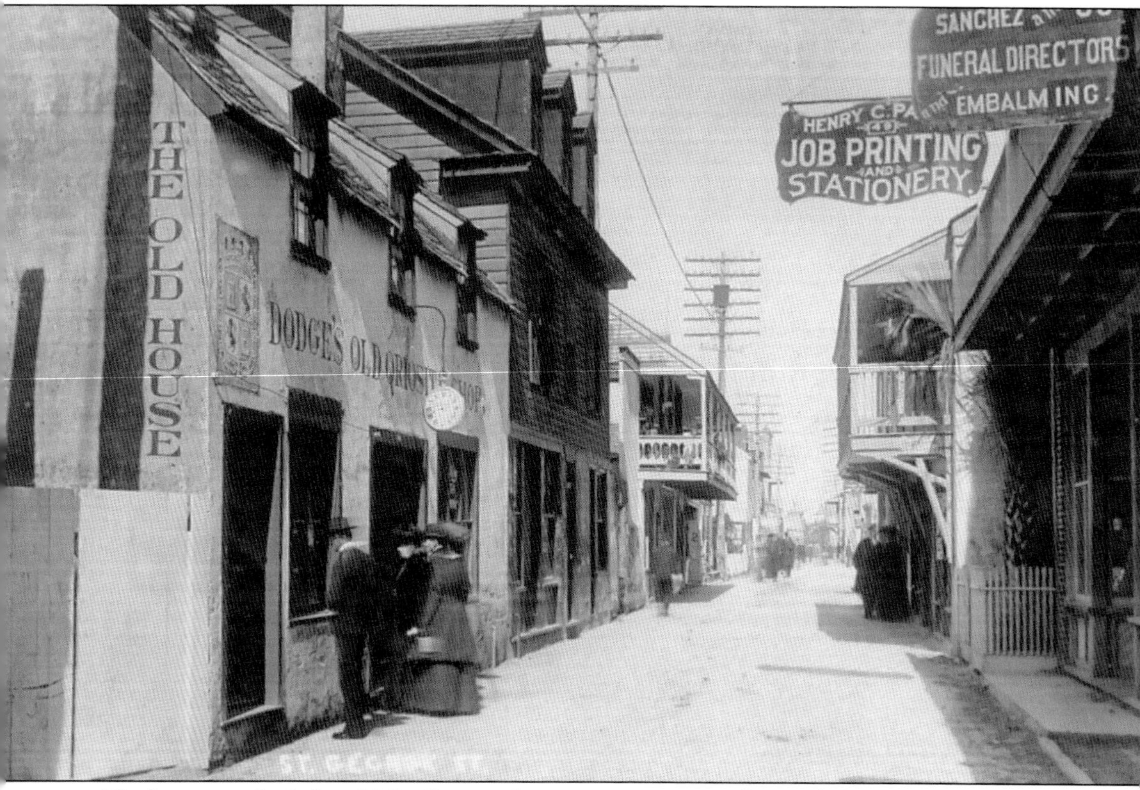

The house on the left at 54 St. George Street was once one of several claiming to be the oldest in St. Augustine. The owner, J. P. Dodge, was a jeweler and watchmaker, as evidenced by the sign over the front door. The two-and-a-half-story home at 52 St. George Street, just beyond the Dodge store, is actually much older, built in 1753–1762 during the first Spanish period. Restored in 1958, it is known today as the Rodriguez-Avero-Sanchez house and is the home of a retail shop. Shown on the right is the printing shop of Henry C. Paffe at 49 St. George Street, next door to the funeral parlor of John W. and Leonard F. Sanchez.

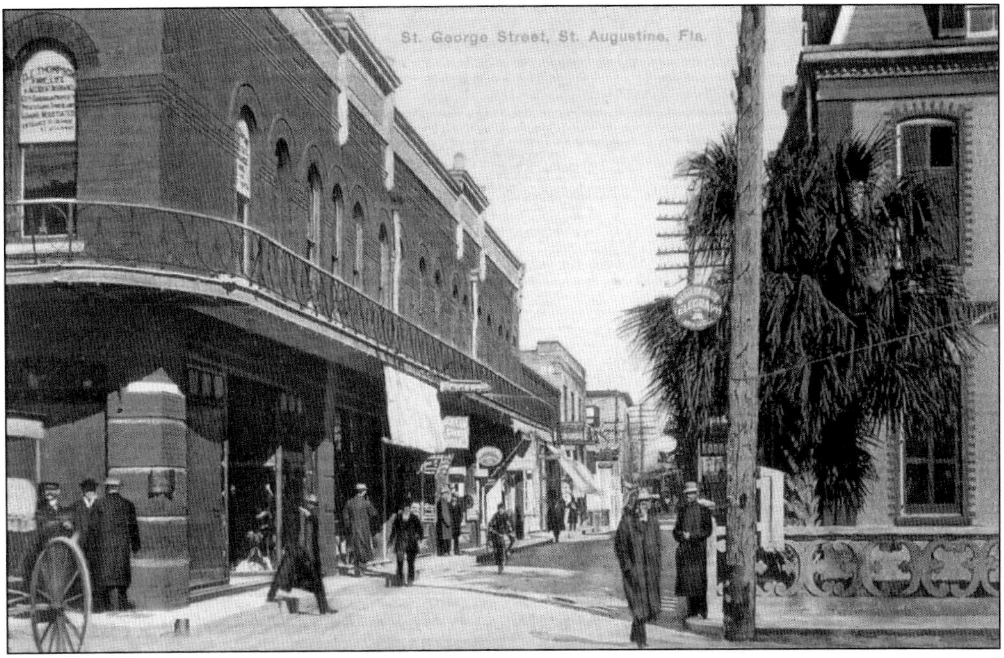

This view of St. George Street, looking north from Cathedral Place, shows the Bishop's Building on the left. The Catholic Church built the red brick structure in 1897 on the grounds of the old St. Mary's Convent. For many years, Genovar's Emporium occupied the ground floor on the busy corner. The Bishop's Building was demolished in 1960, and the site is now a bank parking lot.

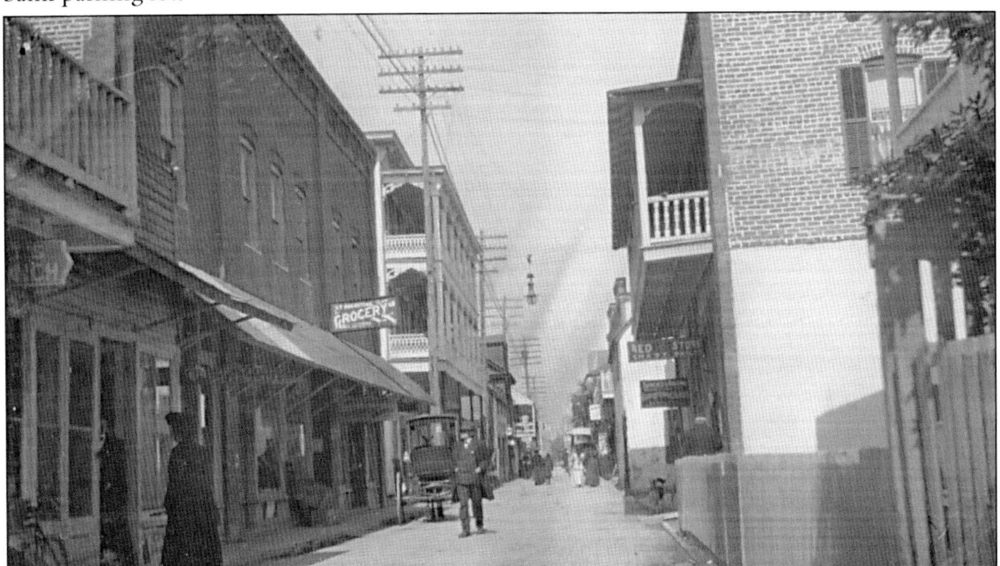

The St. Augustine Grocery Company at 62–64 St. George Street is shown on the left in this view looking north, with the intersection of Cuna Street just beyond the parked carriage. The business was originally owned by William C. Middleton and managed by Leonard L. Simms, who later took over the firm. A 1902 advertisement featured hams, bacon, coffee and apples—all priced at 2 pounds for 25¢.

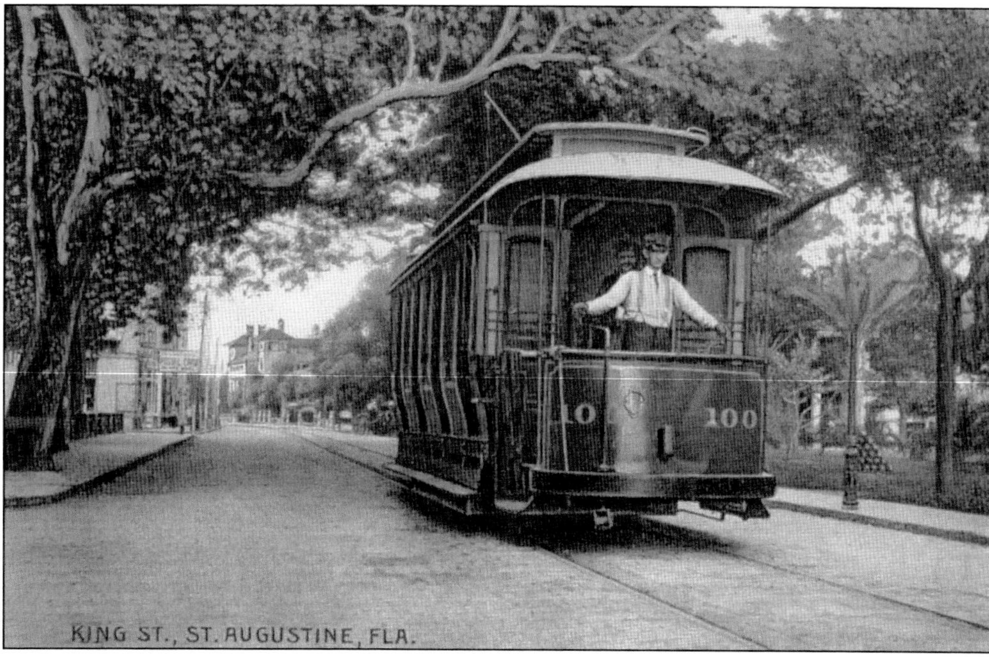

The St. Johns Light and Power Company began laying track in 1906, and St. Augustine's first trolley ran on June 16, 1907. At first, service was limited to the immediate downtown area, but it later expanded to other areas of the city. This view shows trolley No. 100 on King Street at the south side of the plaza.

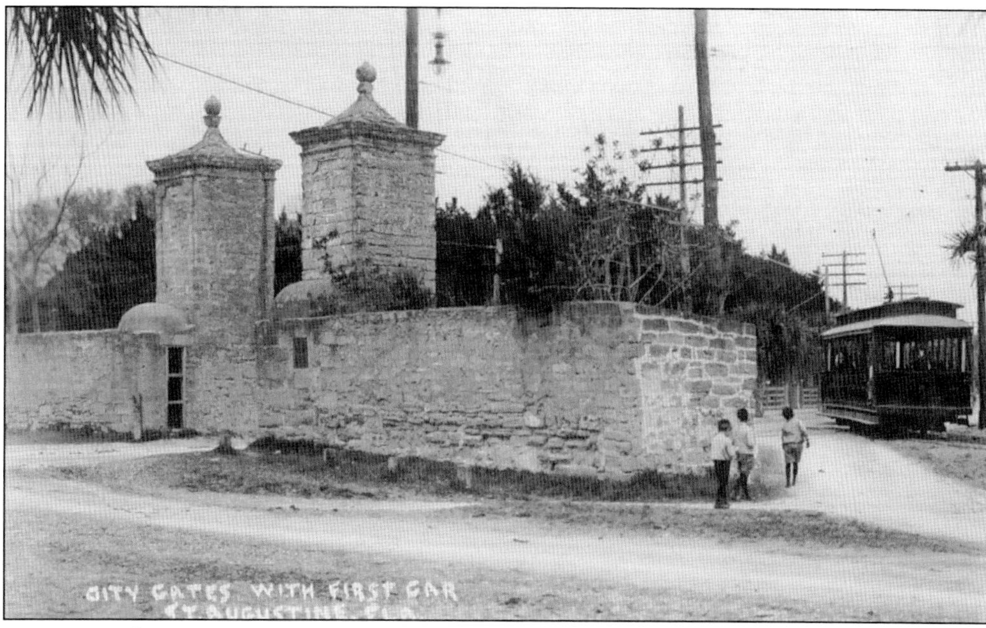

In 1908, trolley service was extended to North City, after the U.S. Army granted permission to run track across the grounds of Fort Marion. The trolley ran north along San Marco Avenue to the Deaf and Blind School at Genopoly Street. Service was also added along Central Avenue to South Street and west on King Street to New Augustine. This view by W. J. Harris shows a trolley at the City Gate.

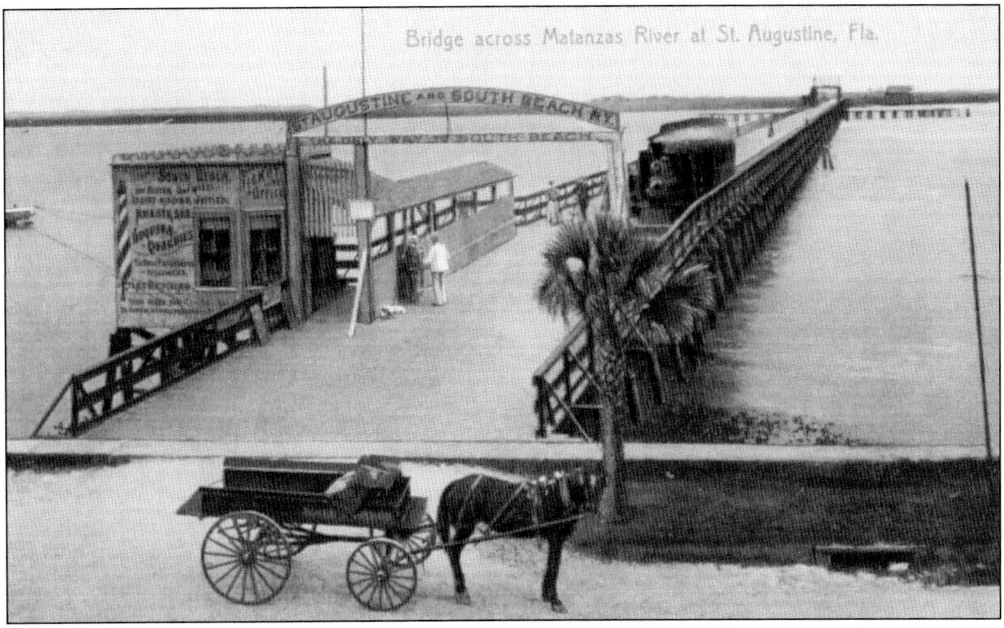

The entrance to the St. Augustine and South Beach Railway was at the foot of King Street, just south of the present-day Bridge of Lions. A wooden bridge with a mule-drawn tram had replaced the ferry across the Matanzas River in 1895. In 1899, a steam engine was used to pull a passenger car over a narrow-gauge railway, carrying visitors to the lighthouse, Whitney's Alligator Farm, and South Beach.

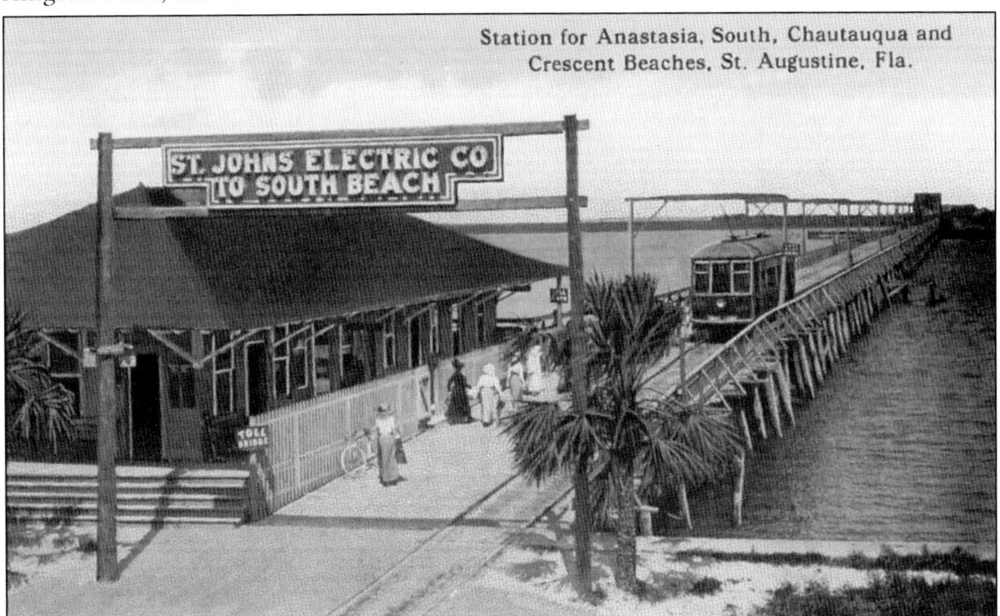

The South Beach Railway went into receivership in 1911 and was taken over by the St. Johns Electric Company, becoming part of their city trolley system. They erected the larger terminal building shown here. When the Bridge of Lions was constructed in 1927, the building was moved onto the county jail property. The terminal building was later relocated to 4700 U.S. 1 North and used as an office building.

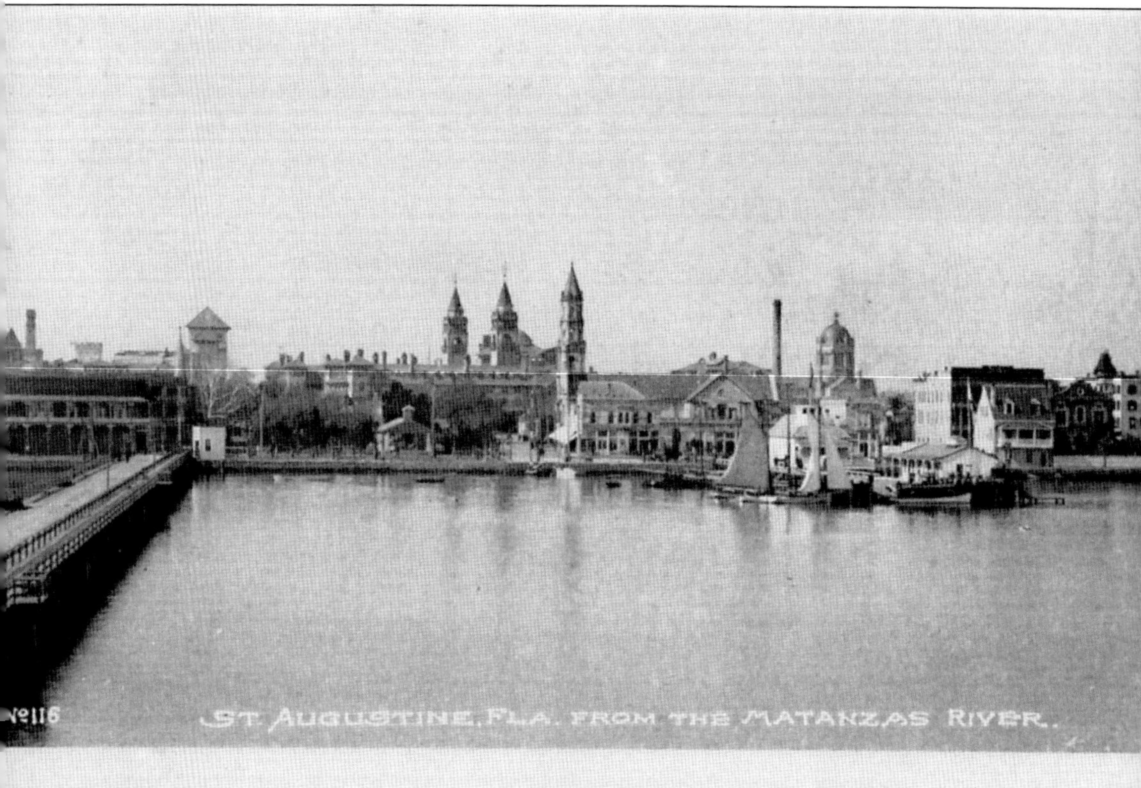

This view of St. Augustine from the Matanzas River shows the Estes Building, 1 King Street, on the left at the foot of the bridge. John Wesley Estes, a native of Cumming, Georgia, operated a large department store he named the Surprise Store. A 1902 advertisement for the store lists "Thompson's Militant Corsets" for $1 and Stetson hats from $1 to $5. The building looks much the same as it did in the early 1900s and is now home to a restaurant and other businesses. To the right are several boats tied up at Corbett's Dock, with the St. Augustine Yacht Club visible behind the sailboat. At the extreme right is the Florida House with its tall Victorian tower.

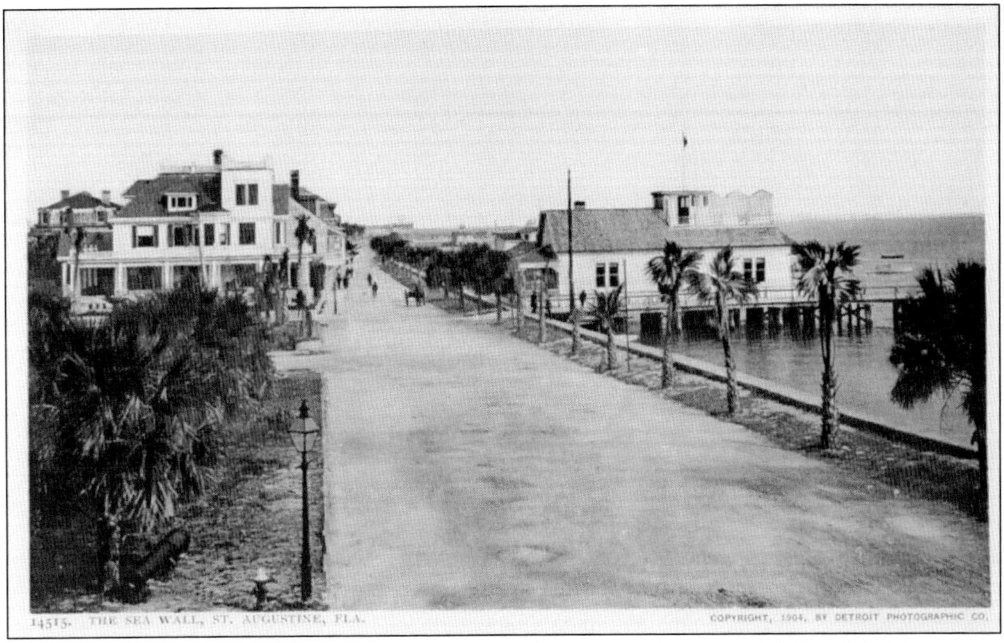

The seawall was built by the U.S. Army Corps of Engineers between 1833 and 1844 at a cost of $100,000 and extended for three-quarters of a mile from Fort Marion to the St. Francis Barracks. This view shows Bay Street (Avenida Menendez) looking north from King Street, with the Hamblen home on the left and the St. Augustine Yacht Club at the right.

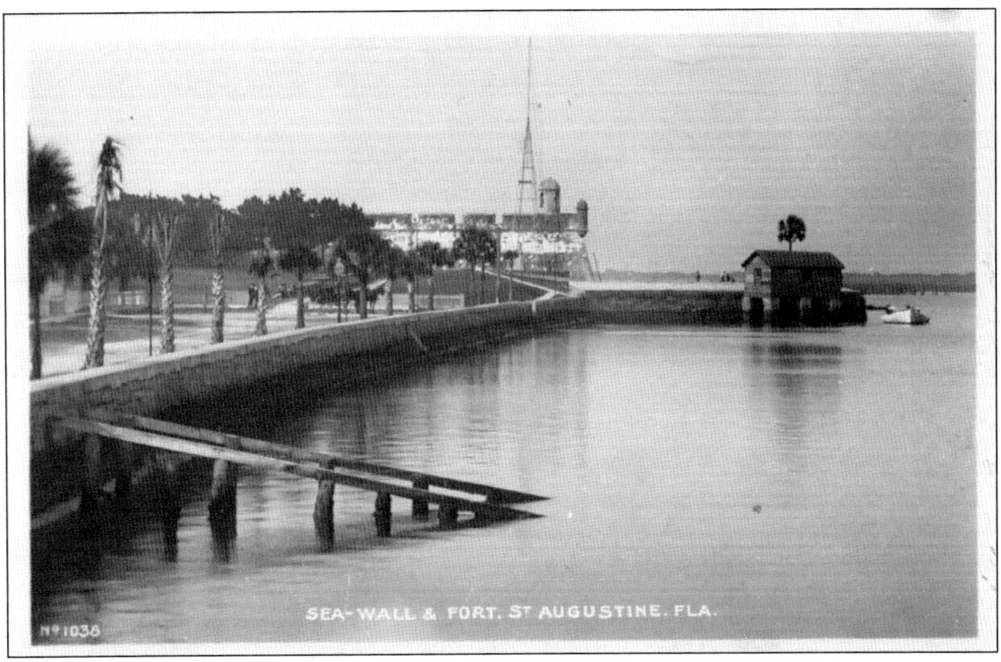

This view of the seawall looking north toward Fort Marion shows the wireless antenna that was in use until the 1920s. The small house on the right held supplies for the lighthouse. The northern portion of the seawall was demolished when Avenida Menendez was widened in the late 1950s, but the original seawall still extends south of the Bridge of Lions to the St. Francis Barracks.

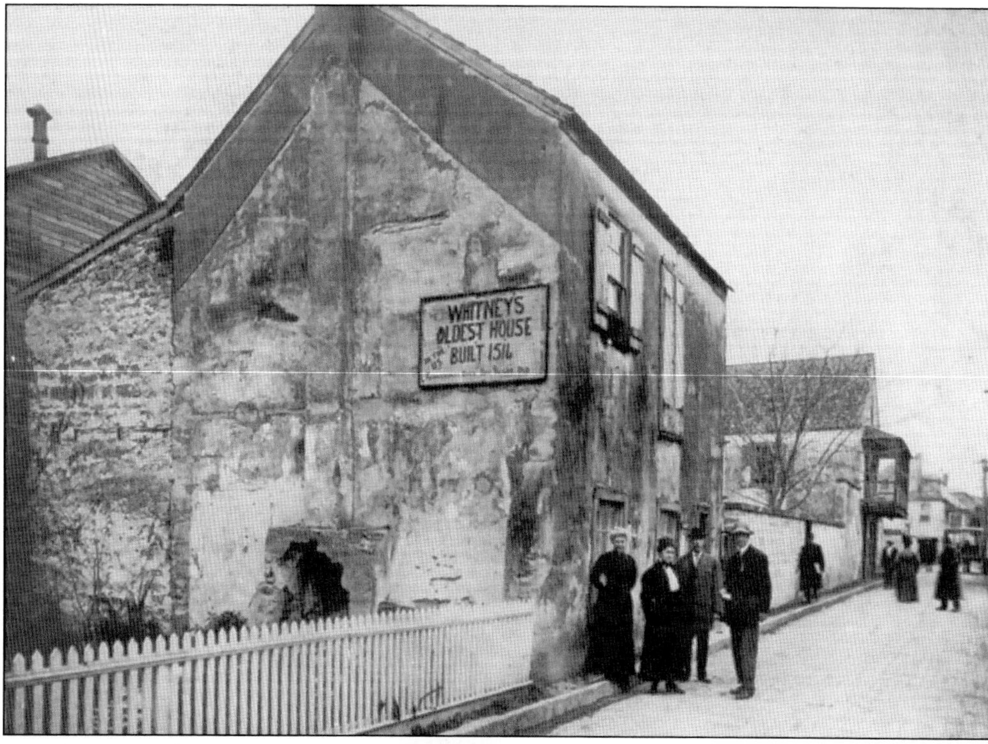

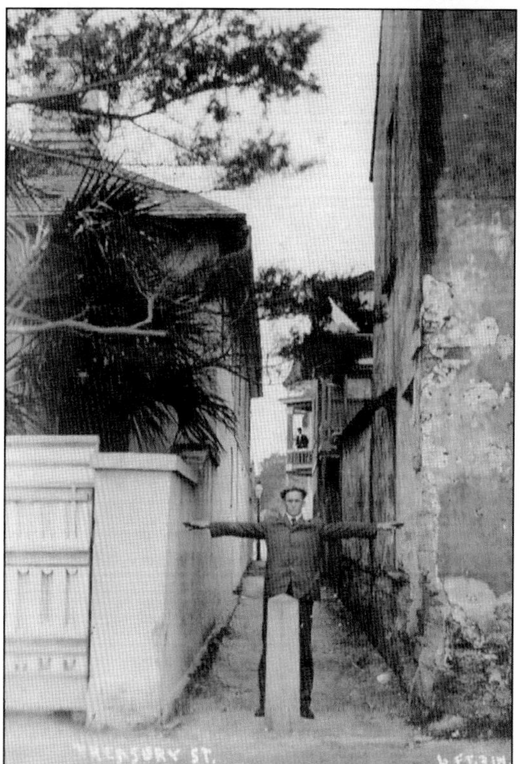

Hospital Street was the location of the Spanish Royal Hospital, which burned in 1818. In 1924, the city council voted to change the name of Hospital Street to Aviles Street because it sounded "more charming." This 1911 view shows Whitney's Oldest House on the left, with the O'Reilly House in the distance. Photographer W. J. Harris is on the right in the group of people in the foreground.

Another Harris view looking west from Bay Street (Avenida Menendez) shows Treasury Street "6 feet 3 inches wide." This scene would be repeated in countless postcards, with arms outstretched to emphasize the narrowness of the street. Treasury Street was so named for the residence of the royal treasurer at the corner of St. George Street, now the Peña-Peck house and home of the Women's Exchange.

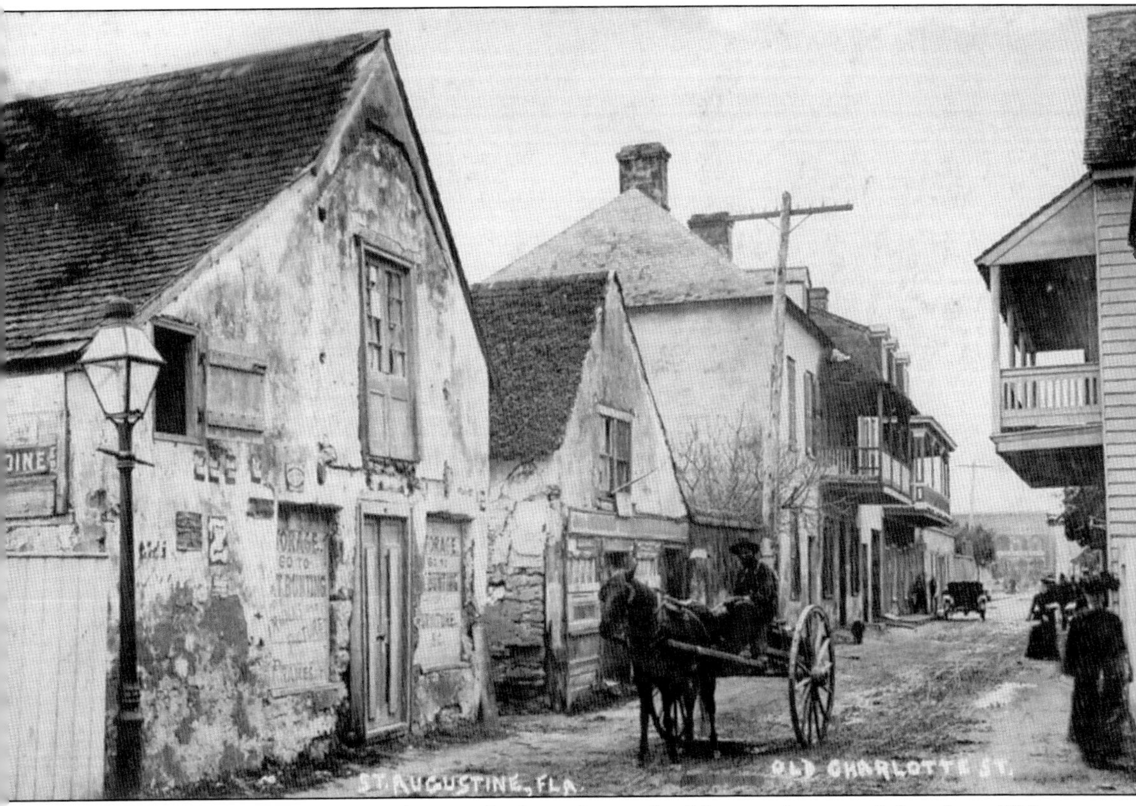

This 1912 view by W. J. Harris shows Charlotte Street, looking south toward the plaza. This scene is one of the most-photographed views of the Ancient City, appearing in countless postcards and hand-tinted photographs of the period. The entrance to Baya Lane can be seen between the two houses on the left, just in front of the horse. Baya Lane has since been closed, and today it is the location of the Charlotte Street entrance to a modern hotel.

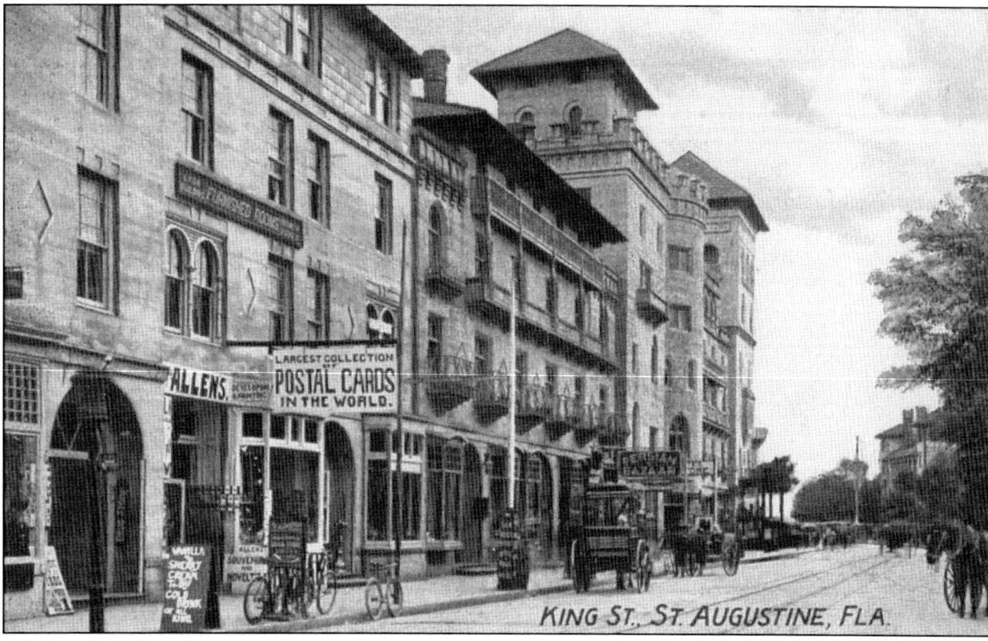

The R. B. Allen Company at 43 King Street advertised itself as having "the largest collection of postal cards in the world." Around 1910, the location was taken over by the Rogero and Pomar Company, operated by Harry Rogero and T. V. "Ted" Pomar, who continued to sell postcards and souvenirs. Today the location is an upscale gift shop in the renovated Lyon Building.

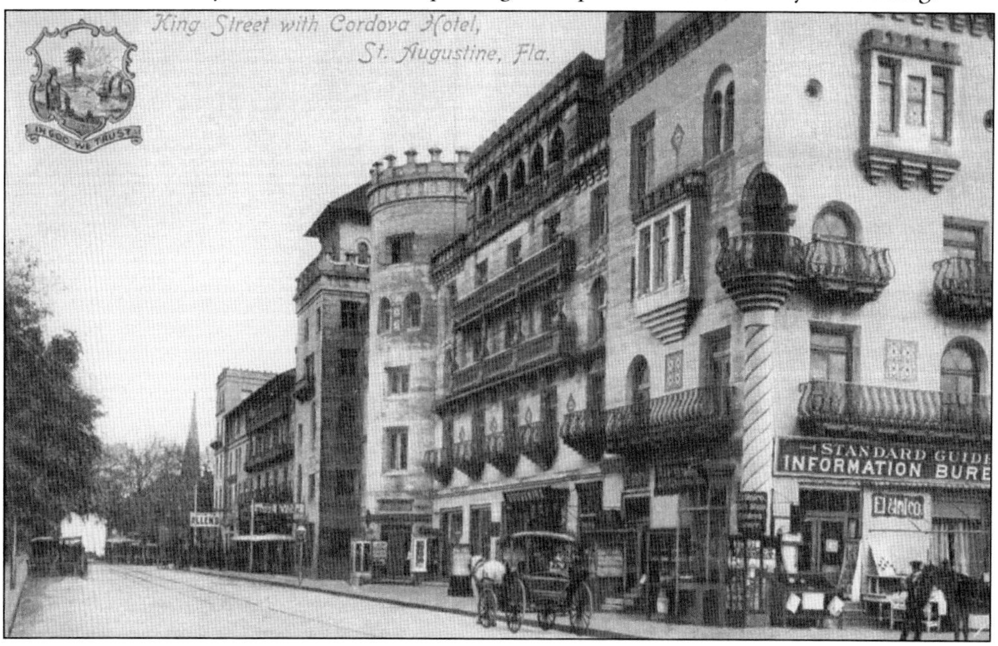

The busy corner of King and Cordova Streets was the location of the Standard Guide Information Bureau, operated by Ward G. Foster and Charles B. Reynolds. Later known as "Ask Mr. Foster," it is the nation's oldest travel agency. It also housed El Unico, a souvenir and postcard shop operated by W. H. DuBois. Today the Cordova corner is the site of the Casa Monica Hotel's coffee shop and café.

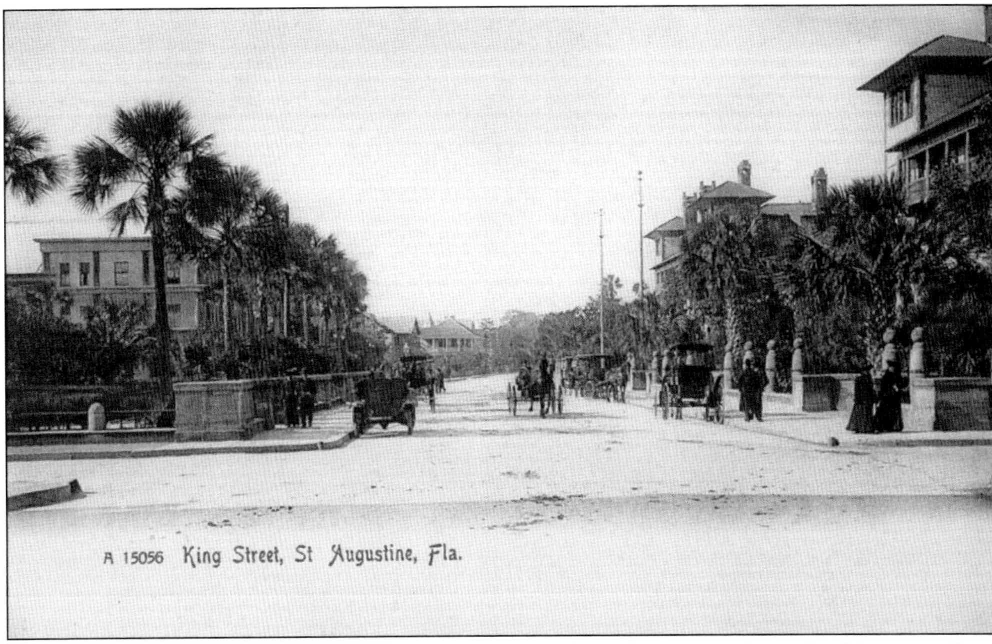

This pre-1907 postcard by the Rotograph Company shows busy King Street looking west from the intersection of Cordova Street. On the right is the Ponce de Leon Hotel, and on the left, just beyond the grounds of the Alcazar, is the Hotel Granada.

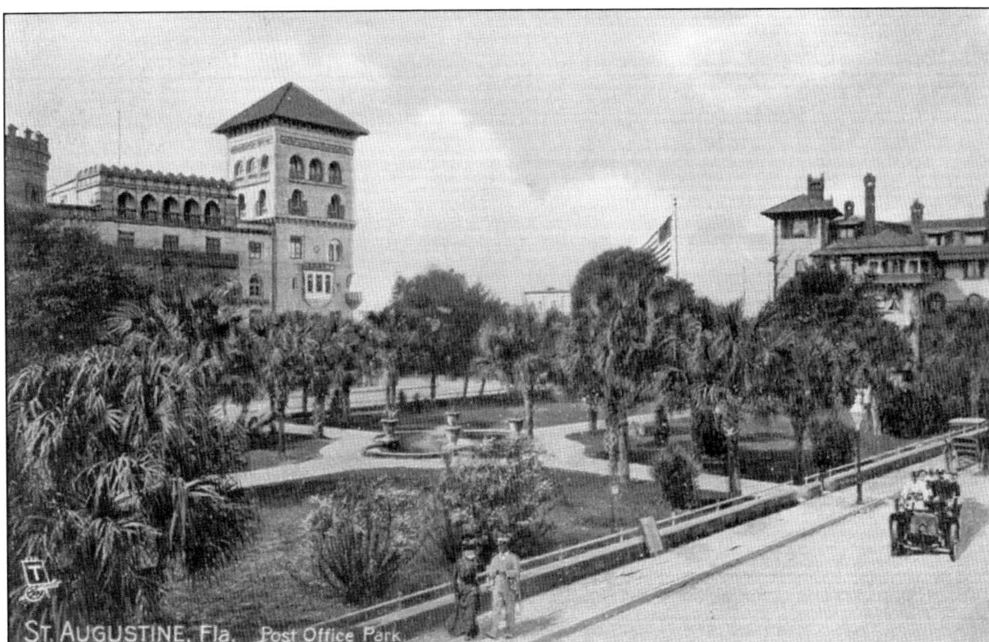

Located just west of the post office, the park with its fountain is shown prior to the 1920 dedication of a memorial to William Wing Loring, Confederate general from St. Augustine. Longtime residents will remember the low concrete fence topped by a metal pipe that surrounded this park for many years. The Ponce de Leon Hotel can be seen on the right and Cordova Hotel on the left.

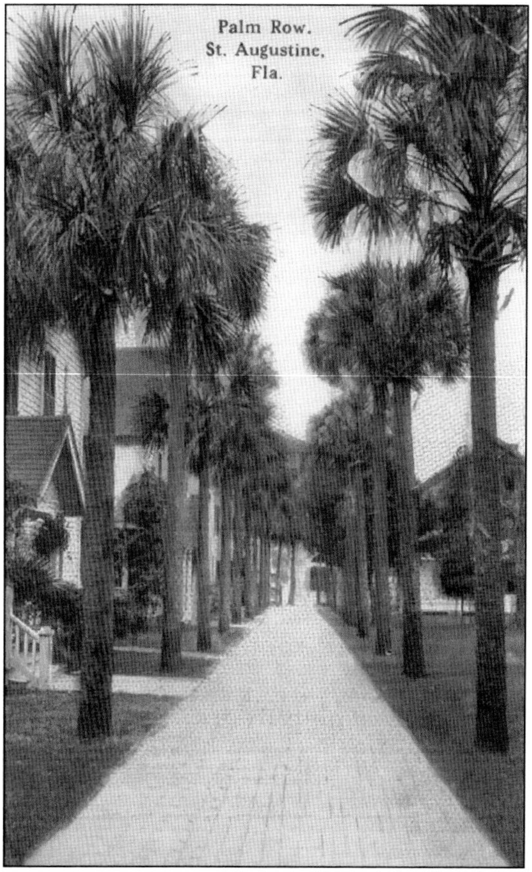

Henry P. Ammidown purchased property between Cordova and St. George Streets in 1904 and constructed a brick thoroughfare between the two streets. He built six Victorian-style homes—original plans had called for 12—and maintained them as rental properties until his death in 1913. He named his development Palm Row, and many of the original palms trees still remain along this picturesque byway.

Taken from Fort Marion (Castillo de San Marcos), this view looking south along the bay front was made prior to 1904. The Bennett House is near the center of the postcard, just above the palm trees. At the left, Capo's Bath House can be seen in the distance along the seawall. On the extreme right is the tall standpipe of the City Water Works on Hypolita Street.

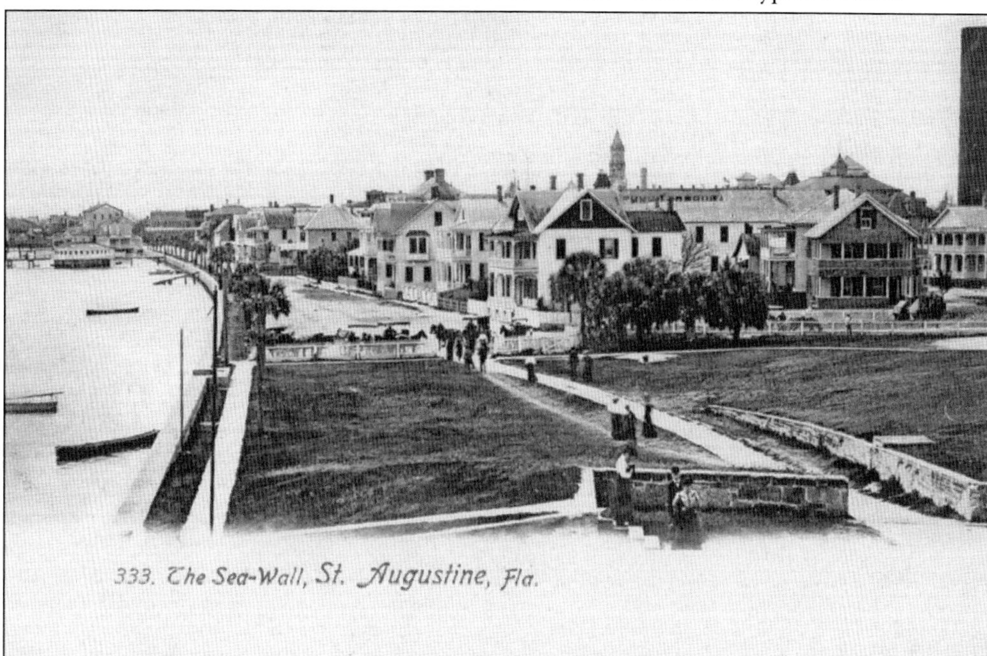

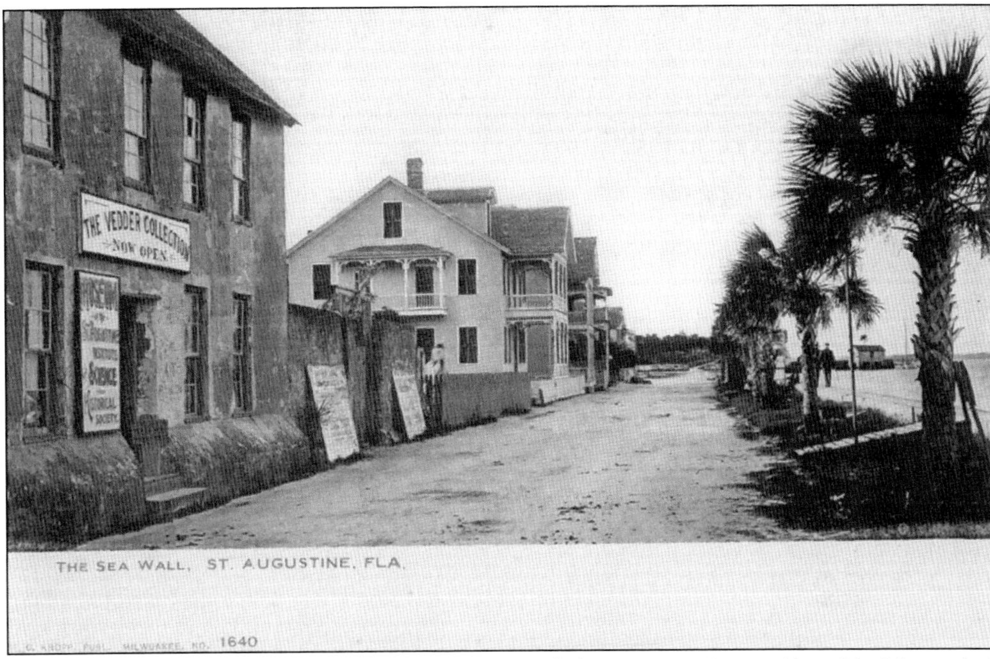

Looking north from Treasury Street, this postcard depicts Bay Street (Avenida Menendez) around 1905. On the left is the Vedder Museum, with a sign reading "Museum of the St. Augustine Institute of Science and Historical Society." Beyond the museum is the Monson House, and the seawall is on the right, just beyond the palm trees.

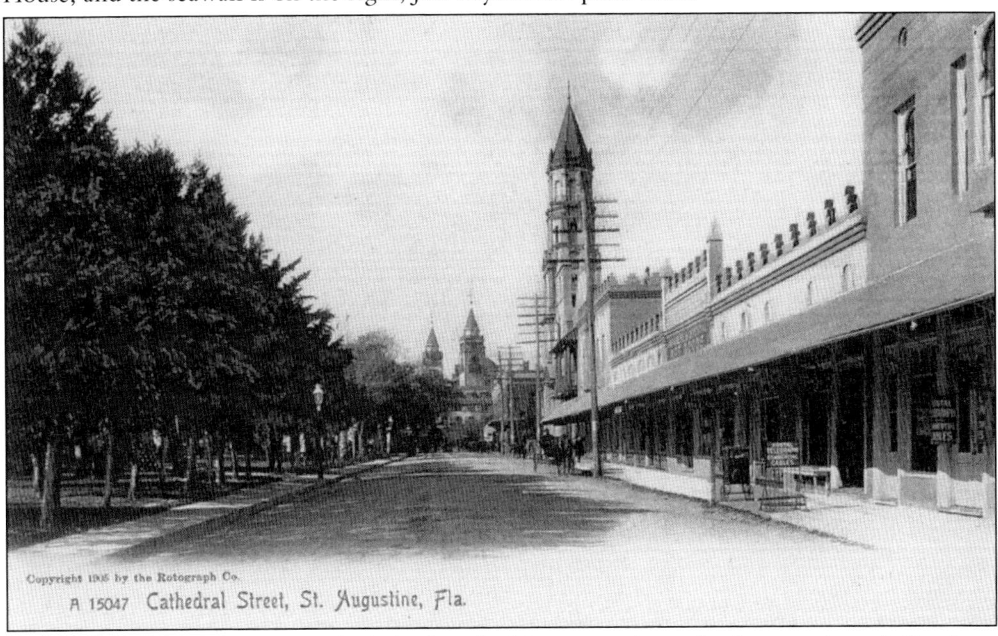

This 1905 postcard shows Cathedral Place looking west from the intersection of Charlotte Street. Capt. Edward E. Vaill built the Moorish Revival buildings on the right, known as the "Vaill Block," after his St. Augustine Hotel was destroyed by fire in 1887. In the 1920s, architect Fred A. Hollingsworth remodeled the two-story portion of the building shown at the far right to its present Mediterranean-style appearance.

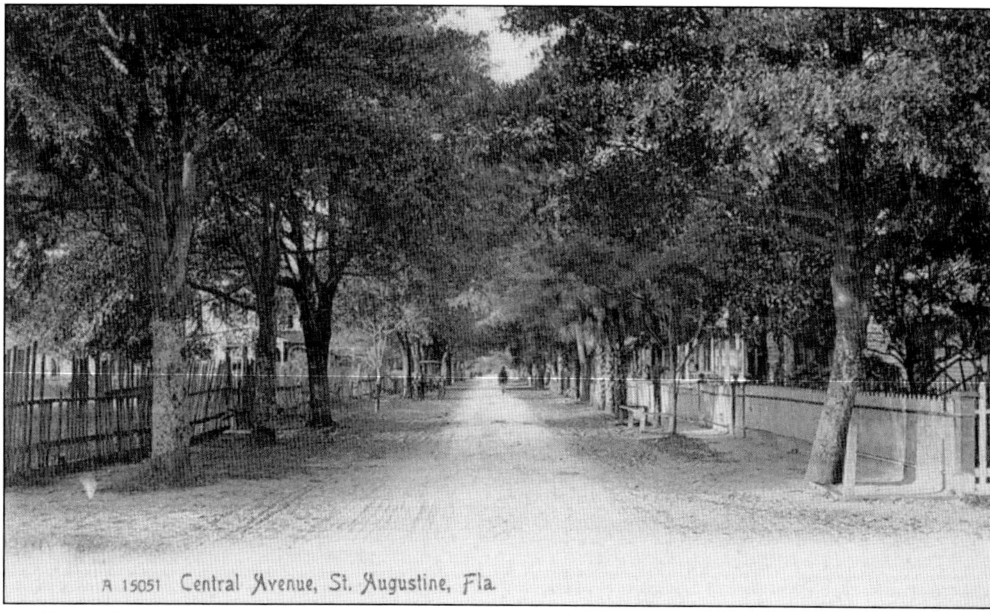

In 1885, the St. Augustine Improvement Company purchased and subdivided the Buena Esperanza tract in today's Lincolnville area. By 1894, more than 30 large houses had been built, and the area became one of St. Augustine's premier Victorian neighborhoods. This 1905 view shows Central Avenue looking south, near the intersection of Bridge Street. The name of Central Avenue was changed to Dr. Martin Luther King Avenue in 1986.

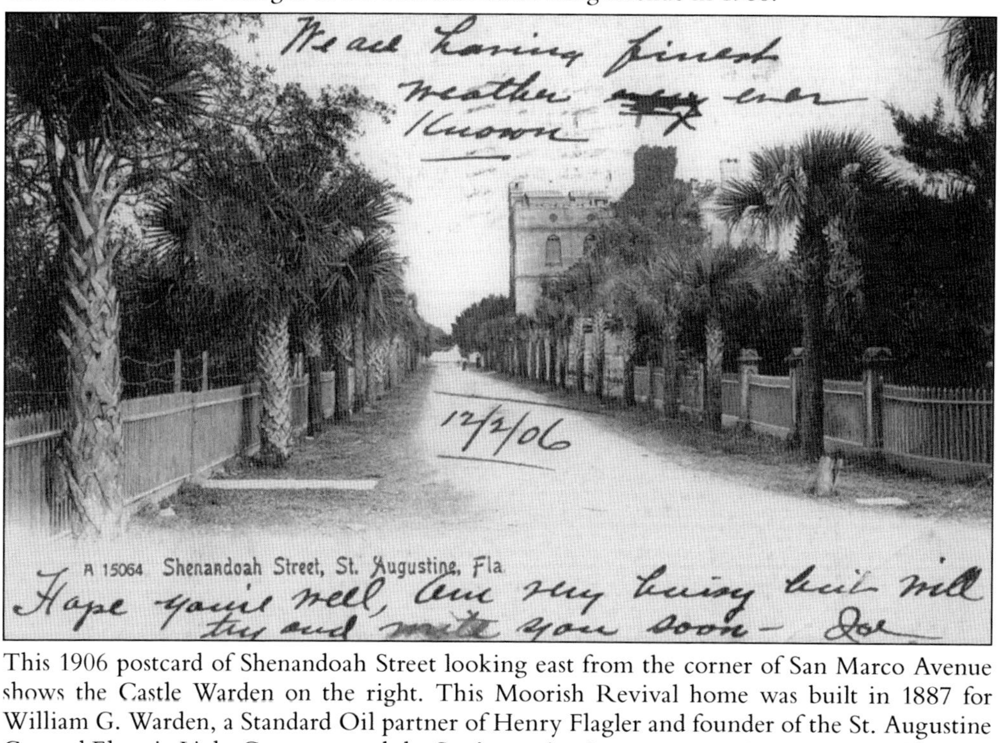

This 1906 postcard of Shenandoah Street looking east from the corner of San Marco Avenue shows the Castle Warden on the right. This Moorish Revival home was built in 1887 for William G. Warden, a Standard Oil partner of Henry Flagler and founder of the St. Augustine Gas and Electric Light Company and the St. Augustine Improvement Company. The building became Ripley's Believe It or Not Museum in 1950.

Seven

Celebrations and Disasters

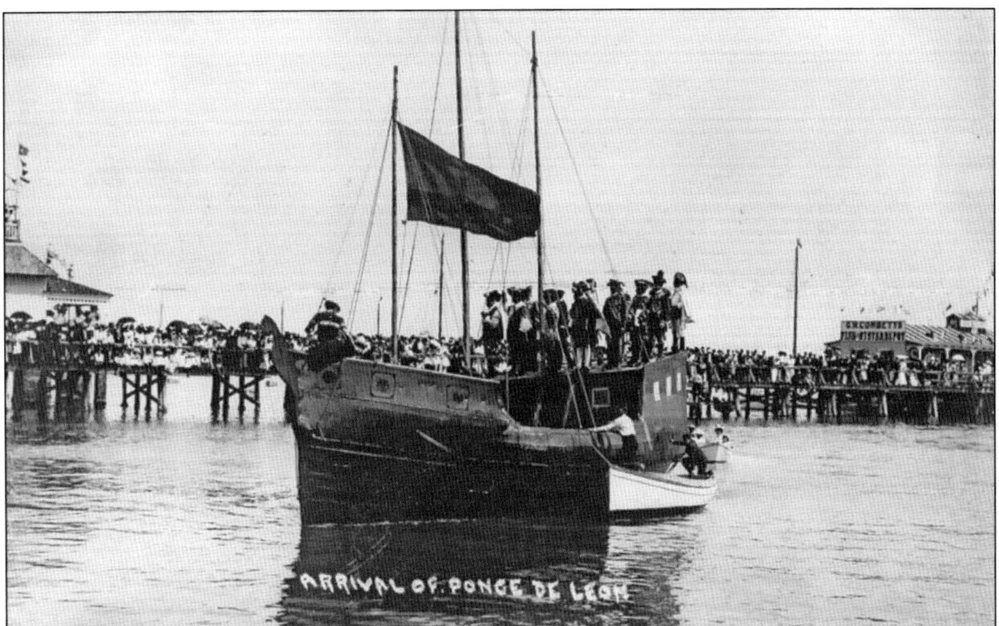

The Ponce de Leon Celebration was first held in March 1883 to commemorate the discovery of Florida. It was held sporadically in the years that followed, but by the early 1900s, local businessmen had organized the event into a spectacular annual festival. Held in early April, it marked the end of the winter tourist season. This view by W. J. Harris from around 1907 shows the arrival of Ponce de Leon and his men on a mock-up of a Spanish caravel that was towed to the waterfront. G. W. Corbett's Fish and Oyster Depot can be seen on the right, with the St. Augustine Yacht Club on the left, both filled with spectators watching the landing.

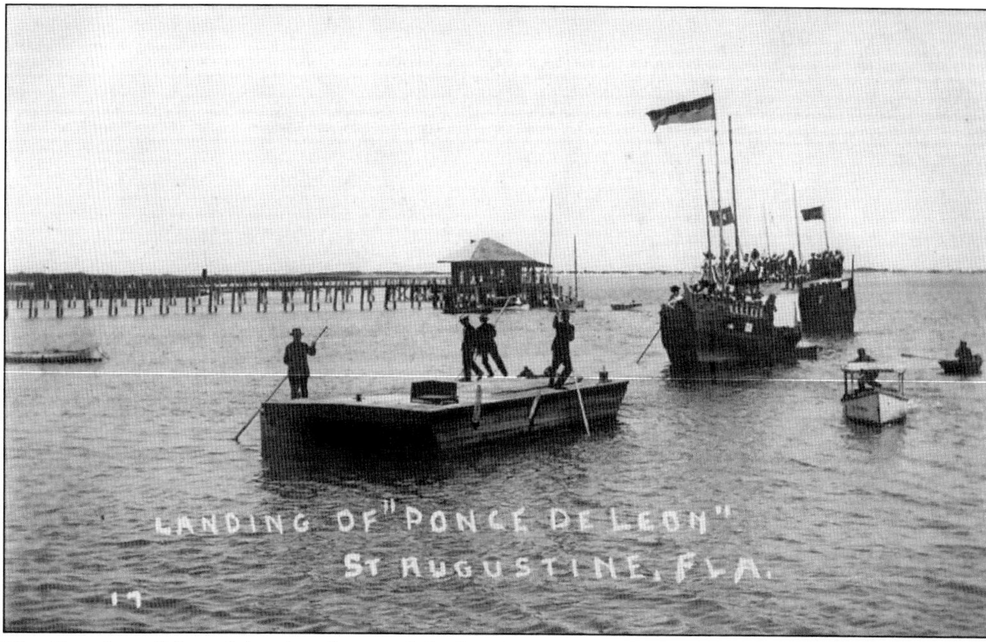

The first day of the celebration featured the landing of Ponce de Leon, the discoverer of Florida in 1513. On the second day, another landing marked the arrival of Pedro Menendez de Aviles, who founded St. Augustine in 1565. In this view, a barge is towing two Spanish caravels to a landing spot on the north side of Fort Marion (Castillo de San Marcos).

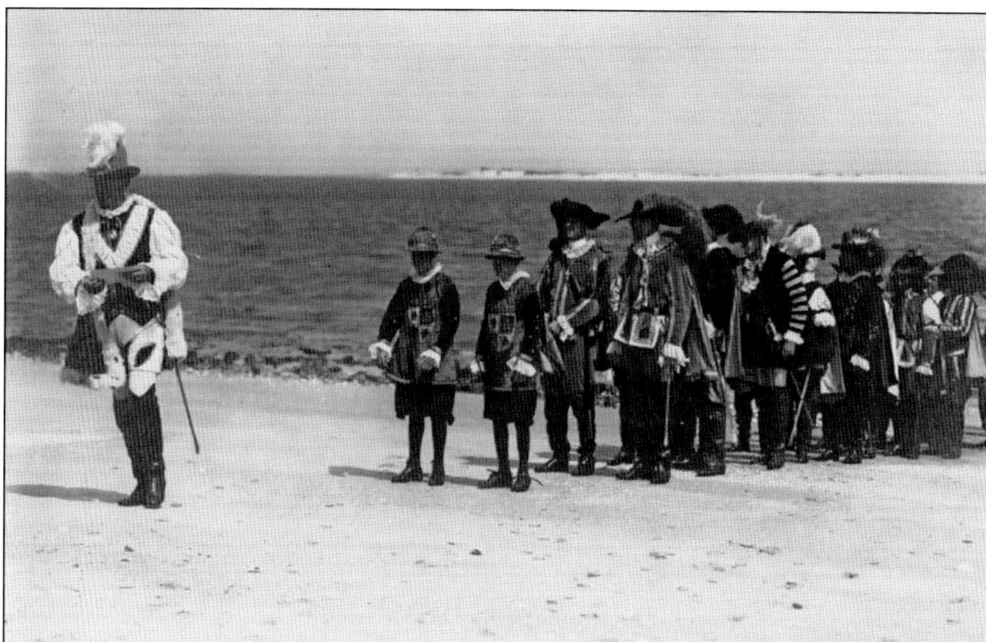

This photo postcard by Blair's Studio is postmarked April 3, 1913, and shows a reenactment of Spanish forces stepping ashore on Matanzas Bay. The Ponce de Leon Celebration was a weeklong event, with civic leaders portraying the key historical figures and townspeople filling the roles of the infantry and mounted forces of the Spanish, British, and Native Americans.

This Blair view shows the H. W. Davis store at 47 King Street decorated for the Ponce de Leon Celebration around 1912. The left window is filled with men's hats, and on display in the right window are the trophies for various athletic competitions held during the festival. The H. W. Davis Company is St. Augustine's oldest clothing store, now operating at 152 St. George Street.

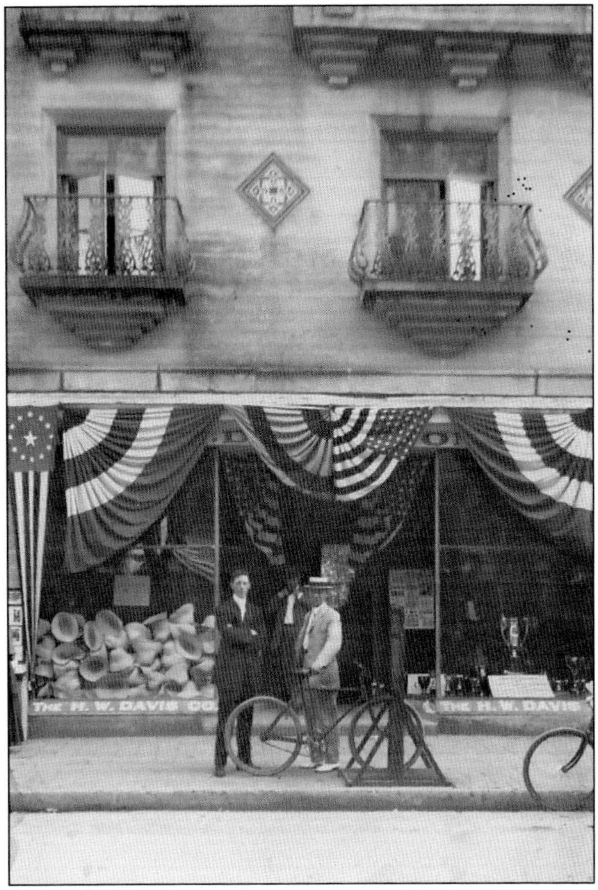

The cigar factory of Candido Meitin was located in the old St. Mary's Convent building at 52–56 Cathedral Place. Meitin was a native of Spain who took over the Garcia and Vega cigar factory in 1907 and also served as a city councilman in that year. The site is now a parking lot at the corner of St. George Street and Cathedral Place.

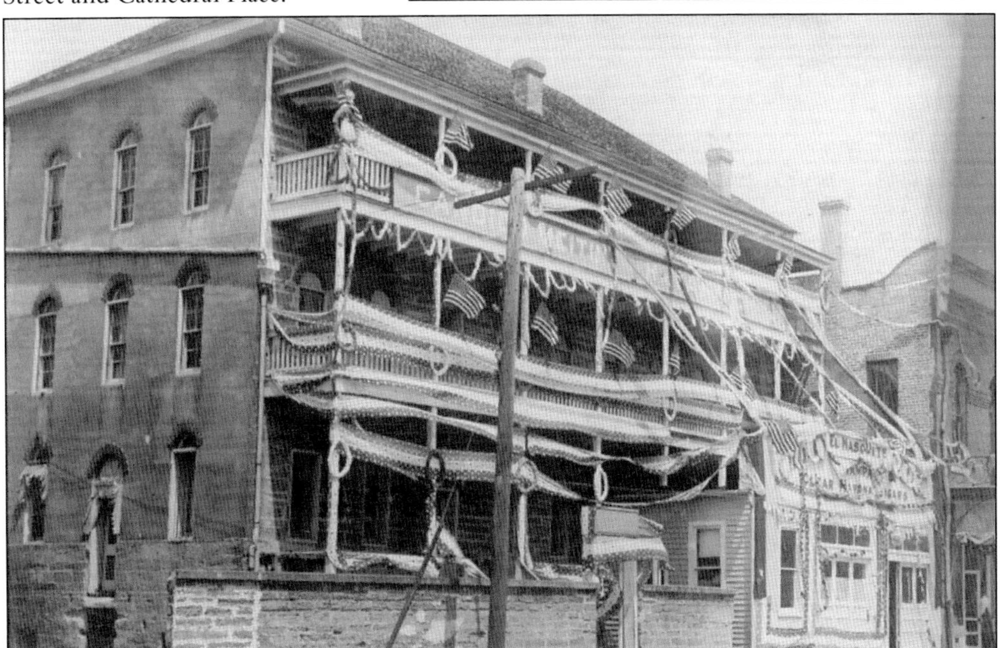

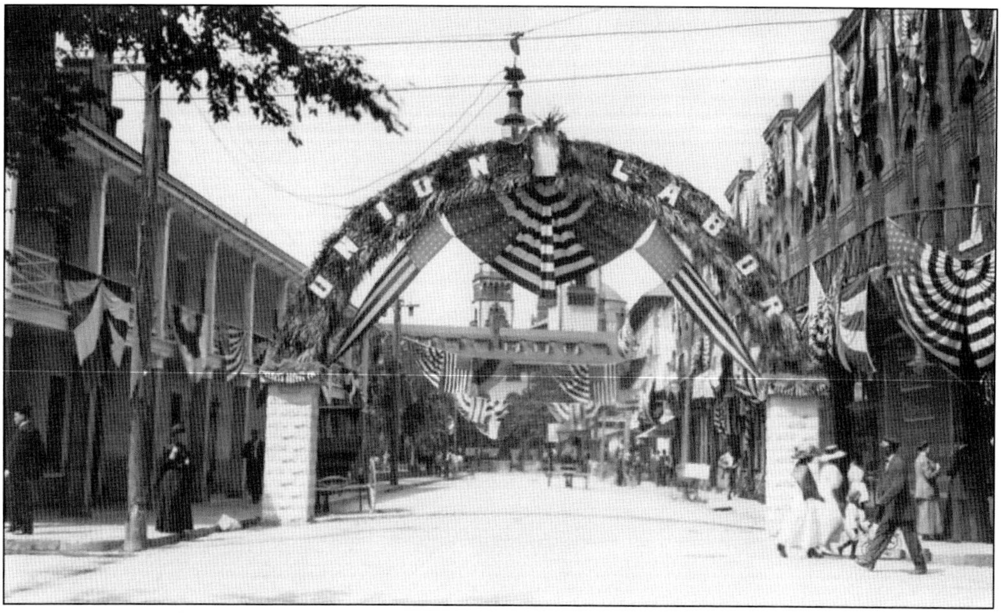

Civic groups and organizations were responsible for decorating certain areas of the city for the Ponce de Leon Celebration. This postcard shows the arch erected by Union Labor over Cathedral Place, looking west from the corner of St. George Street. The Bishop's Building is on the right, and the post office is pictured to the left.

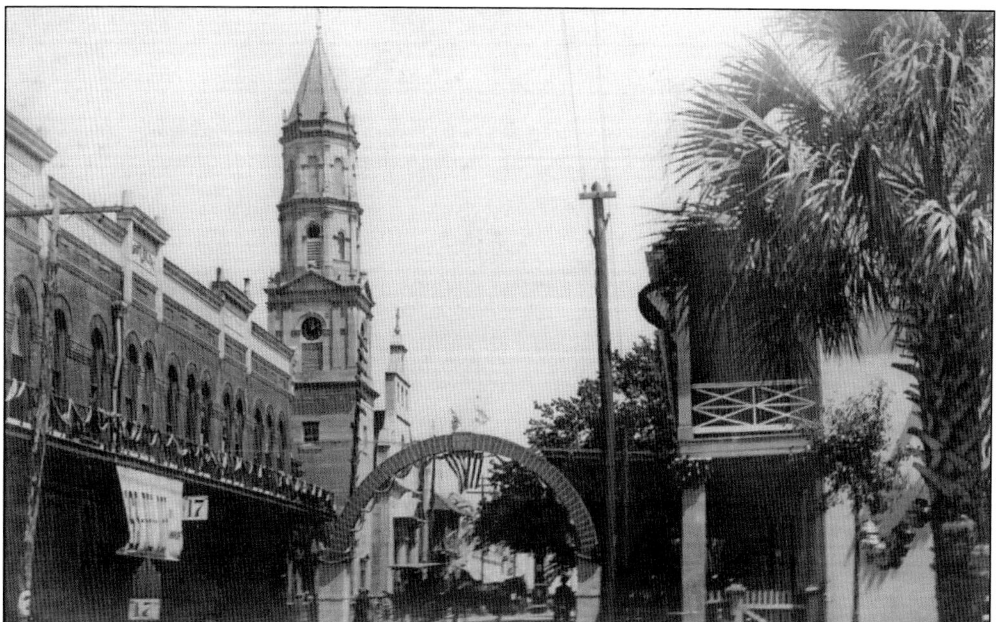

This is another view of the Union Labor arch from a different year's festival than the one shown above. It pictures Cathedral Street looking east, with the balcony of the post office on the right. On the far left, one can just see the newer portion of the Bishop's Building, which incorporated the old St. Mary's Convent into its construction.

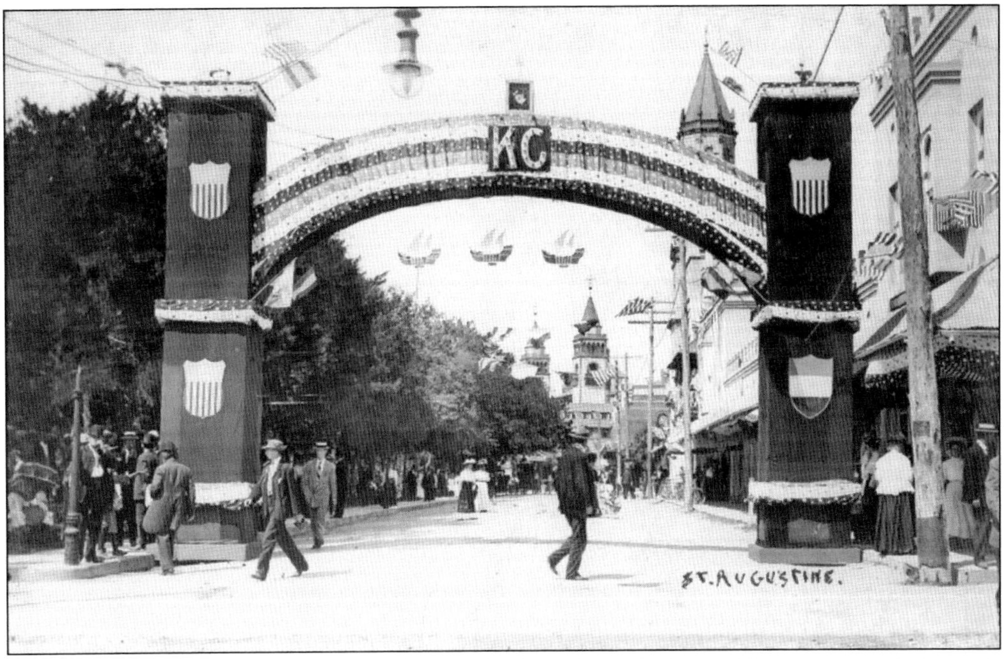

The Knights of Columbus, a fraternal organization of the Catholic Church, erected this arch over Cathedral Place at the corner of Charlotte Street. In this 1907 Harris postcard, the spire of the cathedral bell tower is visible above the arch, with the twin towers of the Ponce de Leon Hotel in the distance and the plaza on the left.

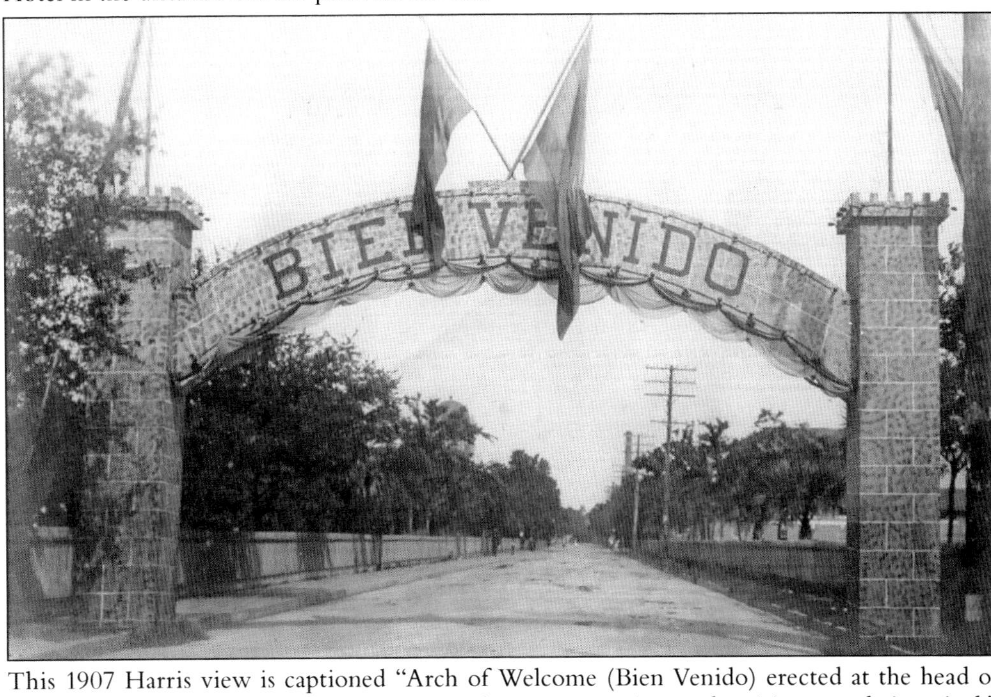

This 1907 Harris view is captioned "Arch of Welcome (Bien Venido) erected at the head of Valencia Street by the Florida East Coast Railway as a greeting to the visitors on their arrival." Valencia Street served as the main thoroughfare into the center of town from the railroad depot on Malaga Street. (Connahey collection.)

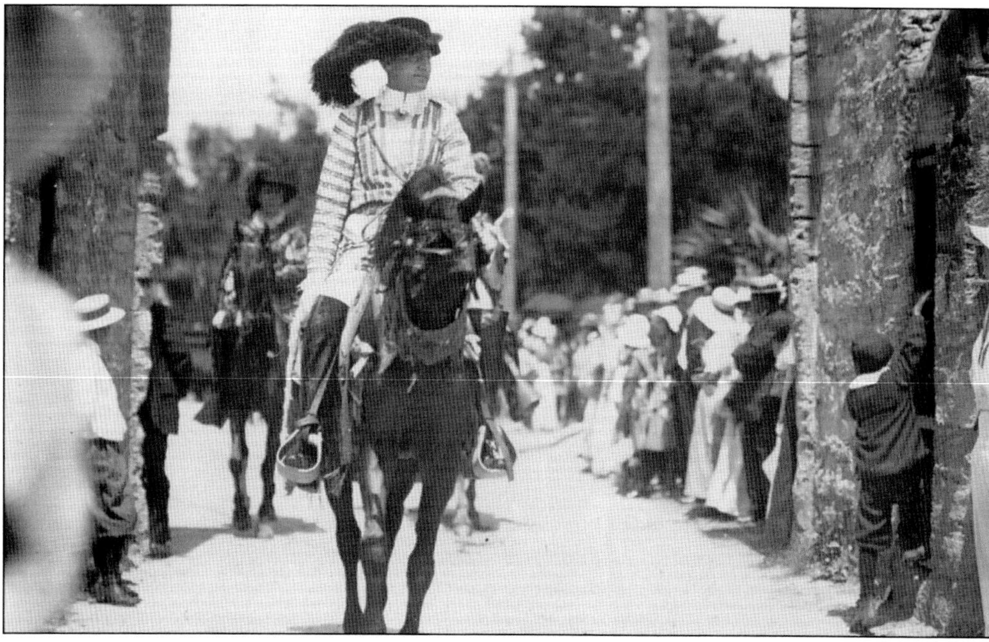

This 1913 view of a horseman riding through the City Gate is captioned "Impersonating Menendez during the Ponce de Leon Celebration." The landings of Ponce De Leon and Menendez were followed by parades through downtown. A reenactment of the attack on Fort Marion by British general Oglethorpe was capped by a "grand pyrotechnic display" on the final day of the celebration. (Connahey collection.)

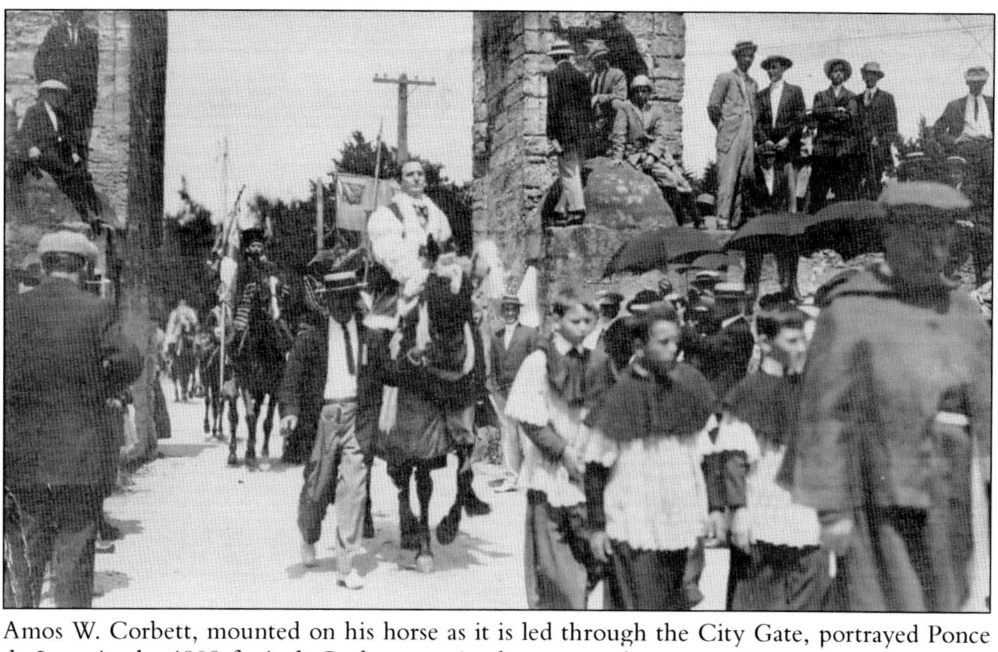

Amos W. Corbett, mounted on his horse as it is led through the City Gate, portrayed Ponce de Leon in the 1909 festival. Corbett was in the grocery business and a member of the fire department, serving as its chief in 1911–1912. In 1913, he was elected mayor of St. Augustine and was in office during the disastrous fire of 1914. In the 1920s, Corbett moved to Miami.

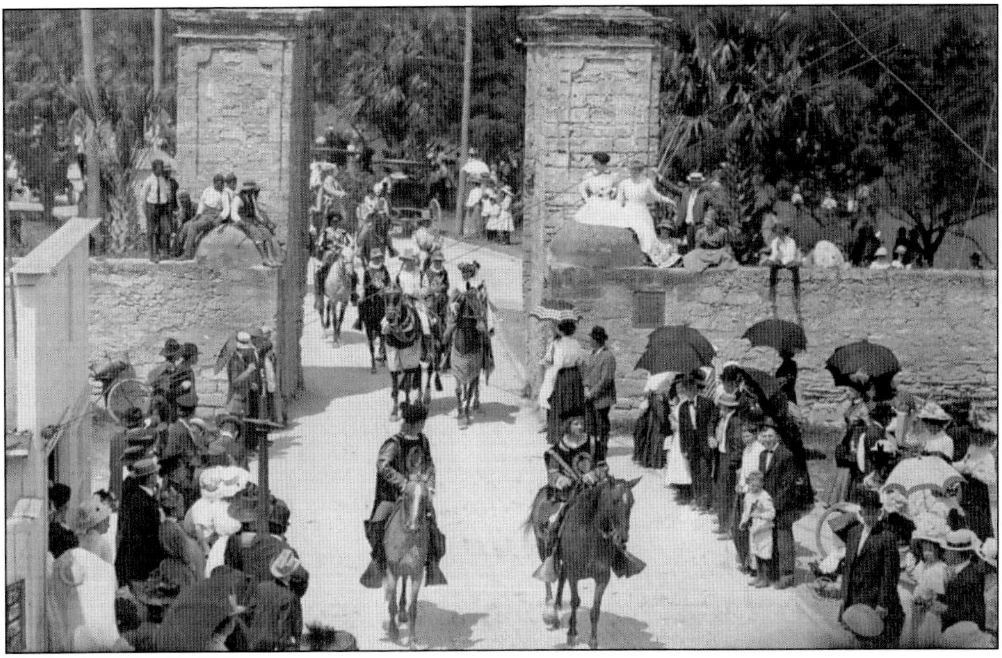

These two views of a parade through the City Gate during the Ponce de Leon Celebration were taken within a very short time of each other. The postcards are undated but are from the years 1907 to 1909. Notice the women sitting atop the City Gate on the right and the black children on the left. The photographer's studio in the left foreground has postcards on display outside the shop. Parades were a daily feature of the Ponce de Leon Celebration, with the highlight being a boat parade on the bay. The Capos' boat, *Pauline II*, led the way around the harbor and carried the band on board. Schools were out during the week of the celebration, and many local businesses held special sales. There were nightly concerts in the plaza and diving and swimming competitions in the Alcazar pool.

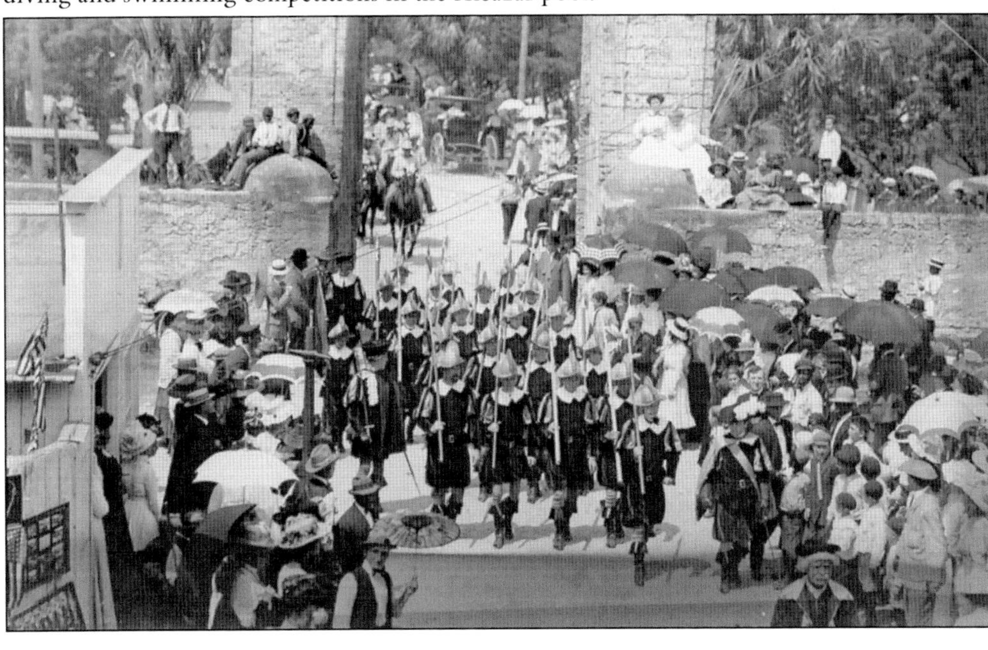

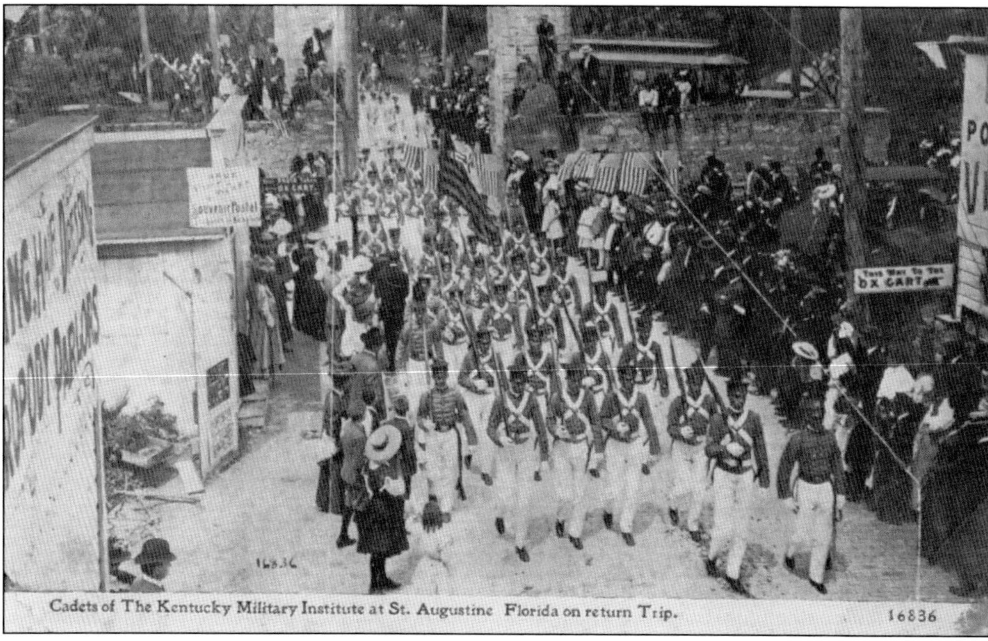

The Kentucky Military Institute had its winter quarters in Eau Gallie, Florida, from 1906 until 1921. Cadets from the institute are shown marching through the City Gate in this postcard made sometime after 1908, the year that the trolley began its run past the gate to San Marco Avenue. While in town to march in the festival, the cadets camped on the parade ground in front of the St. Francis Barracks.

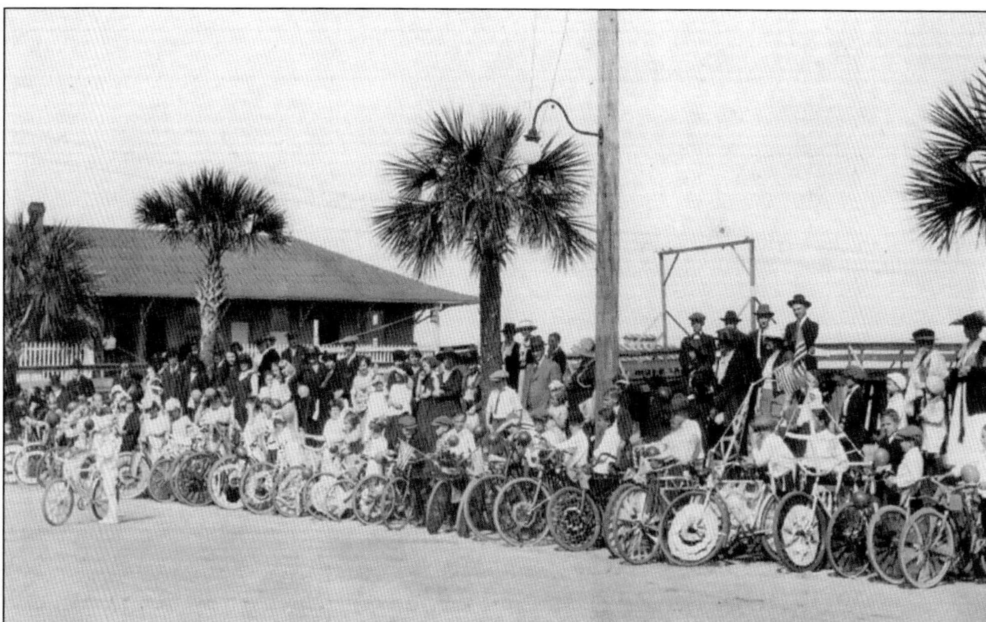

A group of cyclists have decorated their bicycles for the Ponce de Leon Celebration. Behind them is the terminal building for the St. Johns Electric Company on Bay Street (Avenida Menendez), at the foot of the bridge to Anastasia Island. This view was taken sometime after 1911, as overhead electrical wires for the trolley have been installed on the bridge.

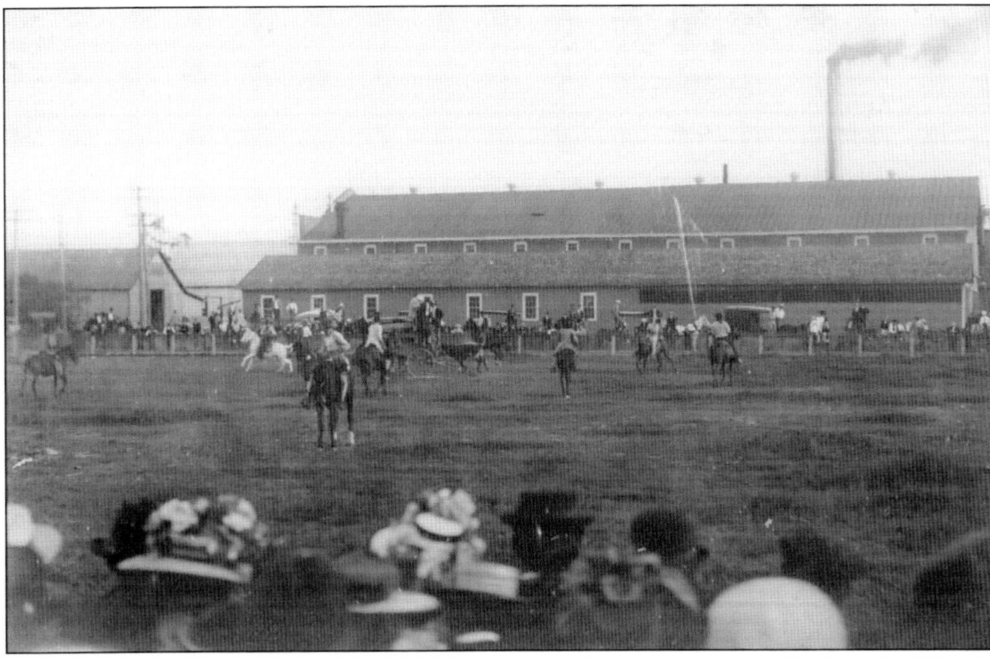

This view is looking south near the corner of King and Riberia Streets. The large building in the background is the St. Augustine Transfer Company, which later became the J. O. Miller Building. Colee's Stables, still located on Riberia Street between La Quinta and Cedar Streets, is the gable-roofed barn on the left. The scene shows riders attacking a stagecoach, one of the reenactments of the Ponce de Leon Celebration.

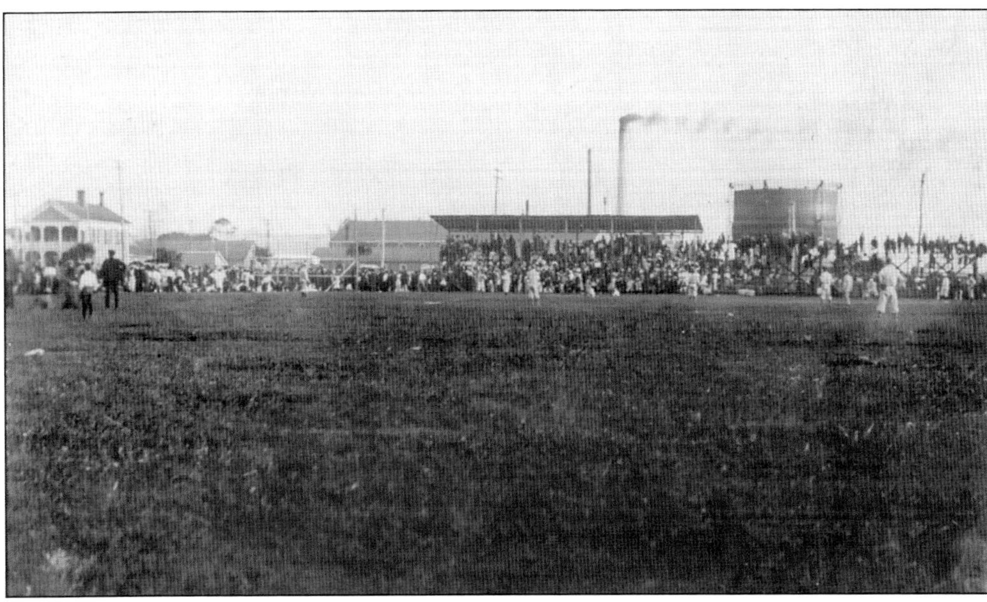

Several baseball games were held during the week of the Ponce de Leon Celebration, featuring the local YMCA team competing against squads from Rollins and Stetson Colleges. This field was near the corner of King and Malaga Streets, on a site later occupied by the FEC office buildings. The large storage tank of the St. Augustine Gas Company can be seen in the background. (Connahey collection.)

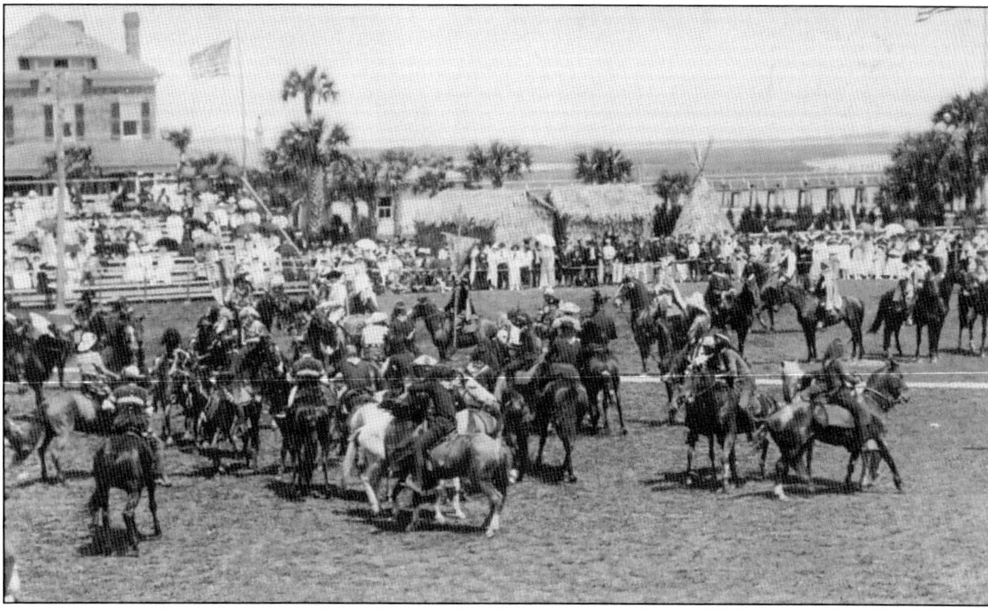

Bleachers were erected on the north side of Fort Marion, and spectators were charged admission to help defray the costs of the festival. Several elaborate battle reenactments were held, including this one with mounted Native Americans going up against cavalry units. Notice the historically inaccurate tepee, never used by the native Floridians. The home of Walter Darrow at 21 Water Street can be seen in the background on the left.

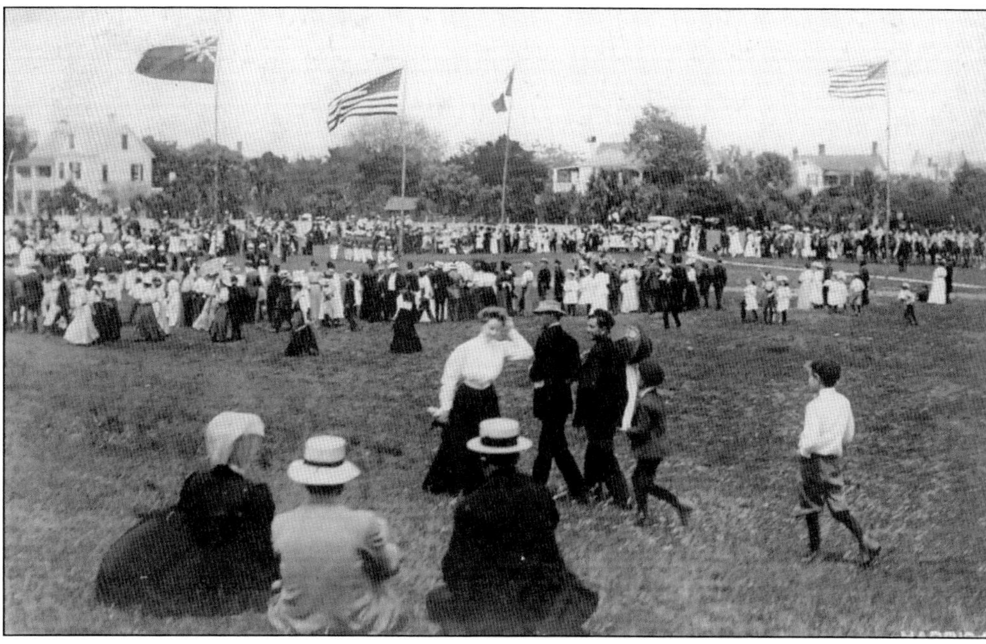

Uniformed marchers parade beneath flags of the competing Spanish, British, and American forces in this *c.* 1907 Harris view. The three spectators in the foreground are seated on the glacis of Fort Marion, looking northward. The home at 28 Water Street is seen beneath the flag on the far right, and the Lucy Abbott house at 22 Water Street is just to its left, behind the large tree. (Connahey collection.)

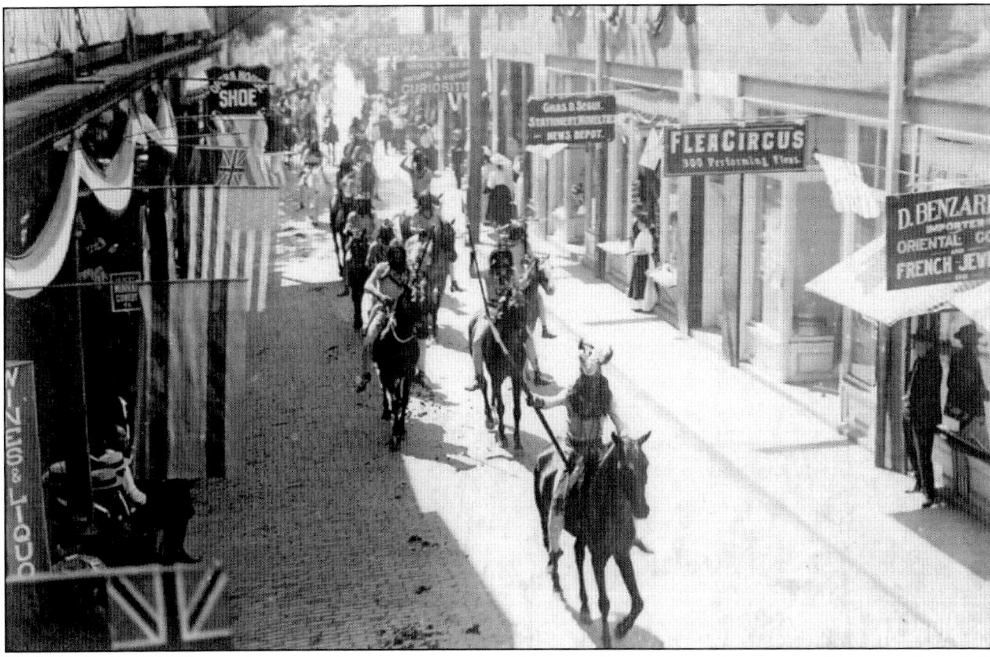

Mounted Native Americans ride north on St. George Street in this postcard from the 1907 celebration. The building on the right with the "Flea Circus" sign has been remodeled with modern storefronts and now houses businesses at 118 to 124 St. George Street. All the buildings on the left, including the Opera House Shoe Store, would be destroyed in the 1914 fire. (Connahey collection.)

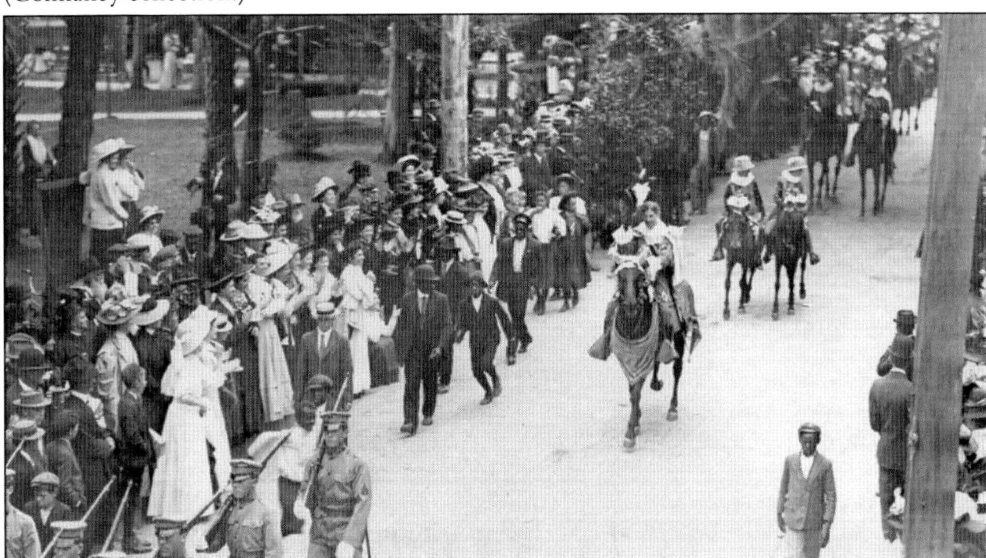

Oscar F. Usina, portraying Pedro Menendez in the 1909 celebration, rides along Cathedral Place at the plaza. Usina worked as a clerk at Genovar's Emporium and later opened Usina Brothers, a souvenir shop at 43 King Street. A battalion of the U.S. Coastal Artillery from Fort Screven (near Savannah), Georgia, marches in front of Usina. During the festival, the enlisted men camped on the grounds of Fort Marion, while the officers were housed at the Ponce de Leon Hotel.

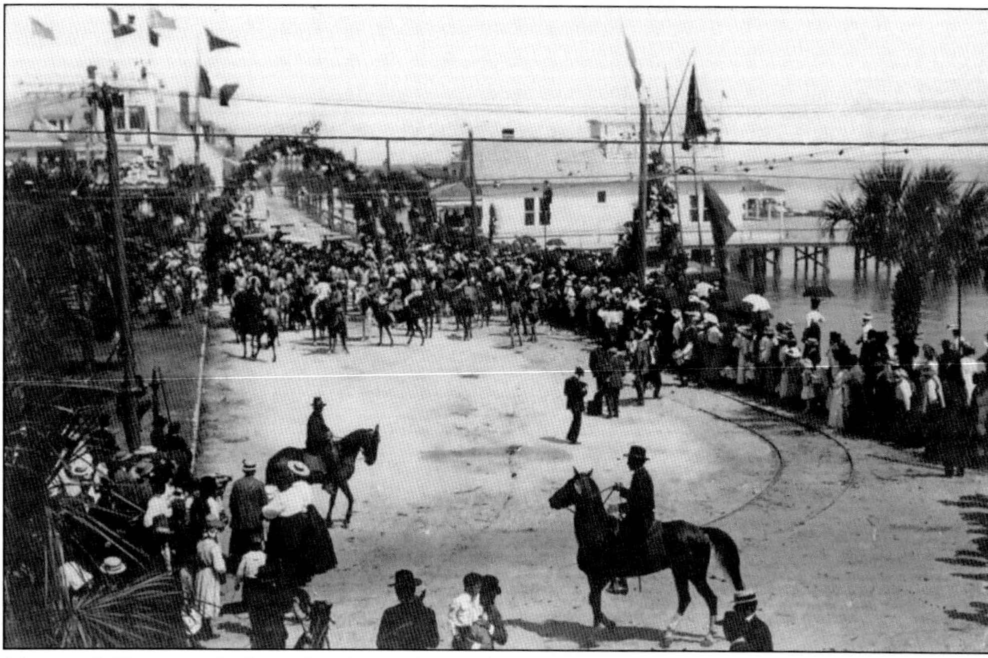

Mounted riders parade along Bay Street (Avenida Menendez) between King Street and Cathedral Place. The St. Augustine Yacht Club is in the center of the postcard, with the Charles Hamblen home (today's American Legion) in the distance on the left. The trolley tracks indicate that this Harris postcard was made sometime after 1907.

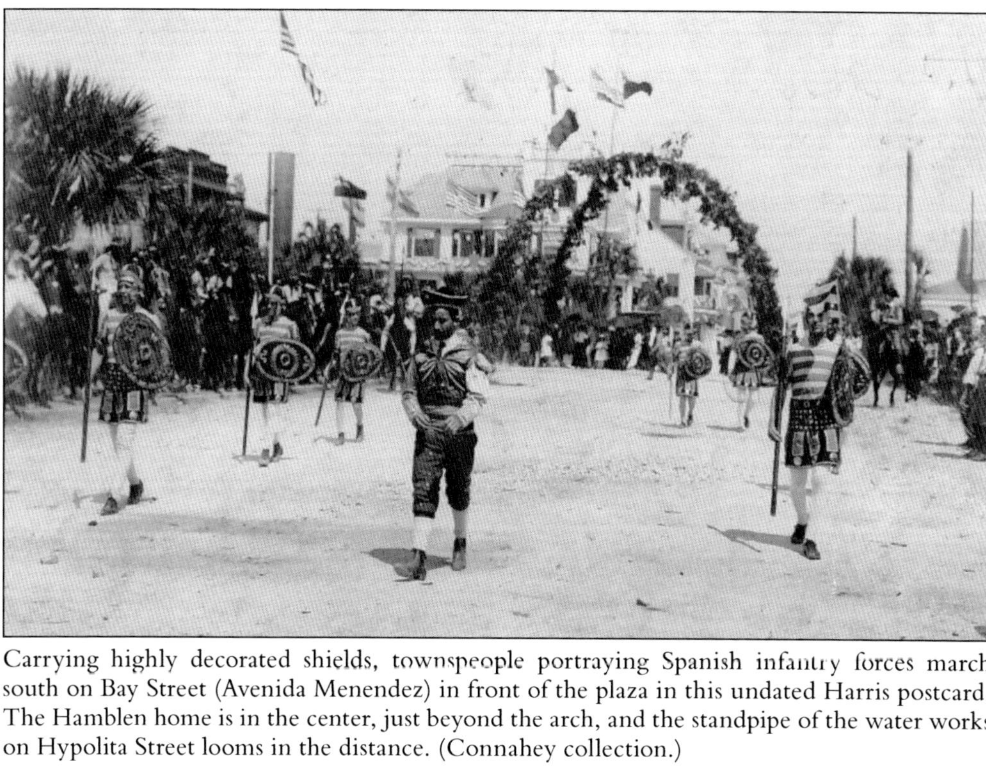

Carrying highly decorated shields, townspeople portraying Spanish infantry forces march south on Bay Street (Avenida Menendez) in front of the plaza in this undated Harris postcard. The Hamblen home is in the center, just beyond the arch, and the standpipe of the water works on Hypolita Street looms in the distance. (Connahey collection.)

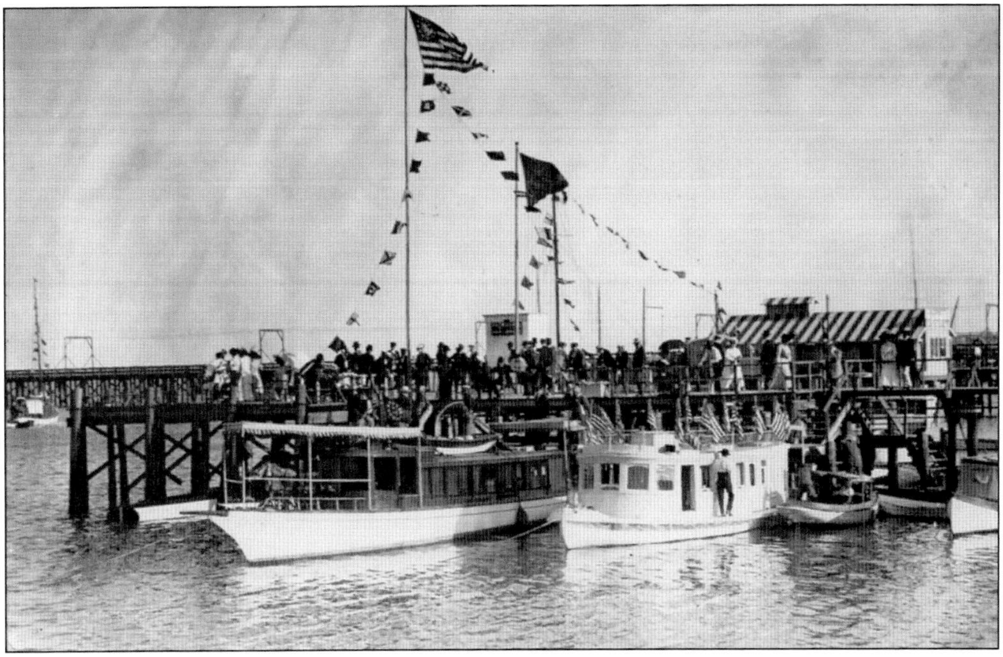

Corbett's Dock, located on the bay front just north of the present-day Bridge of Lions, is decorated for the 1910 Ponce de Leon Celebration. Powerboat races were a popular event and featured a 15-mile race for speedboats. There was also a five-mile handicap race for working boats, won in 1909 by Alvin Drysdale's boat, the *Irvine D.*

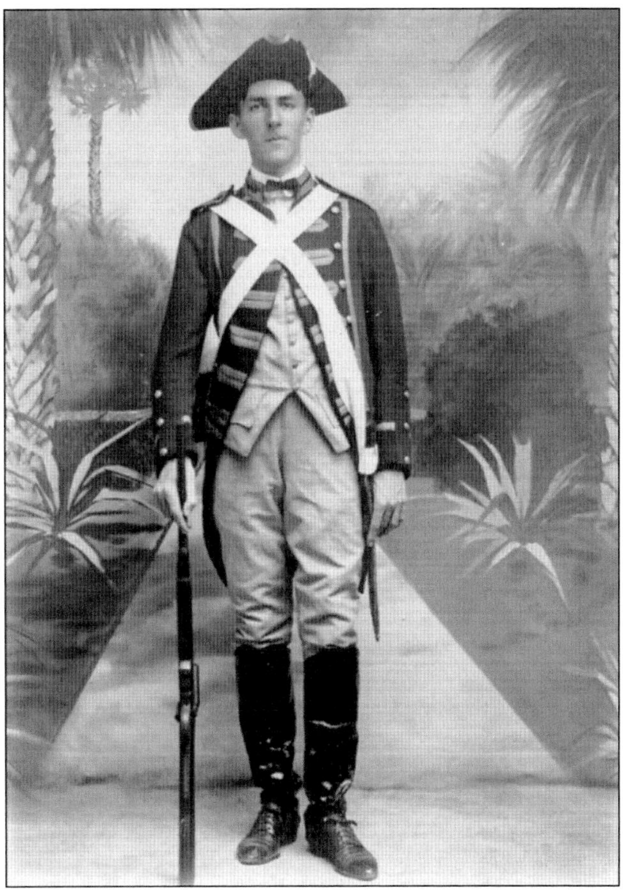

Raymond A. Leggett, one of the many local men who took part in the Ponce De Leon Celebration, is dressed as a British soldier for the 1907 festival. At the time, Leggett was a student and lived at home with his mother, Annie (widow of George W. Leggett), at 119 Cordova Street.

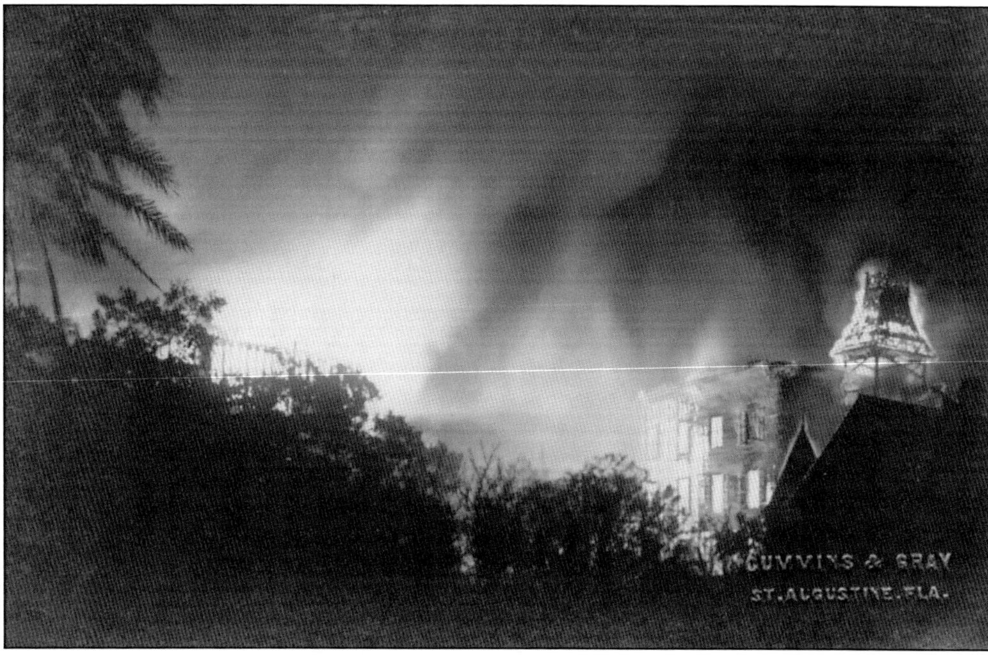

At 12:50 a.m. on April 2, 1914, Patrolman S. A. McCormick reported smoke pouring from the second story of the Florida House, shown here with its Victorian tower ablaze. The conflagration spread quickly, and Fire Chief Charles P. Townsend called for help from Jacksonville. The FEC Railway sent a special train with fire equipment that made the 36-mile trip in a record 37 minutes.

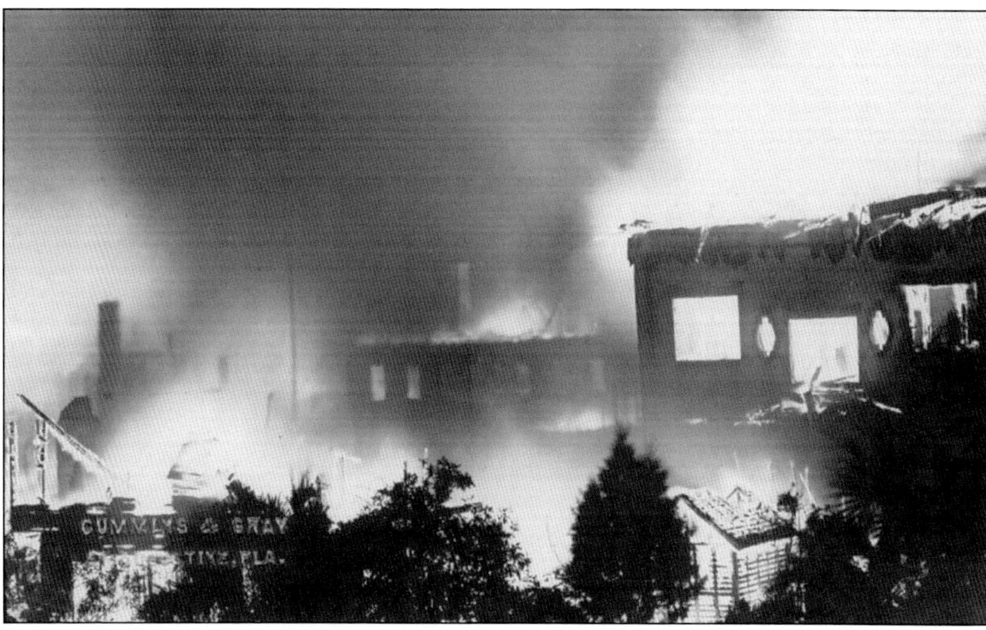

Fire soon engulfed the courthouse, shown here on the right, and spread north to Hypolita Street and east to the bay front. Fortunately the courthouse records were kept in a fireproof vault and were not damaged. The Hotel Magnolia on the west side of St. George Street was saved by the valiant efforts of firemen, including fire squads from the Ponce De Leon and Alcazar Hotels.

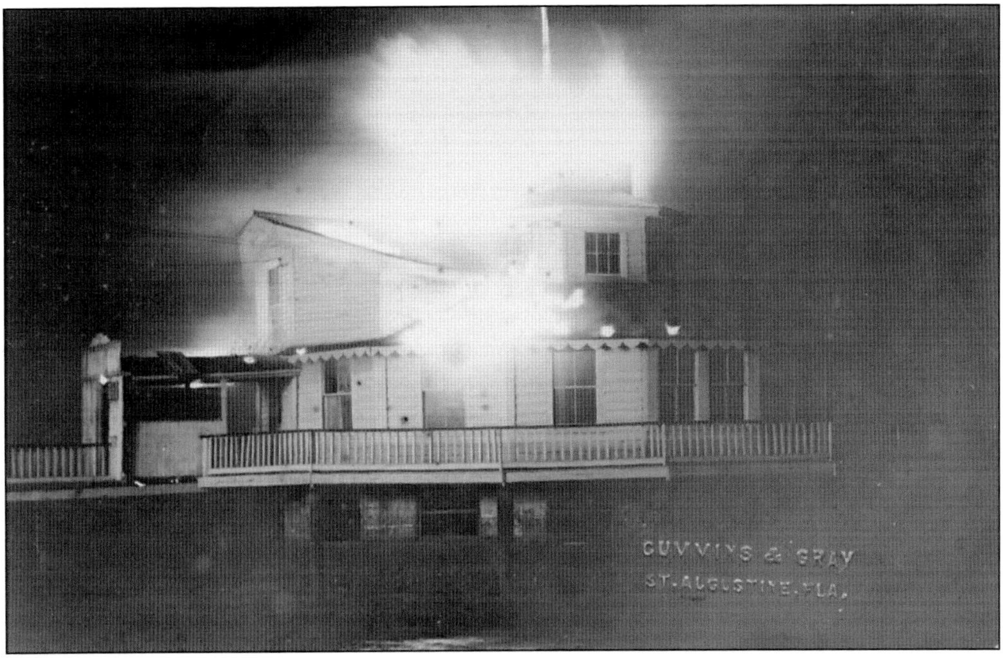

By 1914, Capo's Bath House on the bay front had become the home of the Power Boat Club. Over $30,000 worth of valuable boats were saved from the fire by club manager Charles F. Hopkins Jr., who towed them across the river to safety before flames destroyed the building, leaving only the coquina foundations remaining.

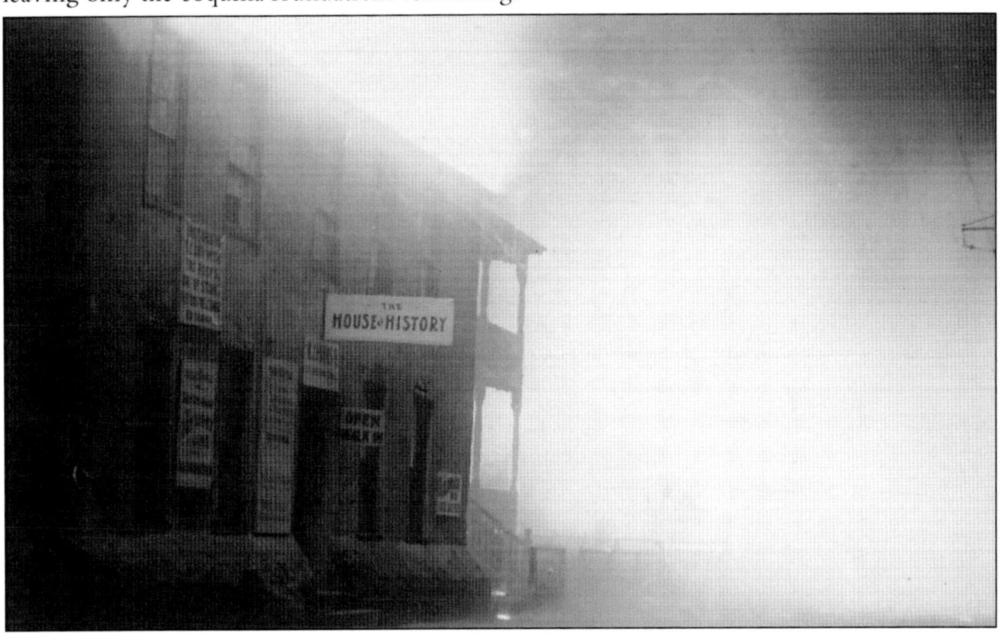

The former Vedder Museum, owned by the St. Augustine Institute of Science (today's St. Augustine Historical Society), fell victim to the fire, and with it went the institute's entire collection of artifacts and documents. In 1912, photographer W. J. Harris had become curator for the institute and had moved his photographic business into the old Vedder building. The fire destroyed his entire postcard and photographic inventory.

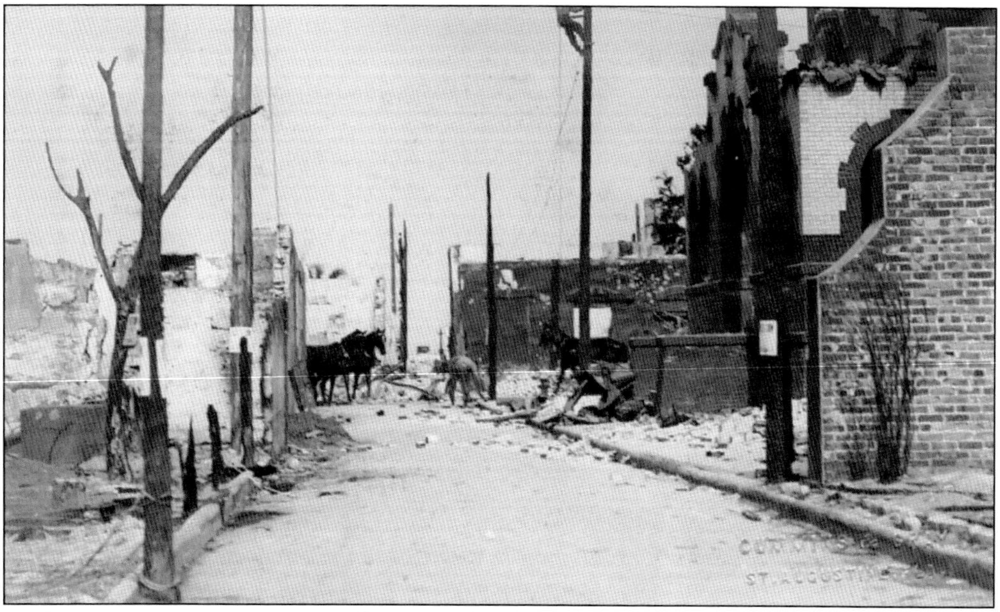

Looking east on Treasury Street, the ruins of the St. Johns County Courthouse can be seen on the right. On the left, very little remains of the wooden Florida House where the fire began. The horses are at the intersection of Treasury and Charlotte Streets. World War I began in Europe in August 1914, and silent film companies used St. Augustine's ruins to depict battlefield scenes of the war.

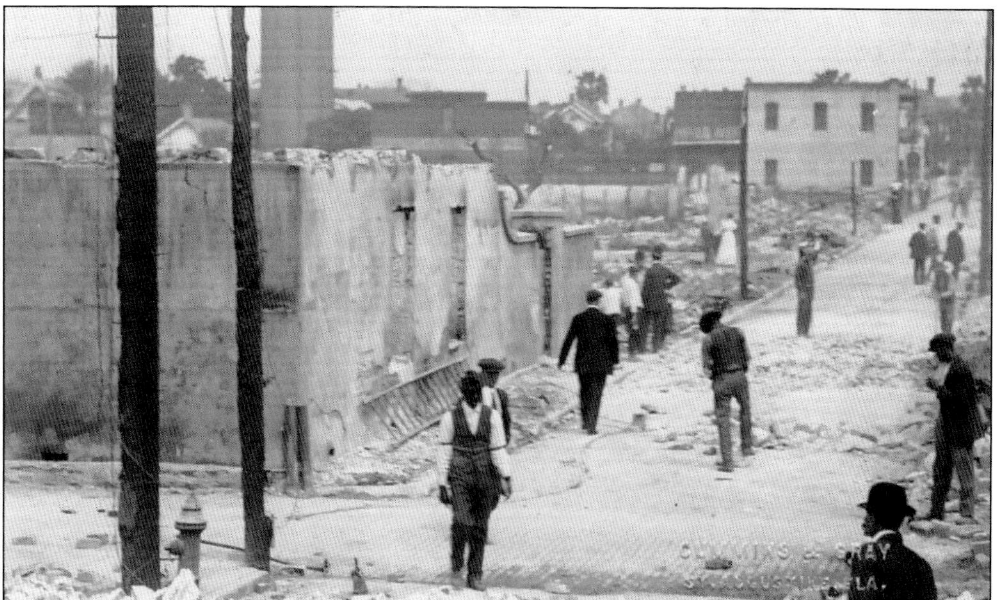

This view looking north from the intersection of Treasury Street shows workers removing debris on Charlotte Street. On the left are the ruins of the Sallas Building, the present location of a real estate company and other businesses. The white two-story building in the distance is the Charles L. Deardorff residence, now a retail shop on the northwest corner of Charlotte and Hypolita Streets.

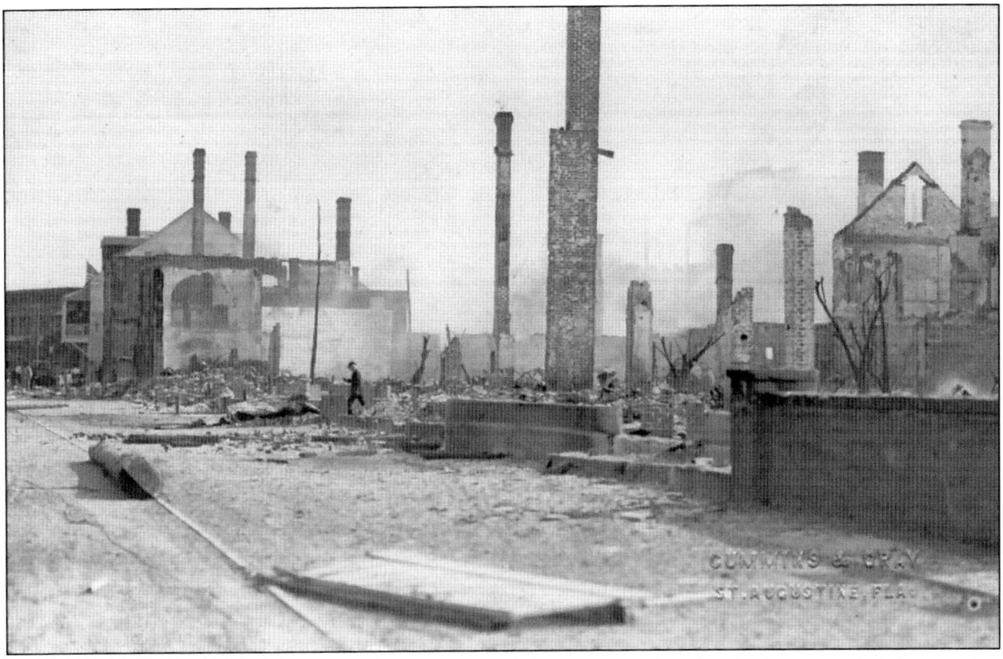

By 1914, photographers Albert A. Cummins and Charles E. Gray had taken over Blair's Studio at 163 St. George Street. All postcards of the fire and its aftermath included in this book are from their studio. This view shows the ruins on Bay Street, looking south from the corner of Hypolita Street. In the distance on the left, the house with the balcony is today a restaurant at 46 Avenida Menendez.

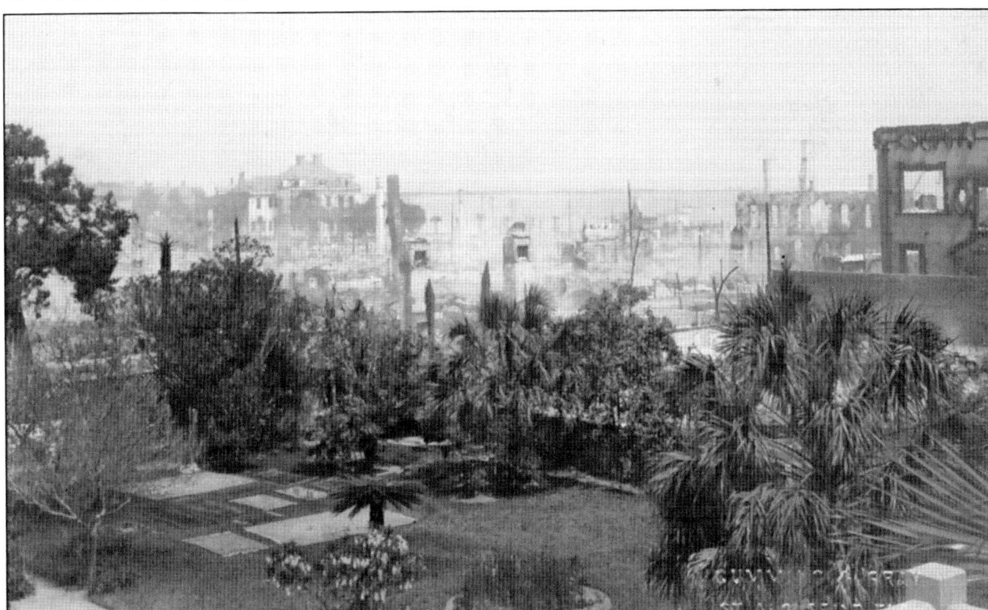

The garden of the Peña-Peck House at the corner of St. George and Treasury Streets is filled with rugs saved from the fire. The fort green and plaza were also piled with personal belongings and guarded by police. At the far right, beyond the wall, is the courthouse, and the ruins of the Florida House are in the center of the view.

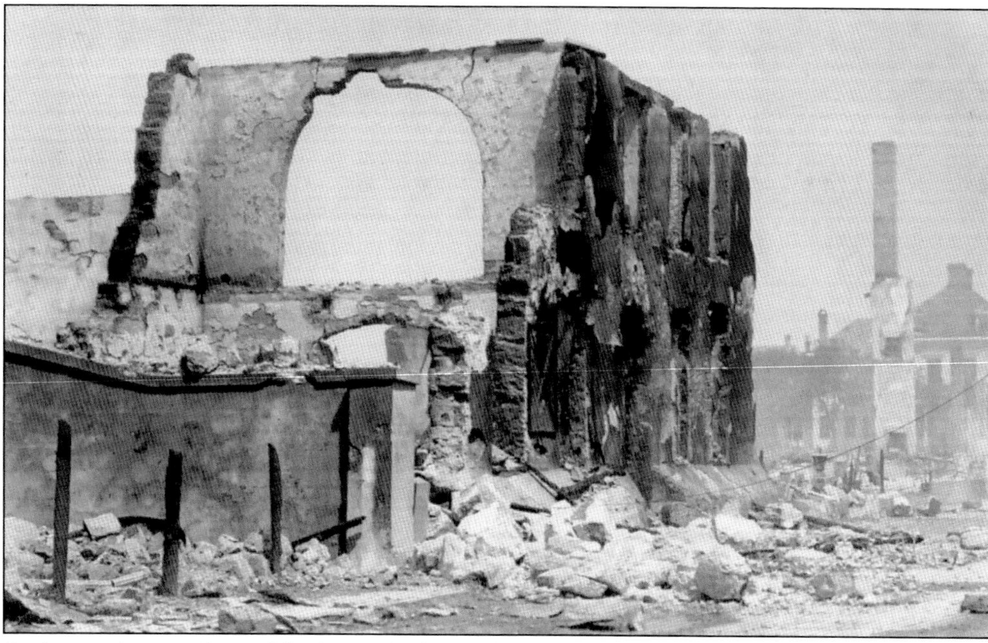

An interesting survivor of the fire is the base of this wall of the Vedder Museum. After the fire, the remaining walls were leveled, but the distinctive coquina escarpment in front remained. The property was sold to the Monson Hotel, and the escarpment became part of the Monson's garden wall. Later motels incorporated the wall into reconstructions of the old house at the corner of Avenida Menendez and Treasury Street.

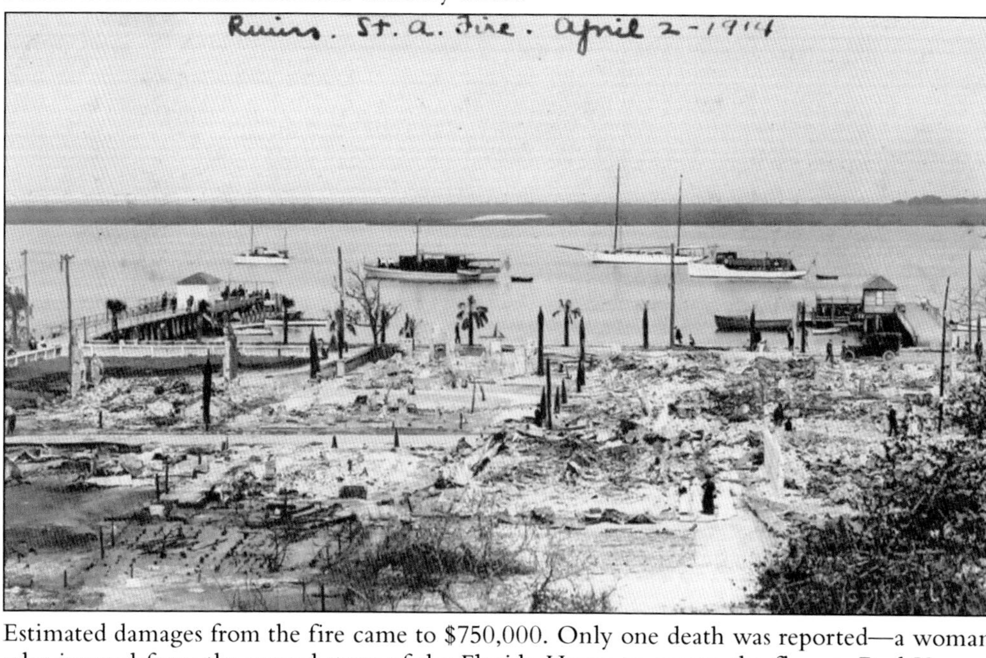

Estimated damages from the fire came to $750,000. Only one death was reported—a woman who jumped from the second story of the Florida House to escape the flames. Fred Young, brother of Florence Monson, was badly burned trying to save guests and their belongings at the Monson House. This view looking eastward toward the harbor was taken after much of the fire debris had been cleared away.

Eight

Photographers and Their Subjects

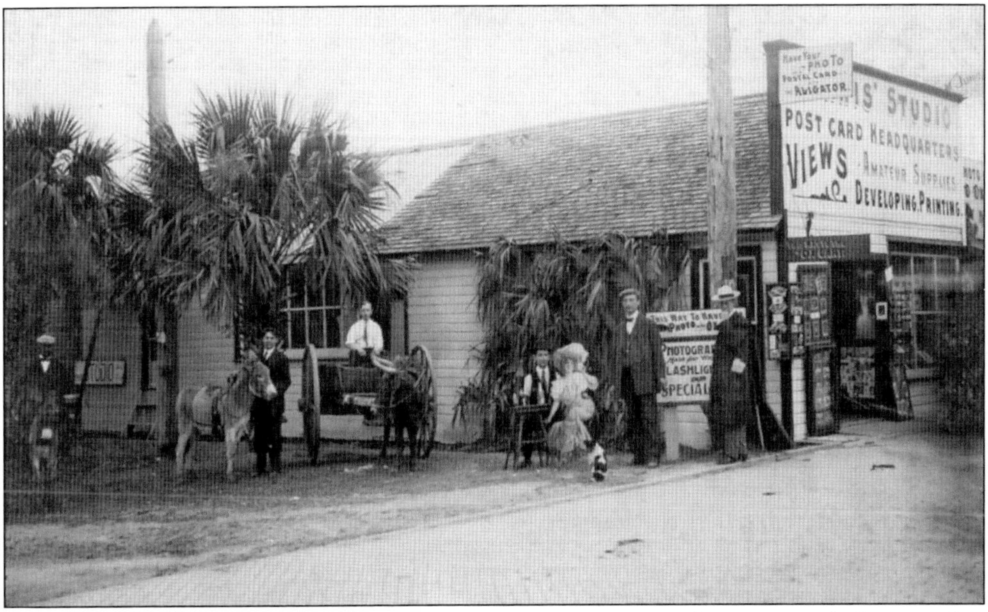

During the first few decades of the 20th century, St. Augustine's most noted photographer was William J. Harris. Born in England in 1867, Harris first came to the city in 1898 and operated the Acme View Company at 84 St. George Street. During the following years, he maintained a studio in St. Augustine in the winter season and spent the summers working at Lake Hopatcong, New Jersey. Around 1909, the Harris studio was located just inside the City Gate at 1 St. George Street as shown in this postcard. Harris specialized in photo postcards of tourists taken in front of the nearby City Gate or inside his studio with visitors posed in a typical Florida scene. Harris's associates are pictured with some of the props used in his photographs. From left to right are two burros, the famous oxcart, and a mock-up of a voluptuous woman. Harris is standing just to the right of his dog, Hypo, named for hyposulfite of soda, a solution used by photographers.

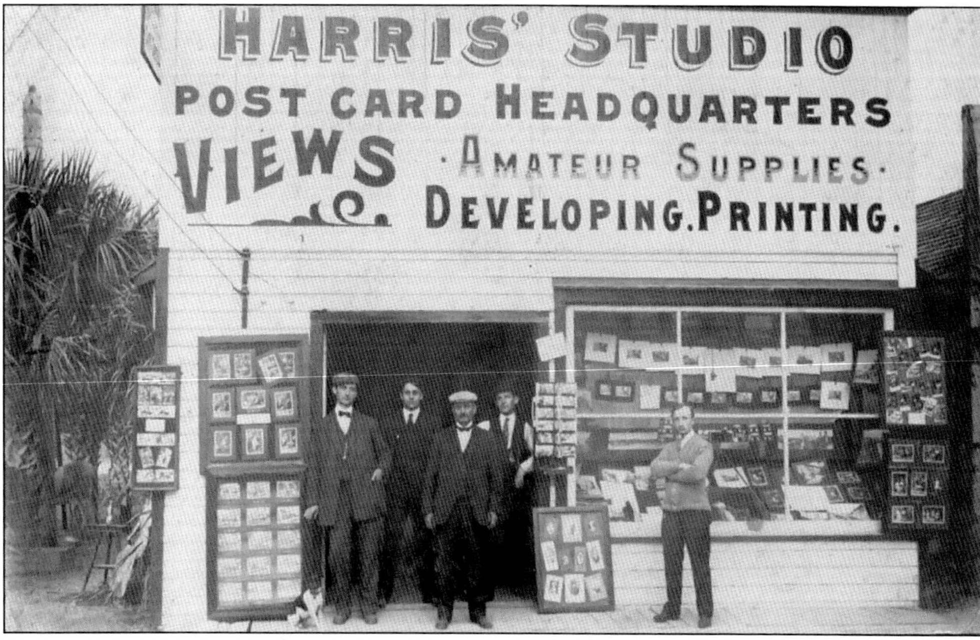

This front view of the Harris studio at 1 St. George Street around 1909 shows W. J. Harris and his fox terrier, Hypo, on the far left. Others, pictured from left to right, are Harris's associates Herb Thrasher, John G. Harris, W. R. Hites, and Albert A. Cummins. In 1911–1912, Cummins would work for the Blair Studio and later open his own studio with Charles E. Gray.

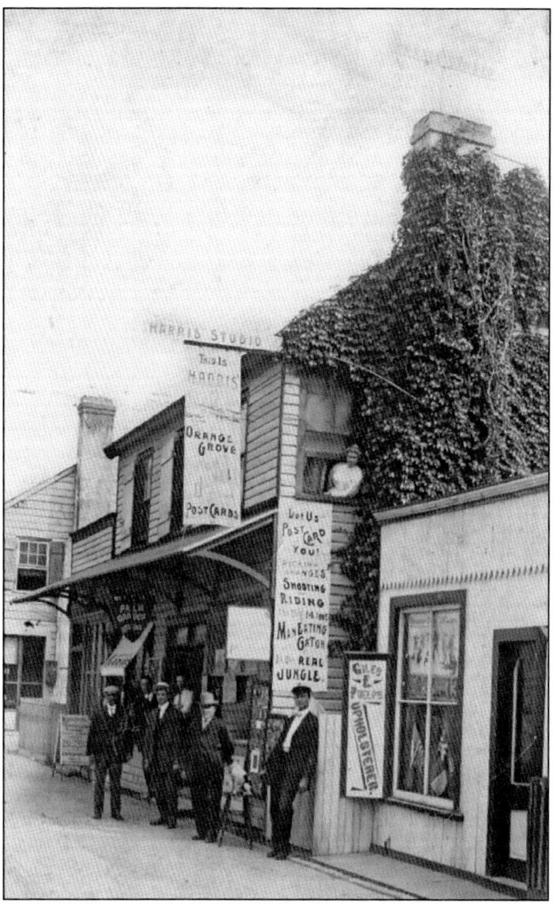

By 1911, Harris had moved his studio a few doors down to 15 St. George Street and now advertised it as the Palm Garden Studio. Harris is standing below the sign that reads "Let us post card you picking oranges, shooting, riding the big 14-foot man eating gator in our real jungle." Notice the woman in the upper window and Harris's dog, Hypo, sitting on a stool next to him.

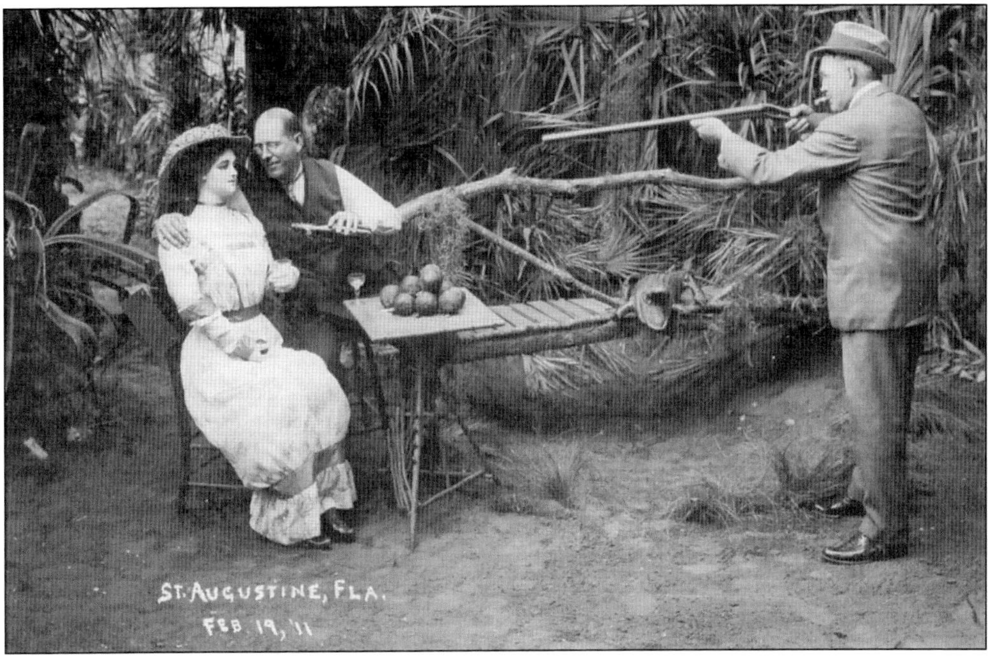

These postcards were both photographed at the "jungle" inside W. J. Harris's aptly named Palm Garden Studio. The upper card, dated February 19, 1911, shows a man plying a female mannequin with liquor, while an angry father or husband aims his shotgun. Notice the small stuffed alligator on the wooden bridge. The bottom card has the same background scene and shows a couple in Harris's "gatormobile," pulled by the stuffed 14-foot man-eating gator. Staged comic scenes such as these were very popular with tourists, and Harris and other photographers supplied thousands of them.

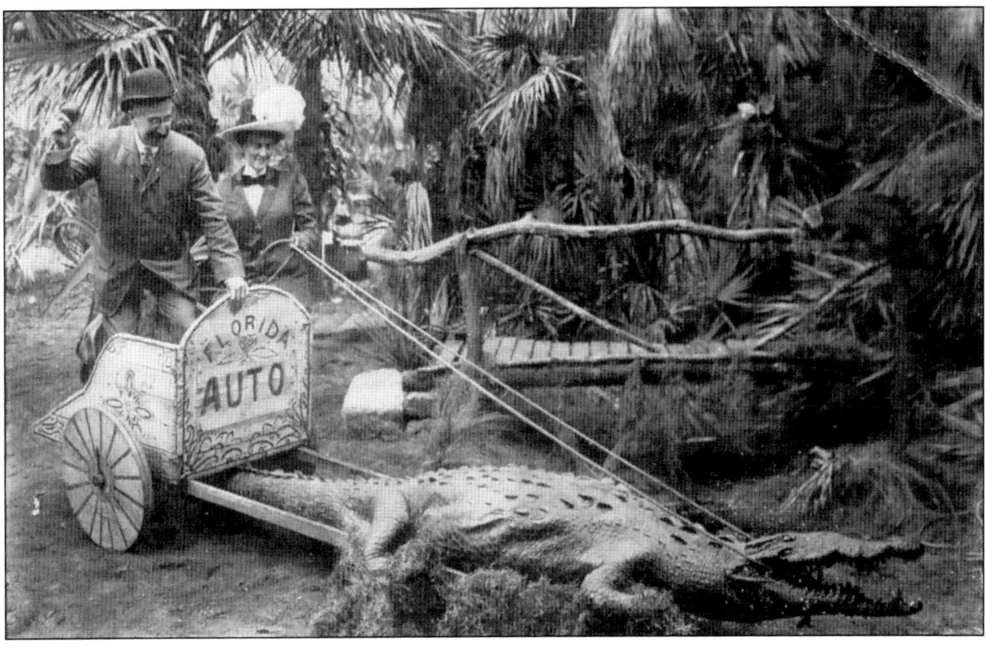

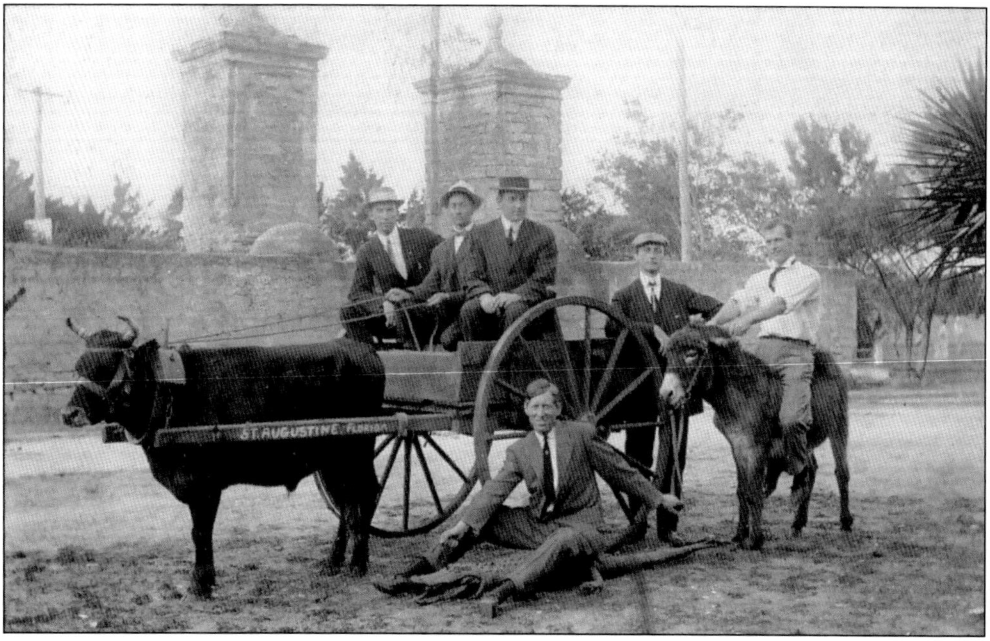

W. J. Harris is standing just behind the wheel of the oxcart in this postcard taken at the City Gate. The oxcart was one of the favorite props for tourist poses in front of the gate, as were the burro and the stuffed alligator also shown here.

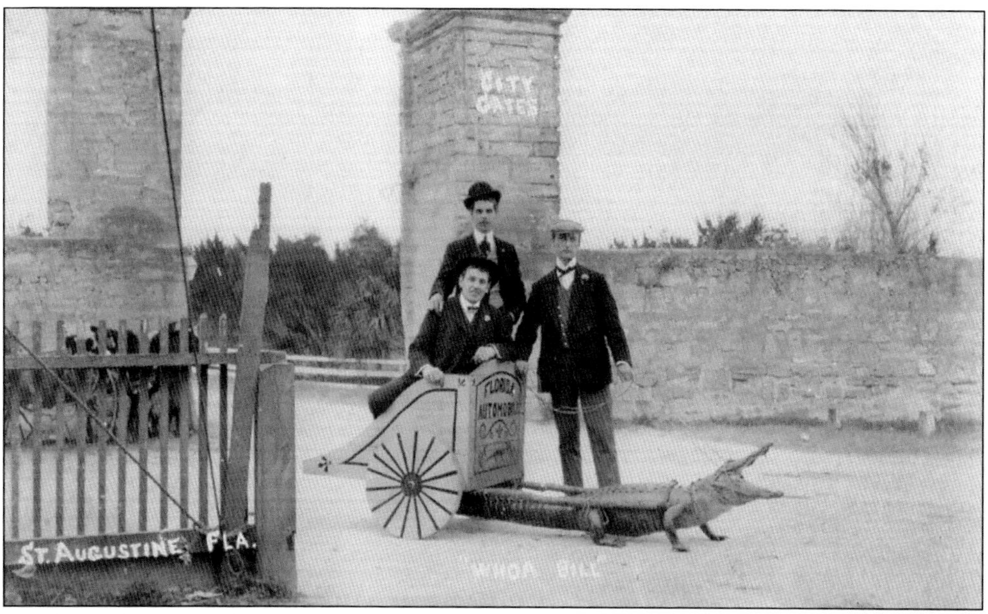

Another of Harris's famous props for tourist photographs was the Florida automobile or "gatormobile," pictured here in front of the "City Gates [*sic*]." Although the two pillars make up only one gate, it was often referred to in the plural, and longtime residents still use that nomenclature. Harris is standing on the right, behind the stuffed alligator.

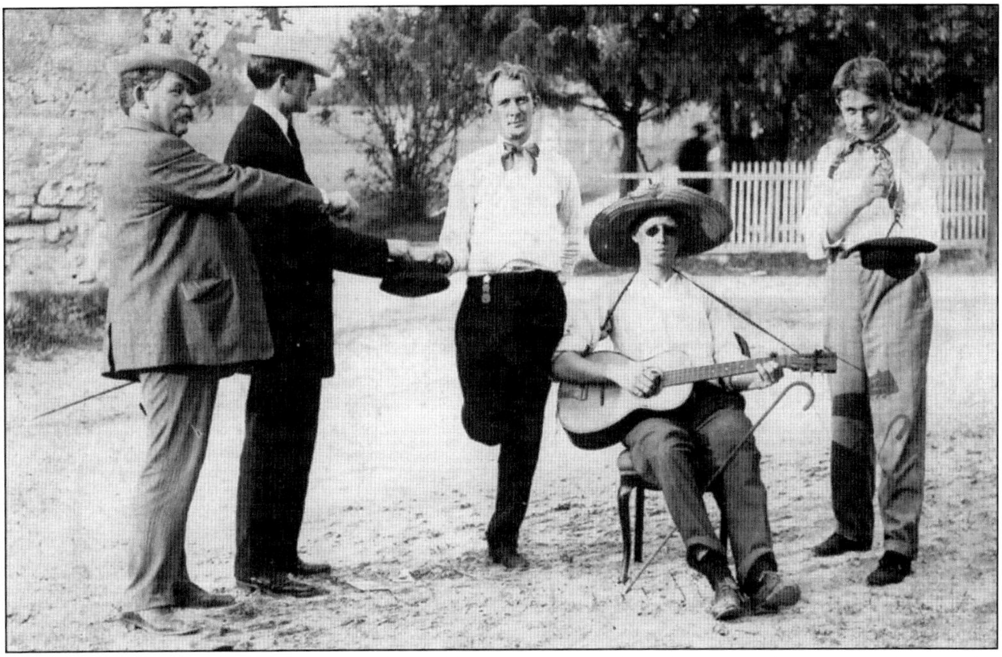

This comic Harris postcard shows three "beggars" near the City Gate. The man playing the guitar is wearing sunglasses, with a cane resting between his legs, pretending to be blind. The second man is standing on one leg, feigning an amputation, while the third man passes the hat. Photographer W. J. Harris is in the dark suit, second from the left, putting money into the hat.

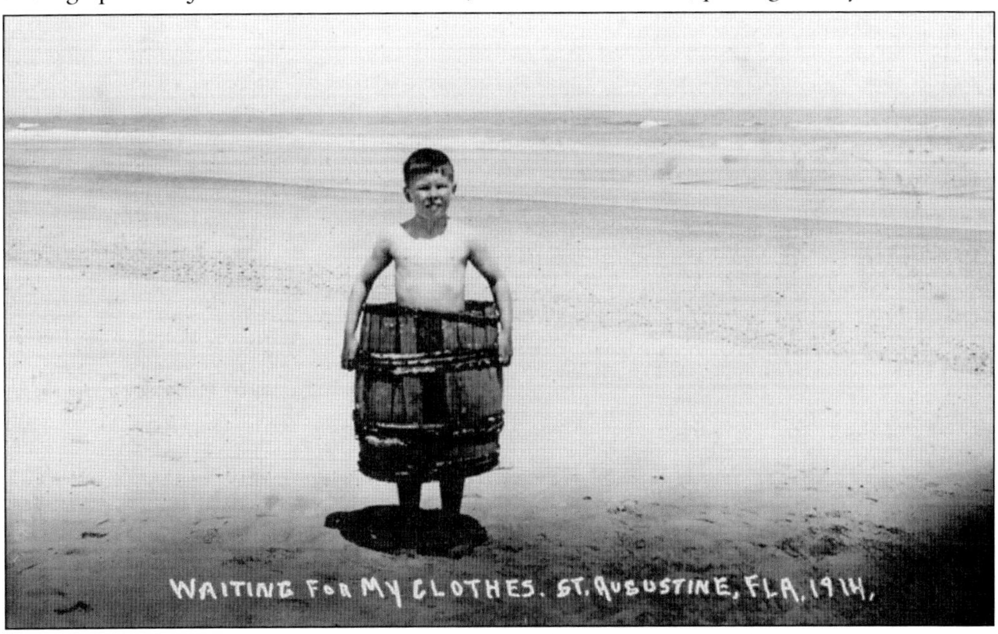

Another novelty card by W. J. Harris shows a small boy holding up a barrel with the caption "Waiting for my clothes—St. Augustine, Fla. 1914." Harris often used his son, Carver, in many of his photographs, but the subject in this postcard is unidentified. Carver Harris also became a photographer and took over his father's tourist business and management of the St. Augustine Historical Society after W. J. Harris's death in 1940.

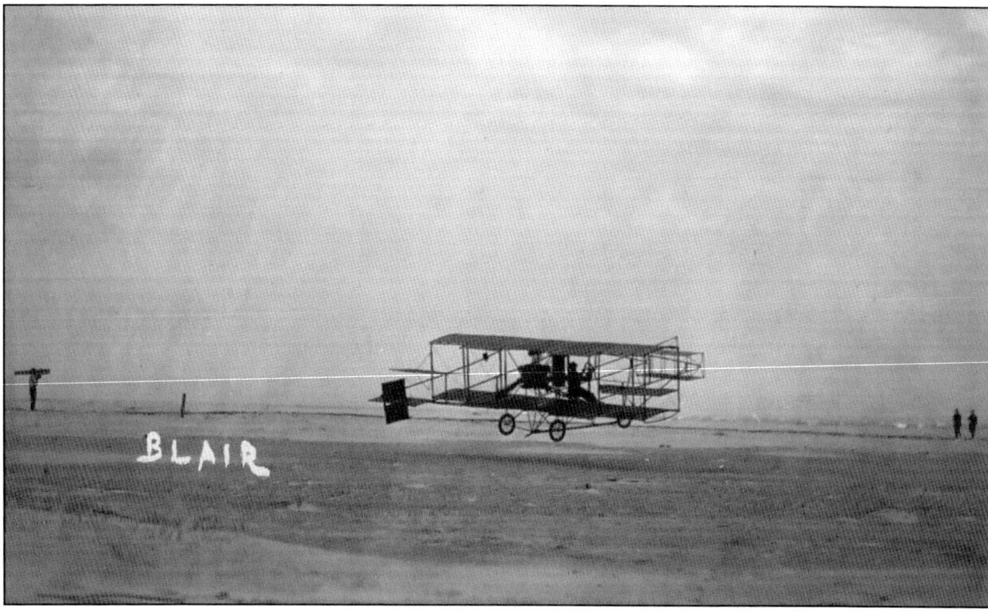

An early Curtiss Pusher biplane lands on the hard-packed sands of St. Augustine Beach in this photo postcard by Lewis W. Blair. The airplane is the "Shooting Star" of Jimmie Ward, who participated in an aviation meet with flyer J. A. D. McCurdy at South Beach on April 2, 1911. Three days later, Ward raced his biplane against several powerboats competing in speedboat championships on Matanzas Bay.

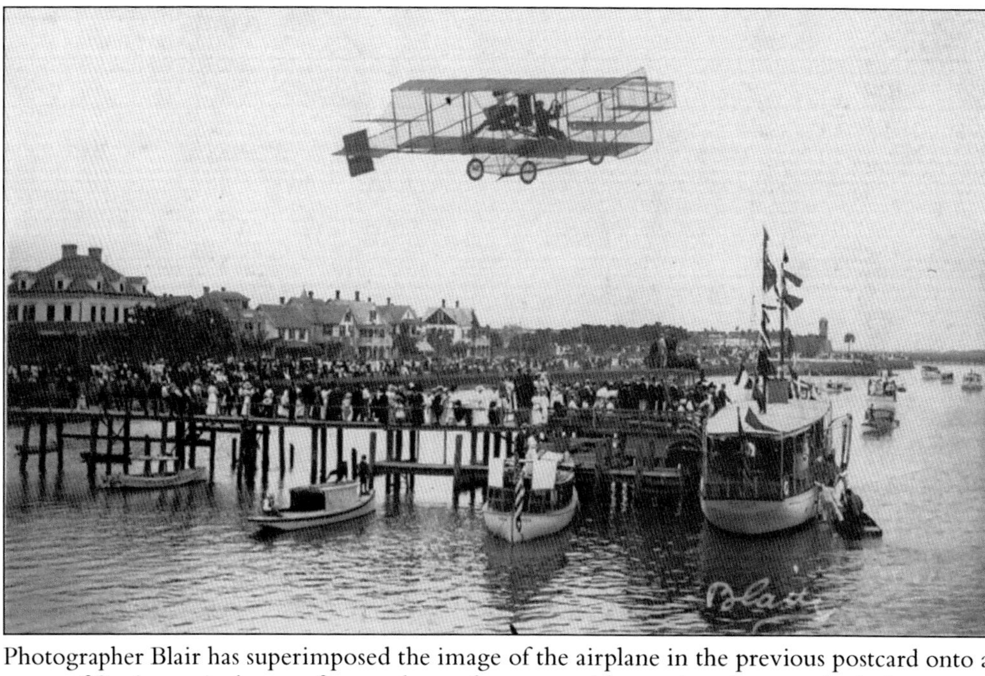

Photographer Blair has superimposed the image of the airplane in the previous postcard onto a scene of St. Augustine's waterfront, where a large crowd has gathered to watch the boat races held during the Ponce de Leon Celebration. At the end of the pier is the motor yacht *Paula*, belonging to J. Stuart Blackton of New York. Blackton owned the Vitagraph Company, and his Elco launch, *Vita*, competed in the races.

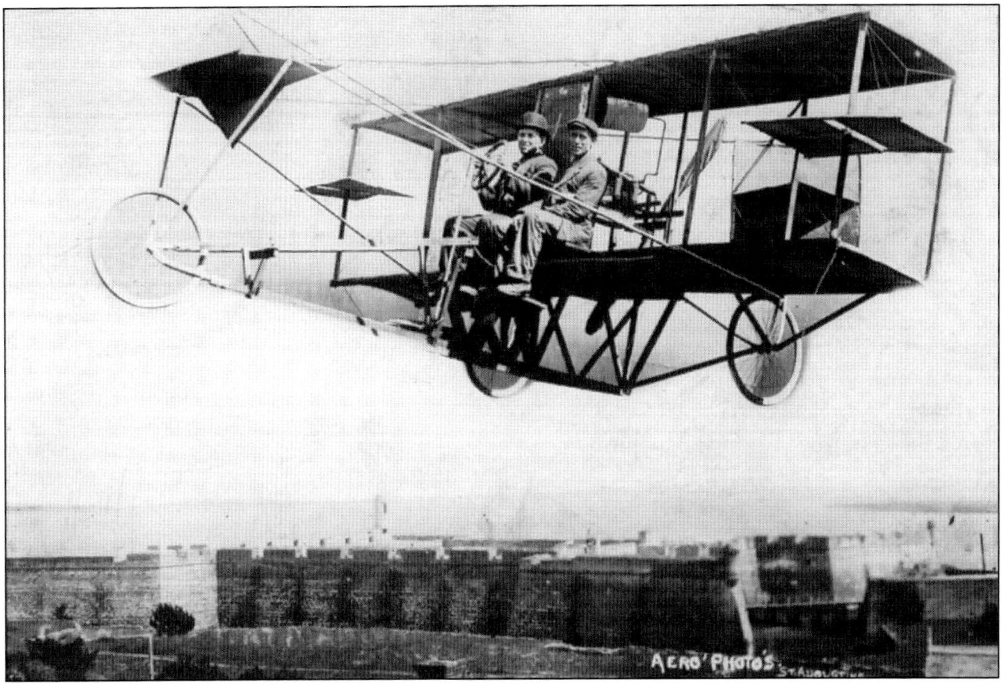

The "aeroplane" novelty postcard was popular all over the United States just prior to World War I. The image of tourists in a mock plane was shot in the photographer's studio and superimposed onto another image so that the visitors appeared to be flying over a famous landmark. This postcard of two men flying over Fort Marion is by an unidentified photographer.

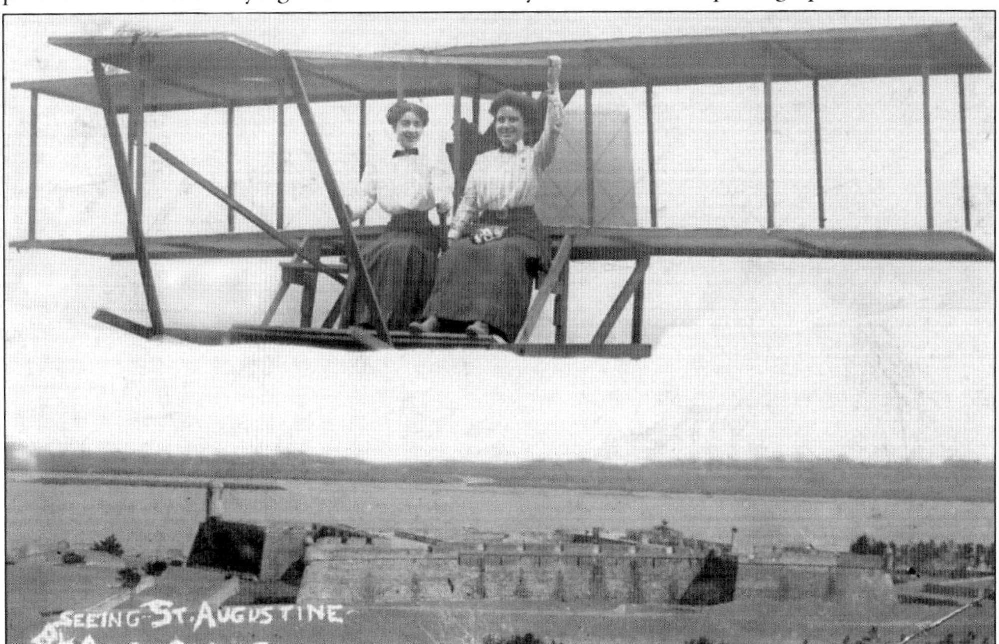

Two women are shown "flying" over Fort Marion in this W. J. Harris card postmarked March 14, 1911. Notice that the "aeroplane" is much less complete that the one shown above, as it has neither engine nor wheels! (Connahey collection.)

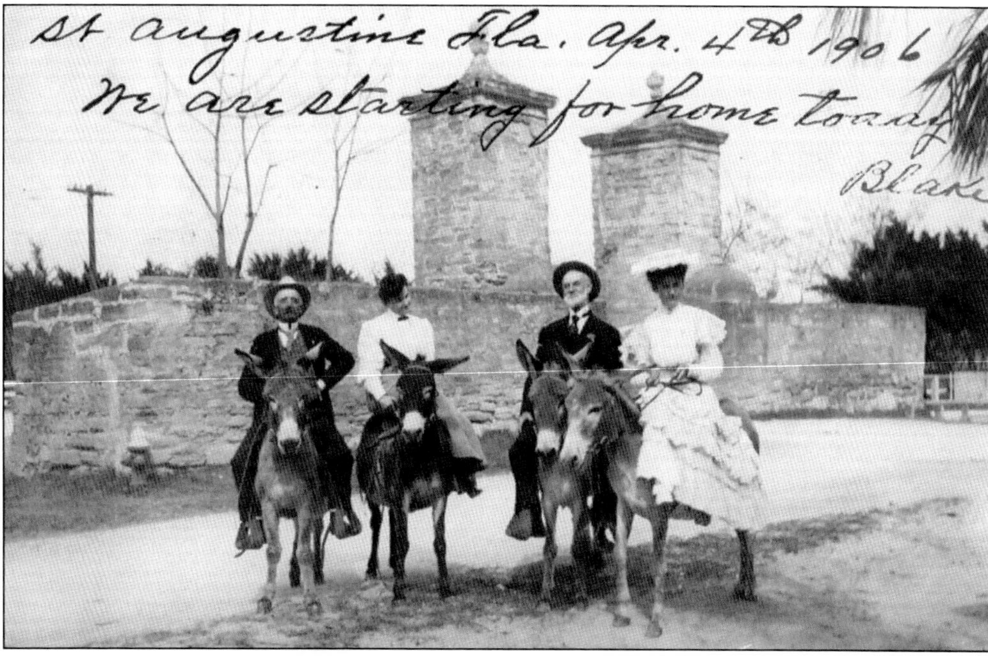

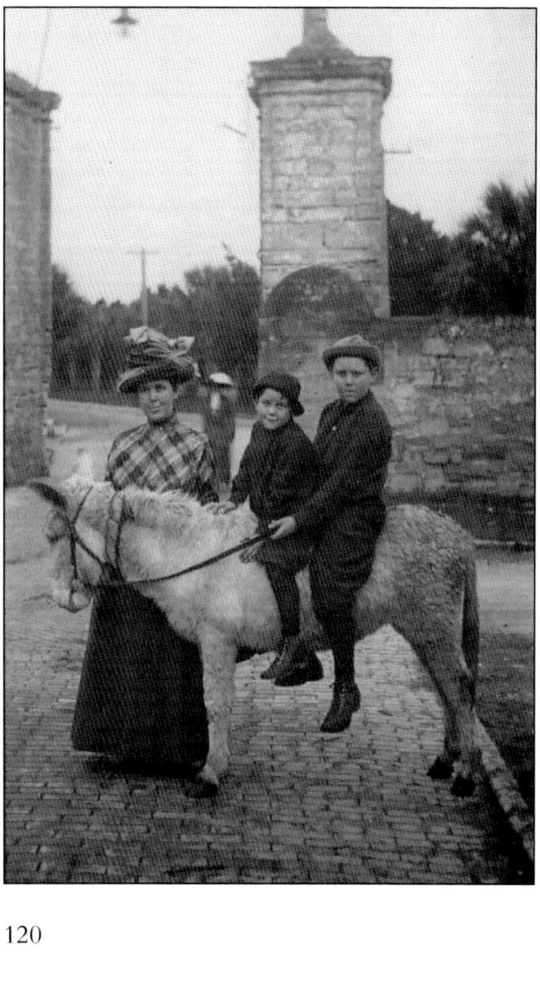

A group of four tourists on burros are posed in front of the City Gate in this photo postcard dated April 4, 1906. The inscription reads, "We are starting for home today—Blake." With postage at only 1¢ and mail delivery twice a day, postcards were a quick and convenient way to send brief messages such as this.

The message on the back of this undated card by photographer Willis A. Kugler reads, "The boys enjoyed the ride on the gentle donkey's back. We are just in front of the old city gates—but little of the wall remains which once surrounded the city."

In addition to his location at 163 St. George Street, photographer Lewis W. Blair also maintained a studio in Garnett's Grove from around 1910 to 1913. Here a group of tourists is posed in one of the giant live oak trees, with the message on the back, "Do you recognize your friends? Taken in the Garnett Grove, St. Augustine, March 8, 1909."

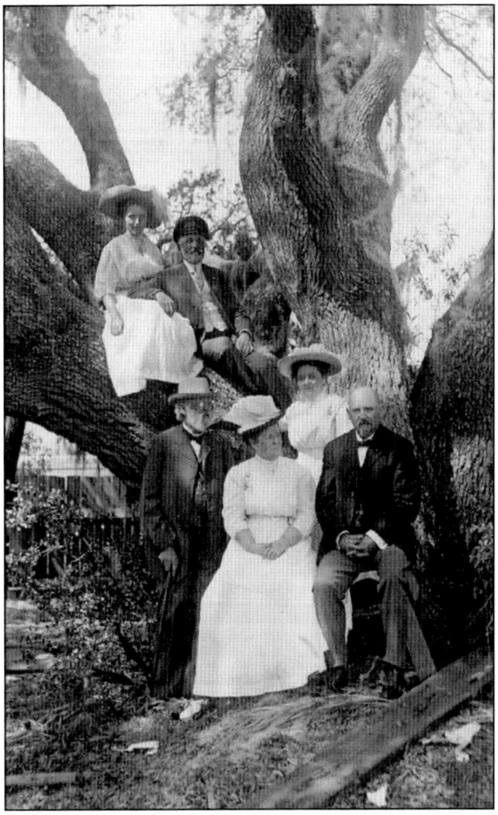

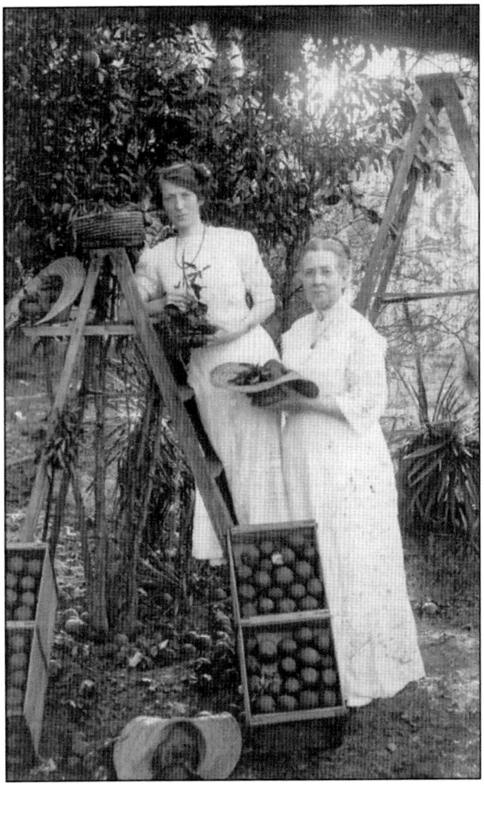

Another popular prop for postcards shot in Garnett's Grove was a stepladder, with tourists posed picking citrus fruit. Oftentimes, the location and date of the photograph was written on one of the ladder's legs. Willis A. Kugler photographed the two women gathering oranges in this undated postcard.

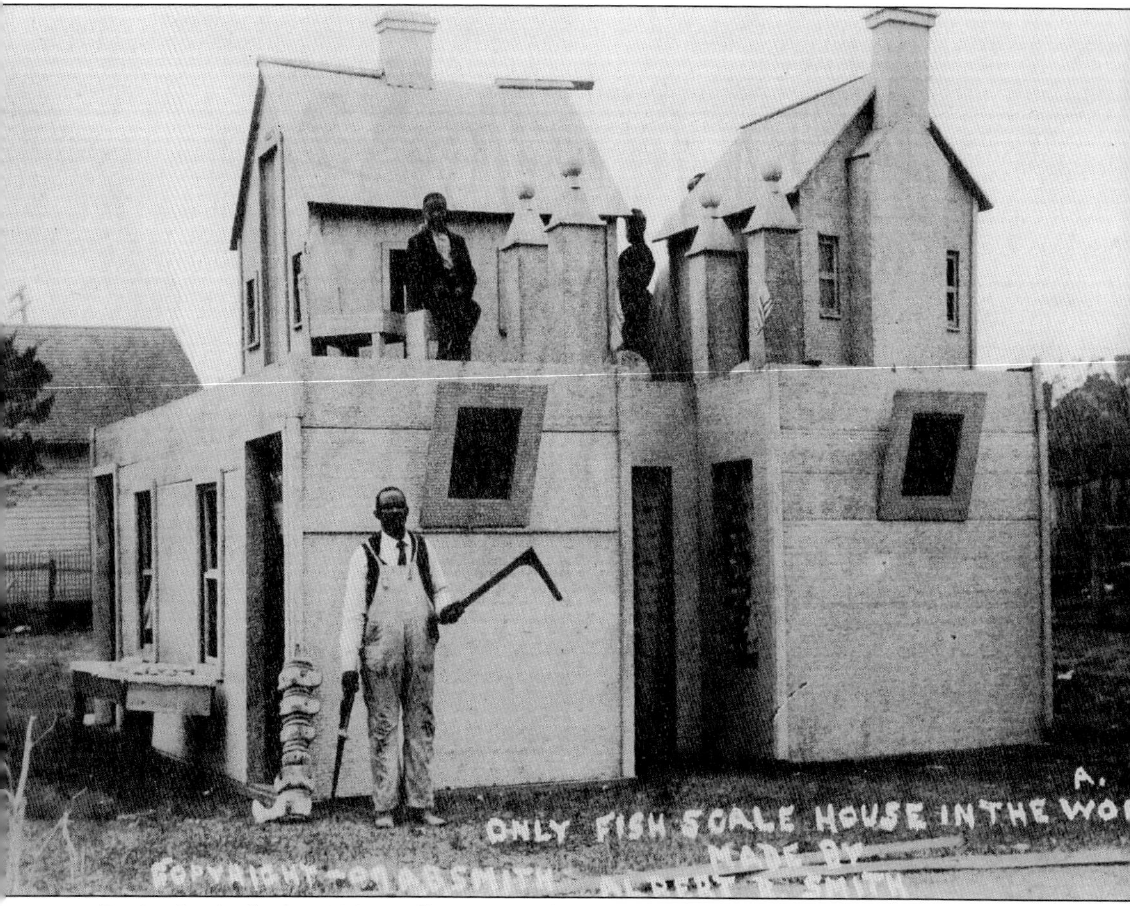

Beginning in the late 1880s, Albert B. Smith began using the large fish scales from black drum to make souvenirs for tourists. He later built this two-story "Fish Scale House," 15 feet by 18 feet and over 12 feet high, with a complete set of furniture made from drum scales and bones. This postcard by W. J. Harris is copyrighted 1907. (Robert G. Goller collection.)

Photo postcards were often used to send pictures of new babies or young children to relatives and friends. This postcard by an unknown photographer shows William Wisner "Buddy" Wilson at three years of age in 1914. Wilson would later become a photographer himself, work as the business manager for the *St. Augustine Record*, and serve as president of the St. Augustine Historical Society.

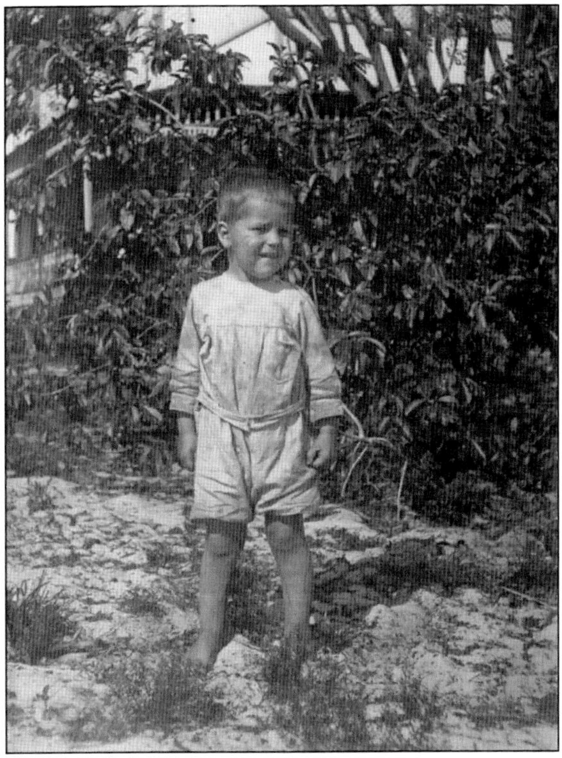

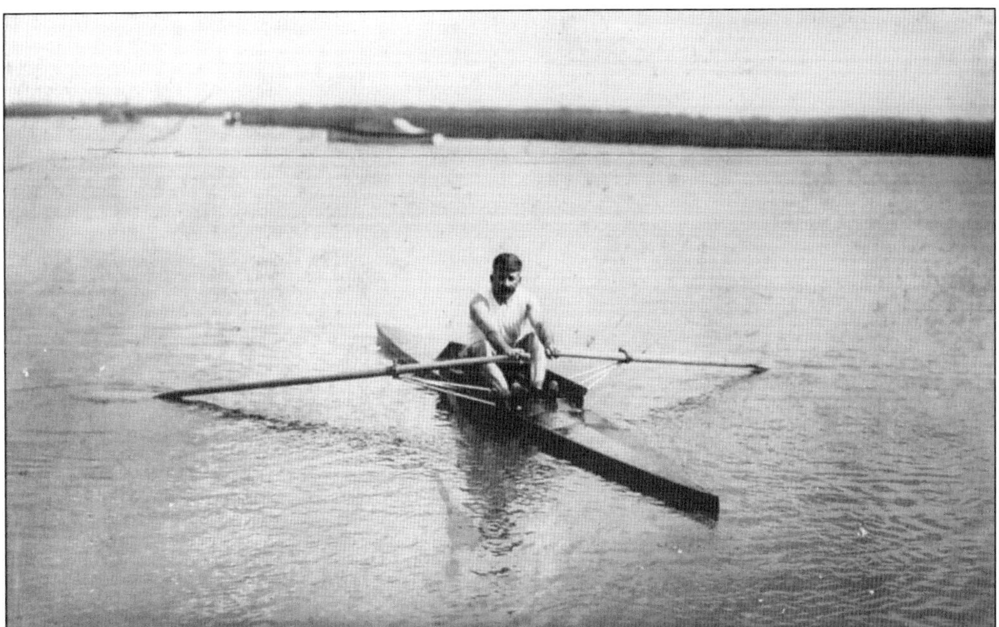

At the dawn of the 20th century, sculling became a popular sport, and rowing clubs sprang up all over the country. Capt. George W. Johnson built this 95-pound scull from newspapers and shellac. He rowed north from St. Augustine to New York City in nine weeks, arriving in mid-July 1908. The boat was then put on display at Whitney's Oldest House, where it could be seen for a fee.

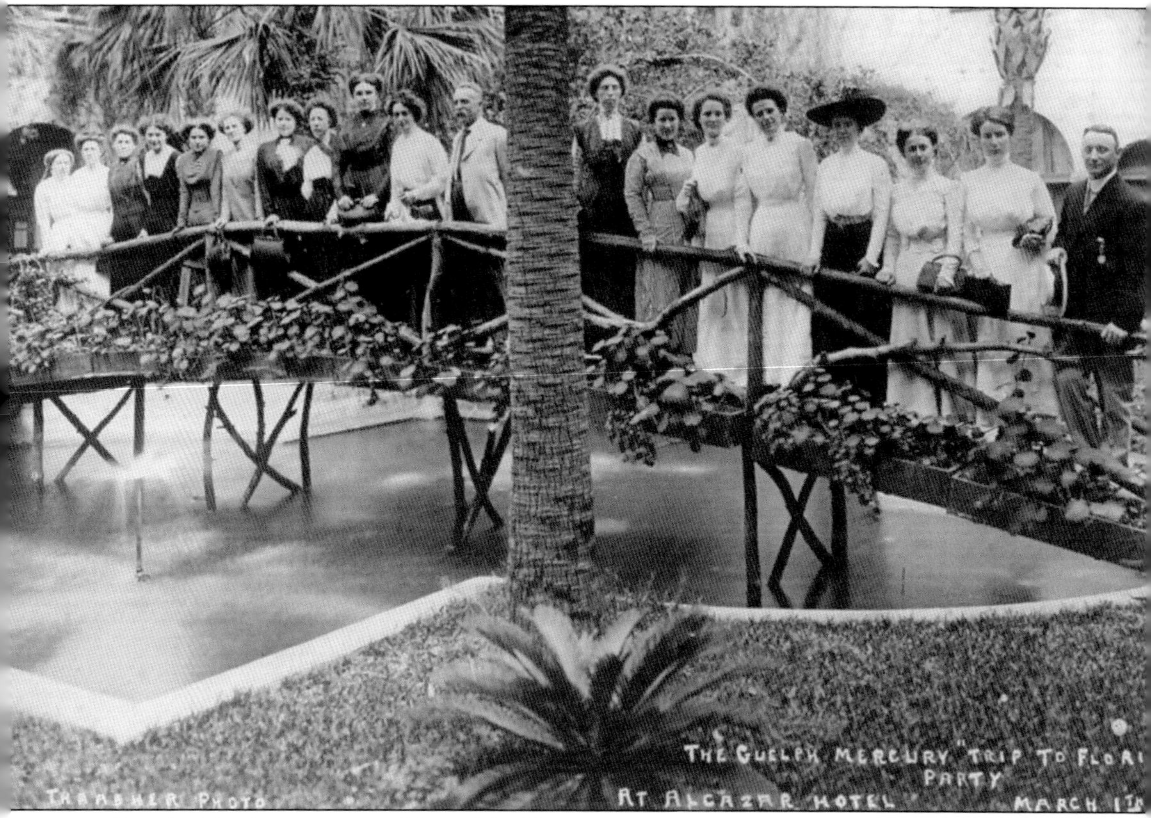

The *Guelph Mercury* is one of Canada's oldest newspapers, serving the Ontario area since 1854. Photographer Herb Thrasher made this postcard of the group's March 1910 trip to Florida, posed on the rustic wooden bridge in the courtyard of the Alcazar Hotel. The courtyard bridge is still a favorite place for photographs and today is the scene of many weddings.

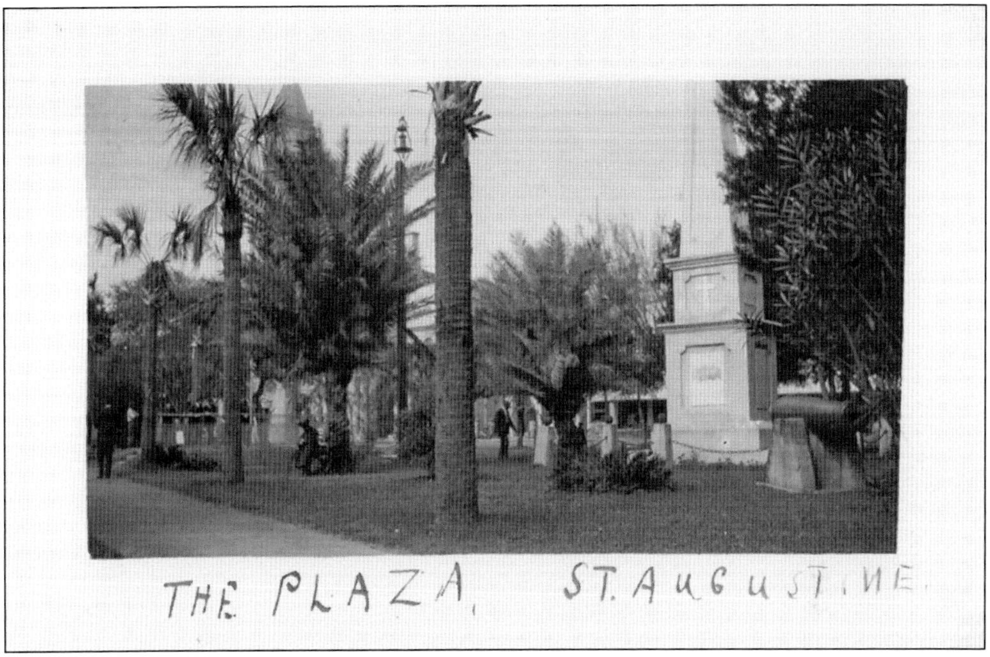

In 1903, the Eastman Kodak Company introduced the No. 3A Folding Pocket Camera, designed for postcard-size film. This camera allowed the general public to take their own photographs and have them printed on postcard backs. These two postcards are examples of those taken by amateur photographers during the early 1900s. The top view shows the plaza and Confederate Monument, erected in 1872 as a memorial to St. Augustine's Civil War dead. The bottom card is mistakenly labeled "Cordova St." but is actually King Street looking east from the intersection of Sevilla Street. The tower of the Cordova Hotel can be seen in the distance on the right, with the familiar fence surrounding the Ponce de Leon Hotel on the left.

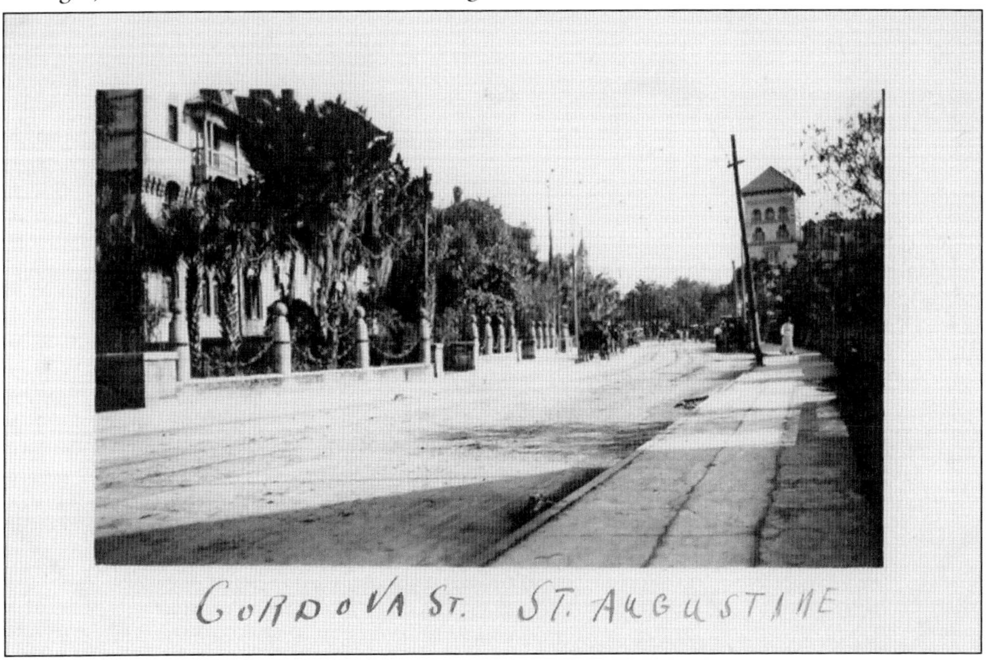

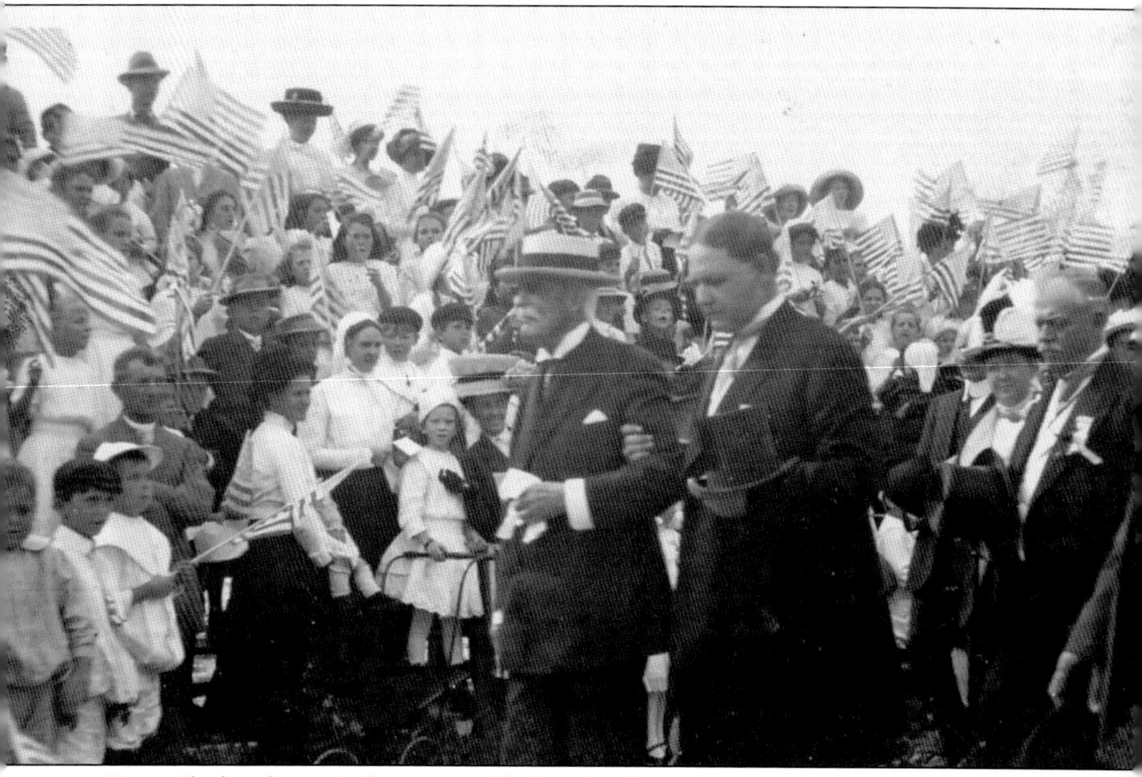

Henry Flagler, shown in the center with the white hat, is escorted by Mayor Joseph N. Fogarty of Key West during the celebration welcoming the first Florida East Coast Railway train into that city on January 22, 1912. In early 1913, Flagler fell down the stairs at Whitehall, his home in Palm Beach, and broke his hip. His health failed rapidly, and Henry Flagler died on May 20, 1913. He is buried beside his first wife and daughter in the Memorial Presbyterian Church in St. Augustine. Dr. Fogarty, pictured above with Flagler, later served as mayor of St. Augustine in 1926–1927—perhaps the only man to hold the same office at opposite ends of the state.

Bibliography

Coomes, Charles S. "The Basilica-Cathedral of St. Augustine, St. Augustine, Florida and Its History." *El Escribano* 20 (1983): 32–44.

Doster, Gary L., ed. *From Abbeville to Zebulon: Early Postcard Views of Georgia*. Athens, GA: University of Georgia Press, 1991.

Goller. Robert R. "North and South with W. J. Harris, Photographer." *El Escribano* 28 (1991): 1–55.

Graham, Thomas. *Flagler's St Augustine Hotels*. Sarasota, FL: Pineapple Press, 2004.

———. *The Awakening of St. Augustine*. St. Augustine, FL: St. Augustine Historical Society, 1978.

Harvey, Karen. *St. Augustine and St. Johns County. A Pictorial History*. Virginia Beach, VA: Donning Company, 1980.

Harvey, Karen. *America's First City*. Lake Buena Vista, FL: Tailored Tours Publications, Inc., 1992.

Jacksonville Historical Society. *Jacksonville in Vintage Postcards*. Charleston, SC: Arcadia Publishing, 2001.

Joyce, Edward R. "St. Francis Barracks: A Contradiction of Terms." *El Escribano* 26 (1989): 71–90.

Morgan, Hal, and Andreas Brown. *Prairie Fires and Paper Moons: The American Photographic Postcard: 1900–1920*. Boston, MA: David R. Godine, 1981.

Nolan, David. *The Houses of St. Augustine*. Sarasota, FL: Pineapple Press, 1995.

Ridolph, Edward A. "Street Railways of St. Augustine." *El Escribano* 24 (1987): 85–101.

Stackhouse, H. H. "The Model Land Tract: The Development of a Residential Neighborhood." *El Escribano* 16 (1979): 25–32.

Waterbury, Jean Parker. "Where Artillery Lane crosses Aviles Street: The Segui/Kirby Smith House." *El Escribano* 24 (1987): 1–37.

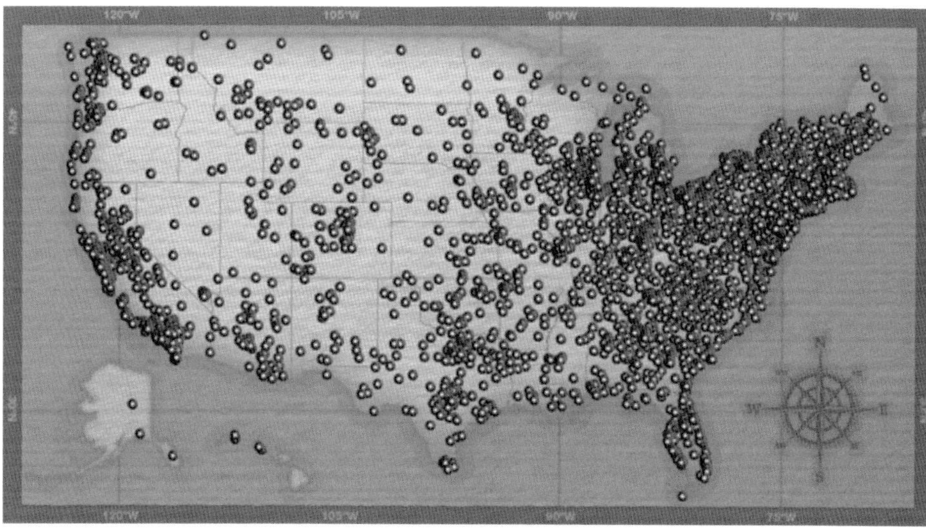